EMPIRE AND ORDER

STUDIES IN MODERN HISTORY

General Editor: J. C. D. Clark, *Joyce and Elizabeth Hall Distinguished Professor of British History, University of Kansas*

Titles include:

Bernard Cottret (*editor*)
BOLINGBROKE'S POLITICAL WRITINGS
The Conservative Enlightenment

Philip Hicks
NEOCLASSICAL HISTORY AND ENGLISH CULTURE
From Clarendon to Hume

William M. Kuhn
DEMOCRATIC ROYALISM
The Transformation of the British Monarchy, 1861–1914

Nancy D. LoPatin
POLITICAL UNIONS, POPULAR POLITICS AND THE GREAT
REFORM ACT OF 1832

James Muldoon
EMPIRE AND ORDER
The Concept of Empire, 800–1800

W. D. Rubinstein and Hilary Rubinstein
PHILOSEMITISM
Admiration and Support for Jews in the English-Speaking World,
1840–1939

Lynne Taylor
BETWEEN RESISTANCE AND COLLABORATION
Popular Protest in Northern France, 1940–45

Empire and Order
The Concept of Empire, 800–1800

James Muldoon
Professor of History
Rutgers, Camden
New Jersey

First published in Great Britain 1999 by
MACMILLAN PRESS LTD
Houndmills, Basingstoke, Hampshire RG21 6XS and London
Companies and representatives throughout the world

A catalogue record for this book is available from the British Library.

ISBN 0–333–65013–1

 First published in the United States of America 1999 by
ST. MARTIN'S PRESS, INC.,
Scholarly and Reference Division,
175 Fifth Avenue, New York, N.Y. 10010

ISBN 0–312–22226–2

Library of Congress Cataloging-in-Publication Data
Muldoon, James, 1935–
Empire and order : the concept of empire, 800–1800 / James
Muldoon.
p. cm.
Includes bibliographical references (p.) and index.
ISBN 0–312–22226–2 (cloth)
1. Imperialism—History. I. Title.
JC359.M86 1999
325'.32'09—dc21   99–13305
                                                CIP

© James Muldoon 1999

This book is printed on paper suitable for recycling and made from fully managed and
sustained forest sources.

10   9   8   7   6   5   4
08   07   06   05   04   03   02

Printed and bound in Great Britain by
Antony Rowe Ltd, Chippenham, Wiltshire

Contents

Preface

A colleague who read this book in manuscript observed that some reviewers will argue that it is 'too stark, too legalistic, and [too focused on] canon law at that'. Another suggested that the book is the result of attempting to compress a three-volume work into a single volume. The easy way around these criticisms is to point out that the publisher set a page-limit for the manuscript. I could of course, have declined to write the book under the conditions that were established and, instead, set out on a scholarly trek that would eventually lead to a multi-volume study.

Instead of declining to examine the concept of empire in a short volume, I decided that writing a short book on a vast topic, as Doctor Johnson said about the contemplation of death, concentrates the mind wonderfully.[1] What is important to say about the concept of empire, what has not been said, what has been underappreciated? What, in other words, is the justification for another volume on empire? It seemed to me that three aspects of the history of the concept of empire deserve fuller attention.

In the first place, there is not a single concept of empire but several. The various meanings of the term contributed, and continue to contribute, to confusion about exactly what is meant when empire is mentioned. Does empire mean a particular place, a unique form of government, a notion of primacy in the temporal order? Does empire refer to a universal government, a basis for world order? Or can it mean a spatially more limited form of rule?

In the second place, the concept of empire was not restricted to the Middle Ages, to be replaced in the modern world by the state. To some extent, the notion that empire was a medieval issue stemmed from the assumption that the term empire referred only to the medieval Holy Roman Empire, an institution that failed to evolve into a state during the early modern era. In fact, however, as European kingdoms were being transformed into states, several were also acquiring overseas territories that were, and are, popularly described as empires.

Finally, the role of lawyers in the developing of ideas about the nature of empire has been generally neglected. All too often the history of political thought has focused on the writings of philosophers, publicists, and other theorists. The study of medieval political thought in particular is approached this way. As a result, the writings of Thomas Aquinas, for example, on political matters, brief as they are, often receive an excessive amount of attention while the writings of the lawyers whose writings were more extensive, and on whom Aquinas drew, have attracted less attention.[2] From the establishment of law schools in the twelfth century on through the eighteenth century, the legally-trained formed a kind of intellectual elite that was deeply involved in politics and government. Alexis de Tocqueville made that point long ago: 'For five hundred years lawyers have taken part in all the movements of political society in Europe.'[3] In recent years, some scholars have pointed to the 'common legal past' that united the lawyers of the continent for eight centuries, until the legal codification movement of the eighteenth and nineteenth centuries transformed the legal world.[4] This book thus stresses, but is not restricted to, what we might label as the lawyers' understanding of empire in medieval and early modern Europe.

The writing of a book of such a large scope is possible only because of the assistance of colleagues and friends who read and commented upon early drafts, suggested topics to explore, provided bibliographical references, and provided opportunities to develop aspects of the book in seminars and conferences. The first stage in the process of developing this book was a request by Professor Giles Constable of the Institute for Advanced Study that I provide a paper for the weekly seminar in medieval studies at some point during my year there. The discussion at that seminar provided a number of stimulating suggestions. A subsequent invitation from Professor Natalie Davis provided opportunity to present a fuller version at the Davis Center for Historical Studies of Princeton University. Finally, Sir John Elliott invited me to present what was becoming an ever longer paper at a seminar at Oxford. In the course of that discussion, someone raised the question of whether the paper was intended as part of a book. At that point I said it was not, because I had another book-length project in mind. Subsequently, J.C.D. Clark, later Hall Distinguished Professor of British History at the University of Kansas, who had attended the seminar, generously invited me to provide a book on the concept of empire along the lines of the seminar presentation for the series of volumes he was editing. Without the suggestions, criticisms, and encouragement of these individuals and the participants in the various seminars, this book would not have been written.

In addition, I owe a great deal to a number of other scholars who read parts of the project. These include Steven Fanning of the University of Illinois, Chicago; Constantin Fasolt of the University of Chicago; John Headley of the University of North Carolina; Cary Nederman of the University of Arizona; James Powell of Syracuse University; and John Robertson of St Hugh's College, Oxford. I have also depended on colleagues at Rutgers, especially Rodney Carlisle, Gordon Schochet and Gerald Verbrugghe, for advice and suggestions. Our department secretary, Loretta Carlisle, has, as usual, provided a great deal of assistance along the way as well.

I also wish to thank two people whose interest and encouragement have provided support over a very long haul. The first is Edward M. Peters, Henry Charles Lea Professor of Medieval History at the University of Pennsylvania, who has been a friend, guide and occasional goad, for thirty years. The other is my wife, Judith, without whom I would never have persevered in this project or in others.

Finally, I wish to dedicate this book to the memory of the late Margaret Gibson, a wonderful friend, a fine scholar who introduced me to the glories of Oxford and who left us too soon.

Introduction

It is wrong, certainly, to write and interpret on the basis of a static, timeless conception of the imperial office.[1]

Having surveyed the political thought of the fifteenth and sixteenth centuries, Quentin Skinner began the final chapter of his massive work *The Foundations of Modern Political Thought* with the following comment:

> By the beginning of the seventeenth century, the concept of the State – its nature, its powers, its right to command obedience – had come to be regarded as the most important object of analysis in European political thought.[2]

This statement reflects a widely held and not inaccurate belief that the fundamental political structure of the modern world is the state, 'the sole source of law and legitimate force within its territory, and ... the sole appropriate objects of its citizens' allegiances'.[3] The modern state is sovereign, occupies a fixed, contiguous territory, has a common law and language, perhaps even a state religion, and, by the twentieth century, is usually occupied by a people officially claiming a single national heritage. Europe consists of a congeries of sovereign nation-states, all legally equal and sovereign, no state being superior in any manner to any other.

Modern Europe thus stands in stark contrast to medieval Europe, at least to medieval Europe as generally perceived in the twentieth century. In this view, a somewhat paradoxical one, medieval Europe was feudally decentralized, even anarchic, at the local level but theoretically united in a Christian world order at the top.[4] Successful medieval rulers represented dynasties that had over centuries acquired a variety of lands, privileges, and rights. Their domains were ramshackle constructions in which kings vied with the Church and with the great nobles for control and in each segment of which the ruler governed according to local custom and practice. On the other hand, medieval political theorists are often said to have focused on the creation of a unified Christian society, Christendom, that incorporated all Christian lands into a single over-arching structure headed by the pope or the emperor.[5] The conflict between popes and emperors

1

that characterized so much of medieval political thought was then a
battle over who would lead Christian society.

A generation ago, in one of the most important textbooks in political thought, George Sabine asserted that for medieval political
thinkers

> The government of the world is therefore shared between a spirit-
> ual and a temporal power, each having its proper jurisdiction and
> marked off from the other by a line not too hard to trace. This
> single world-wide society may be called, with only a difference of
> emphasis, either a commonwealth or a church. ... The controlling
> social conception is that of an organic community in which the
> various classes are functioning parts and of which law forms the
> organizing principle.[6]

Sabine distinguished even more clearly between medieval and
modern political thought in his Table of Contents when he labeled
the chapters dealing with medieval political thought as 'The Theory
of the Universal Community', while the chapters dealing with
modern thought were identified as 'The Theory of the National
State'.[7]

Taken together, the conclusions of Sabine and Skinner frame the
orthodox opinion about the contrast between medieval and early
modern political thought, namely that while in the Middle Ages political thinkers focused on a universal Christian society, early modern
thinkers focused their attention on the more narrowly constructed
political unit known as the state. In practical politics, the consequence
of this change in the focus of political thought paralleled the
transformation of Europe from a universal society to 'a series of
independent, secular, sovereign states'.[8]

According to this model, the crucial stage in the passage from
medieval to modern government came with the writing of two books,
Machiavelli's *Prince*, written in 1513 (published in 1532), which
defined the state, and Jean Bodin's *The Six Books of a Commonweal*,
published in 1576, which for the first time defined sovereignty as the
core of the modern state.[9] As Sabine declared: 'a systematic statement
of Machiavelli's philosophy needed the conception of sovereign power
which Bodin and Hobbes added to it'.[10] This is not to say that the state
was suddenly sovereign, unchallenged in its authority from without
and from within the kingdom, but only that for the first time sovereignty was identified as one of the defining characteristics of the state.

It became a goal toward which rulers could strive as they transformed their feudal holdings into modern states.[11]

It is worth noting that the views of Skinner and Sabine are not unique to the twentieth century. As far back as the eighteenth century, writers were describing the differences in governance and political structure between the Middle Ages and the modern world in similar bipolar terms. William Robertson's life of the Emperor Charles V, first published in 1769, began with a justly famous 'View of the Progress of Society in Europe' that emphasized the emergence of the modern state as one of the most important developments of this period of history.

> Government, however, was still far from having attained that state in which extensive monarchies act with the united vigour of the whole community, or carry on great undertakings with perseverance and success. ... [But in] The kingdoms of Europe, in the present age ... the prince, by the less violent but no less effectual operation of the laws and a well-regulated government, is enabled to avail himself of the whole force of the state, and to employ it in enterprises which require strenuous and persevering efforts.[12]

Robertson's heroes were Henry VIII (1509–47) and Francis I (1515–47) because each developed his kingdom rather than seeking after glory 'in continual wars, which not only exhausted and oppressed his subjects, but left him little leisure for giving attention to the interior police and improvement of his kingdoms, the great objects of every prince who makes the happiness of his people the end of his government'.[13] Their contemporary Charles V symbolized the failings of medieval rulers who failed to create states as modern men understand them. They collected lands and glory abroad instead of creating modern governmental structures at home. Robertson also argued that Charles V did not formulate a 'chimerical project of establishing an universal monarchy in Europe', a vision that some critics claimed to see in his activities.[14] Nevertheless, in his opinion, the flaw in Charles V's government was his failure to recognize the need to create a modern state, limited in size and centralized in power. Robertson's Charles V is a tragic story of overweening ambition that failed to appreciate the coming of the modern world.

Seeing the history of medieval and modern political thought as a linear process that went from some form of universal community, Church or empire, to the state, a transition that occurred around

1450–1500 leads, however, to a misunderstanding of the relationship between medieval and modern political thought and practice because it focuses too narrowly on the writings of a few theorists whose relationship to the political realities of their own day is problematic. For example, it is common to identify Thomas Aquinas as '*the* one great thinker of the Middle Ages' but, as Brian Tierney has observed, this 'is an invention of modern neo-Thomism'.[15] Likewise, to equate Dante's conception of a universal empire with the mainstream of medieval political thought is to place too much emphasis on a conception of politics that one scholar has described as 'original and peculiar'.[16] Although medieval political thinkers did devote a good deal of attention to the issue of a universal Christian society, medieval thinking about politics and government had a broader scope and was more diverse than that.[17]

One scholar who has recognized the links between medieval and modern thought on empire and empires is Anthony Pagden. His *Lords of All the World: Ideologies of Empire in Spain, Britain and France c. 1500–c. 1800* deals with the way in which one medieval concept of empire, the universal Christian empire, shaped the outlook of the great imperial powers of the early modern era as they expanded overseas.[18] Pagden's emphasis on universal empire, however, leads him to underplay the importance of other concepts of empire that existed in the Middle Ages. He also fails to appreciate that the creation of overseas empires and the continuing use of imperial language created a serious problem for those who were transforming medieval dynastic possessions into modern states. Could the emerging states also be empires?

Pagden's recognition of the continuing use of medieval imperial language in the early modern world connects him to an increasing interest among medieval historians in the relation between medieval and modern European expansion.[19] This interest has been especially great in the study of medieval political thought. For the past fifty years, medieval historians have broadened the study of medieval political thought by paying attention to two important aspects of political development, the history of governmental institutions and the history of law, especially the history of canon law.[20] They have studied the development of institutions that prepared the way for the modern state, arguing that many of the institutional elements of the modern state existed before the language to describe it existed. As Gaines Post wrote:

> Indeed, I sometimes think that one of the principal errors of modern scholarship on medieval law and institutions has been that

of interpreting [the development of the state] in accordance with contemporary notions. I prefer rather to find out if there was a *medieval* conception of the state. ...[21]

Other medievalists have pointed out that Machiavelli and Bodin, as well as many other early modern political thinkers, used the contemporary political world as a base for theoretical analysis of the state, but they did not invent the state or sovereignty. A number of years ago a medievalist placed Machiavelli's *Prince* firmly within the medieval tradition of the *speculum principis*, that is, the guide for the moral ruler. More recently, another concluded: 'Bodin's conception of sovereignty was unthinkable without the work of his predecessors.'[22]

Many medieval historians have followed the lead of J.N. Figgis, who argued that 'we must bear in mind that in political theory many of the medieval arguments and methods subsisted until the eighteenth century'.[23] Gaines Post, Brian Tierney and Francis Oakley in particular have developed Figgis's line of argument, asserting that the foundations of modern political thought are to be found in medieval governmental institutions and legal thought. From the perspective of medievalists, Skinner's *Foundations* rest upon a substructure developed over the previous five centuries.[24] As medievalists see matters, there is more continuity with and development from medieval political and legal thought and institutions than has been generally recognized. Indeed, even some of their vocabulary had medieval roots. While the foundational structures of the modern state rest in the Middle Ages, the concept itself, that is the language employed to describe these structures and what they created, is a clearly modern one. Although the term *status* has a medieval history, the term entered the vocabulary of politics with its modern meaning only with Machiavelli in the sixteenth century.[25] As a result, it did not carry with it much medieval intellectual baggage.[26]

Reflecting an understandable tendency among scholars to seek out the new, the innovative, the different, the theory of the state long attracted the attention of students of political thought because it represented the future. Medieval political thought and institutions did not, however, move into the modern era along only one path, the development of the state. What is sometimes forgotten is that alongside the new and the innovative the old and the traditional generally continue to operate and even to develop for a period of time. This appears most tangibly in the history of technology. For example, the finest and fastest sailing ships, the nineteenth-century clipper ships, emerged only after the steamship had appeared. Furthermore, sailing ships, even wooden ones, continued to play a major role in the American maritime industry into the early decades of the twentieth century, competing successfully with steel-hulled vessels for decades. The old and the new often operate side-by-side for generations, even centuries, belying the popular belief that the new, and presumably better, automatically displaces the old quickly.[27]

Applying to the study of political thought the principle that innovation does not immediately drive out the traditional, we can see that alongside the emergence of the state, institutionally and theoretically, was the survival and even the expansion of what might be loosely termed imperial government, a form of government most obviously associated with, but not restricted to the medieval Holy Roman Empire, a term that had a long history and a variety of meanings. Indeed, rather than being simply the history of the development of the state, the history of political thought and institutions from 1500 to 1800 (or, perhaps, 1300 to 1800) can be more fruitfully understood as a conflict between two forms of government, a comparatively new one, the emerging nation-state, and an old form in the process of transformation, imperial government.[28] Even a scholar of an older generation, J.W. Allen, who saw the Reformation as causing a sharp break in the institutional structure of Europe, could assert:

> It is an error to suppose that the sixteenth century saw the development of much that was strikingly new in political philosophy. ... All through the century the main divisions of late medieval opinion were reproduced. This was a necessary consequence of the fact that the basic assumptions made in the sixteenth century were the same that had been made by medieval thinkers.[29]

One might add that much the same could be said of the seventeenth and even of the eighteenth centuries.

In fact, to assume that in political terms medieval Europe was some kind of universalist political society while early modern Europe was a collection of sovereign states, each controlling a specific, limited, territory misses the point that it was in the early modern era that European explorers, traders, missionaries, and settlers were gaining control of lands in the Americas, Asia, and elsewhere, creating, among other problems, a significant problems of governance. How were these newly acquired lands to be ruled? What would be the relation of the

European monarchs to their subjects who chose to settle in the newly discovered lands? Would the indigenous inhabitants of the new worlds be treated as the equals of the ruler's European subjects? A whole series of political problems, some new, some old, appeared or reappeared as European rulers sought to deal with the problems of governance that Columbus and his successors had caused them. In other words, the problem of imperial governance grew in the sixteenth, seventeenth, and eighteenth centuries, rather than disappeared.

From the very beginning of large-scale European overseas expansion in the sixteenth century, there was a tension between the state which was clearly emerging and imperial government which may have seemed on its deathbed in the fifteenth century but was alive and well in the sixteenth. The state was generally small, consisting of contiguous territory and with a comparatively homogeneous population that made possible the identification of the nation with the state by the nineteenth century. State theory stressed concentration of power and uniformity of laws, governmental structures, religion, even language. The state was a response to the large dynastic accumulations of disparate territories that medieval dynasties had created. These dynastic accumulations, loosely termed empires, however, consisted of a number of territories, each with its own laws and customs, its own political, economic and social structures, perhaps even its own religion. As H.G. Koenigsberger has pointed out, rather than being labeled states or empires, these early modern collections of political units should be termed 'composite states or monarchies', reflecting the disparate nature of the various elements.[30]

Those scholars who have focused their attention on the emergence of the state have neglected two important aspects of early modern political thought. In the first place, the emergence of a political universe composed of sovereign states led to the development of international law as a logical consequence of the need to regulate relationships among them in order to avoid a Hobbesian world where men 'are in that condition which is called war; and such a war, as is of every man against every man'.[31] Robertson believed that because of the emergence of states, 'the affairs of different kingdoms [were] becoming more frequently as well as more intimately connected, [so that] they were gradually accustomed to act in concert and confederacy, and were insensibly prepared for forming a system of policy in order to establish or to preserve such a balance of power as was most consistent with the general security'.[32] In fact, however, it was quite clear to Robertson's contemporaries that the European states were not naturally evolving a system of peaceful world order. The development of international law from the appearance of Hugo Grotius's great work *The Law of War and Peace* in 1625 and climaxing in the eighteenth century in the work of Pufendorf, Wolff and their contemporaries indicates just how central the theoretical problem of creating world order was to intellectuals and officials.[33] In many ways, the international-law thinkers of the seventeenth and eighteenth centuries were following in the tradition of medieval theorists of world order who had based such an order on either papal or imperial leadership. International-law thinking of the seventeenth and eighteenth centuries suggested a secularization of medieval ecclesiastical thought about the relations that should exist among nations and how conflicts between nations should be handled.[34]

A second problem associated with the emergence of the state that generated theoretical and practical problems of a larger order was the problem of the relationship between European states and their possessions in the New World. What would be the relationship of the Spanish Americas to the crown of Castile, for example? The existence of a large indigenous population caused one set of problems. The creation of an American-born population of Spanish parentage, the *criollos*, caused another.[35] In British North America, a similar situation prevailed. The American Revolution was a consequence of the failure of the English government and the colonial English population to agree on the nature of their relationship.

In a general sense, the problem of state-formation within Europe developed parallel to the formation of European overseas empires. The history of political thought and practice was thus not a linear movement from universalism to particularity, from Christendom and empire to the state, a movement whose dividing line came at some point in the fifteenth or sixteenth century. Instead, the history of political thought from the Middle Ages to the eighteenth century was the story of two forms of governance, the state and the empire, in tension. Furthermore, as the history of international law demonstrates, the emergence of the state, the conquest of the New World, the establishment of trading relations with Asian societies, and the development of European colonies overseas all contributed to the development of legal and political theories that would create a world legal order to regulate relations among states.

The present book is a contribution to a larger history yet to be written, the history of theories of world order from the Middle Ages to the twentieth century. The focus here is on the history of the concept of empire (or of empires) in the Middle Ages and the relation of the several medieval concepts of Empire to subsequent discussions of empires in the early modern world. In a sense, this volume serves as preliminary to Richard Kroebner's *Empire* and Anthony Pagden's recent *The Lords of All the World*, the most extensive discussions of the concept of empire presently available in English.[36] Although Kroebner's work did discuss ancient and medieval notions of Empire, his primary aim was to discuss the origins of the British empire, not to discuss the concept of empire in general. Likewise, Pagden's focus is on the concept of empire as it developed after the beginning of the European encounter with the peoples of the New World and is concerned with the writings of numerous publicists, philosophers, and travellers but not with the lawyers. The present volume will stress the importance of medieval lawyers and legal ideas in the development of both the state and the concept of empire. Medieval lawyers, canonists and Romanists or civilians, provided much of the basis for all subsequent discussion of both the state and empire. A good deal of scholarly effort has been devoted to the canon lawyers in the past forty years, leading to the need to reconsider the development of political thought in light of the way in which theologians and philosophers, the usual sources of political theory, used legal materials.

Finally, this book will argue that there were several medieval conceptions of what constituted an empire, a situation that had important practical consequences for the language of politics in the early modern world. One of the striking aspects of the history of the concept of empire is that in the period from the sixteenth to the eighteenth centuries, neither the Spanish nor the English monarchs officially referred to their possessions as empires or to themselves as emperors. This failure to employ the most obvious terms to identify their possessions and themselves was deliberate, as the discussion among Spanish intellectuals for a term that would adequate describe their monarch's possessions suggests.[37] Why not use the terms empire and emperor? One reason was that these terms came freighted with meanings that made their use in contemporary political discourse awkward. If a Spanish monarch, Philip II (1556–98), for example, had chosen to refer to himself as an emperor and his possessions as an empire, how would his uncle Ferdinand I (1556–64) who bore the title of Holy Roman Emperor of the German Nation have reacted? Or, to use another example, if Philip II had declared himself emperor, how would that have affected his relationship with the score of individual kingdoms that he ruled?

The terms emperor and empire led to dialogues of the deaf because the various participants in political discourse could – and did – use these terms with different meanings. One way to appreciate this problem at the end of the period being discussed is to consider a debate about the nature of empire that took place in Boston on the eve of the American Revolution. Beginning in 1775, two Boston lawyers, old friends and colleagues, Daniel Leonard and John Adams, outlined the nature of the emerging conflict between the colonies and England in terms that reflected the tension between state and empire. Employing the pseudonym Massachusettensis, Leonard wrote a series of essays defending the royal government's view of the relationship between the colonies and the mother country. Leonard asserted that there was a British Empire to which the inhabitants of New England were subject and that the sovereign authority of that empire was located in the English Parliament.

> However closely we may hug ourselves in the opinion, that the parliament has not right to tax or legislate for us, the people of England hold the contrary opinion as firmly. They tell us we are a part of the British empire; that every state, from the nature of government, must have a supreme, uncontrollable power, co-extensive with the empire itself; and that this power is vested in parliament.[38]

If the colonies are not subject to the authority

> of parliament, Great Britain and the colonies must be distinct states, as completely so, as England and Scotland were before the union or as Great Britain and Hanover are now.

If that is the case, the king of Great Britain 'appears in a new capacity, of king of America, or rather in several new capacities, of king of Massachusetts, king of Rhode Island, king of Connecticut, etc. etc'.[39] That, so it appeared to Leonard, was the *reductio ad absurdum* to which those who would deny the reality of the British Empire would lead their followers. Either the jurisdictions of the King of Great Britain and the Parliament of England were coterminous, or there was no coherent political unit that contained all of the territories that the King of Great Britain ruled in his various capacities. Leonard supported, or at least accepted as a fact, the development of a coherent English – or British – state of which Massachusetts was a subordinate part.[40] Leonard's position was, so to speak, the modern view, based on a notion of the state as sovereign.

Leonard's essays, published in the *Massachusetts Gazette and Post-Boy* beginning in the fall of 1774, caused John Adams, polemicist, revolutionary and future president of the United states, writing under the pseudonym Novanglus, to respond with another series of essays. According to Adams, Massachusettensis was absolutely wrong about the jurisdiction of Parliament.

... the terms 'British Empire' are not the language of the common law, but the language of newspapers and political pamphlets; ... the dominions of the king of Great Britain have no power coextensive with them. I would ask, by what law the parliament has authority over America?[41]

Adams pointed out that the charters establishing the British colonies in North America made no mention of any connection with the Parliament. The colonists only 'owe allegiance to the person of his majesty, King George III., whom God preserve' with the consequence that 'our allegiance to his majesty is not due by virtue of any act of a British parliament, but by our own charter and province laws'. Consequently, 'If it follows from thence, that he appears [as] 'King of Massachusetts, King of Rhode Island, King of Connecticut, &c'. this is no absurdity at all. He will appear in this light, and does appear so, whether parliament has authority over us or not'.[42] Adams might have added that the title of King of Great Britain itself was created only as a consequence of the Act of Union that joined Scotland to England in 1707.[43] The new title reflected the fact that the monarch was now the ruler of the entire island of Britain and the English Parliament the Parliament of the entire island as well.[44] No such act had brought the American colonies under the jurisdiction of that Parliament.

Furthermore, as if to complicate matters further, Adams and Leonard also pointed to the fact that the English monarch was said to possess imperial authority. For Leonard, 'allegiance to the imperial crown' was expected of the inhabitants of Massachusetts.[45] Adams, however, asserted that 'This language, "the imperial crown of Great Britain," is not the style of the common law, but of court sycophants.'[46] What Adams seems to have overlooked was that English law did include the term 'imperial crown'. Henry VIII had employed the phrase 'imperial crown' in several acts that had asserted his kingdom's independence of papal jurisdiction.[47] The phrase subsequently appeared in an act of Elizabeth I that responded to the papal bull ordering Catholics to withdraw their allegiance to her.[48] These early uses of the phrase emphasized the independence of the Church of England from papal jurisdiction and the royal claim to be Supreme Head of the Church of England.

At the beginning of the eighteenth century the Act of Settlement (1701) that arranged for the succession of the House of Hanover to the throne of Great Britain employed imperial language in two senses. In the first place, it excluded Catholics from 'the imperial crown of this kingdom', securing the throne for the Protestant descendants of James I (1603–25).[49] In this way, the Act of Settlement was following the lead of the Tudor monarchs who associated imperial status with independence from the papacy. Elsewhere in the same document, imperial status was seen in another way.

> That in case the crown and imperial dignity of this realm shall here-after come to any person not being a native of this kingdom of England this nation be not obliged to engage in any war for the defence of any dominions or territories which do not belong to the crown of England without the consent of Parliament.[50]

When the Elector of Hanover ascended the throne as George I (1714–27) at the death of Queen Anne (1702–14), by the terms of the Act of Settlement, legally and constitutionally, the only connection between the United Kingdom of Great Britain and the Electorate of Hanover was the fact that the same individual was king in one and elector in the other. Hanover in no way became part of the imperial crown.[51]

Subsequently, Declaratory Acts asserting the jurisdiction of the English Parliament over Ireland (1719) and the North American colonies (1766) stated that the people in each case 'were dependent upon the imperial crown and Parliament of *Great Britain*'.[52] Here the term imperial was used to emphasize that the jurisdiction of the English Parliament extended to all territories that the king of England possessed, though not to those he possessed in his capacity as Elector of Hanover.

What makes these statements especially interesting is that Adams and Leonard were both correct; that is, each used the term empire in a way that was generally accepted. For Leonard, the widespread pos-sessions of the English monarch certainly fitted one definition of what constituted an empire. On the other hand, Adams was correct in denying the existence of the use of the terms emperor and empire in the common law. The related term imperial did, however, exist in royal statutes such as the Declaratory Act. In this usage, however, the term meant that the English monarch was sovereign, not subject to the jurisdiction of any other ruler. The debate between Adams and Leonard thus provided several distinct meanings for empire and related terms, each with its own history.

We might wish to view the ways in which Adams and Leonard employed the terms empire and imperial as nothing more than the partisan views of opposing polemicists who happened to be well-educated lawyers, and to dismiss them as lacking any substantive content. To do so, however, would be to fail to recognize that in these few words Adams and Leonard summed up several of the fundamental problems of political and legal thought and practice that had affected European public life from the sixteenth to the eighteenth century. Those issues included the nature of empires, the nature of the state, the nature of sovereignty, and the relationship between a ruler and the various elements that comprised his territories, as well as the relationship among the ruler's possessions. The American Revolution was not after all simply the rejection of English rule by a group of unhappy colonists. The Americans, such as Adams, and the British, whose views Leonard reflected, had fundamentally different conceptions of what Leonard called, in the loosest possible sense, the British Empire.

At first glance, the debate between Adams and Leonard might seem to be only a semantic one that arose because the British colonists who lived in North America needed some theoretical basis for their revolution. That is, whether one chooses to label it an empire or not, the British North Americans clearly belonged to a political unit headed by the King of England and his Parliament. The nature of the machinery that directed this structure may have been in doubt, but the existence of the structure, whether called empire or something else, was not in doubt.

While such a conclusion would appear a sensible one, it is not accurate. For example, although the King of England had been also the King of Scotland since 1603, it was only with the Act of Union of 1707 that Scotland came under the jurisdiction of the English Parliament.[53] Likewise, until 1800, there was a separate Irish Parliament whose relationship to the English Parliament had long been a matter of dispute.[54] Furthermore, there were the palatine counties of Chester and Durham which had a unique legal and constitutional status.[55]

Then there was the Electorate of Hanover, whose ruler since 1714 was also the King of England. It was well known that the English Parliament had no jurisdiction in Hanover. As Adams pointed out in the *Novanglus* essays, what appears to be the British Empire is in fact a collection of territories joined only by the fact that a particular individual who happens to be the King of England rules each of them; in other words, the empire was really only a personal monarchy. The English Parliament had jurisdiction in some of these lands but not others. The *Novanglus* essays provided a history written to demonstrate the truth of Adams's assertion that there was no British Empire, only a collection of territories joined only by the person of the monarch, a dynastic accumulation of lands that had developed haphazardly over several centuries.

Elsewhere in Europe during the sixteenth century, at precisely the same time that monarchs such as Philip II were attempting to centralize and rationalize their variegated European possessions, moving, however slowly, in the direction of a state structure, they were also becoming rulers of distant lands that could not be easily brought into the emerging state structure.[56] The problems that these overseas possessions created were not resolved until the nineteenth century. The revolutionary movements that transformed Spain's American possessions into independent countries largely resolved the issue of imperial governance for the Spanish, while the Durham Report of 1839 provided the English government with a plan for dealing with the administration of those colonies whose population was largely or entirely English in origin. From the sixteenth to the eighteenth centuries the rulers of European kingdoms faced two distinct governmental problems. Within Europe there was the problem of unifying the disparate possessions that ruling dynasties had acquired over centuries into nation-states, while at the same time these rulers were involved in acquiring new territories overseas that could not readily be fitted into the nation-state model. Furthermore, the emerging political order raised an old problem, the settlement of disputes between rulers, in a new context, one in which there was no official, pope or emperor, who could lay claim to a mediating role. In particular, conflicting claims to the newly discovered regions of the world generated a demand for rules to govern the behavior of European governments overseas, a demand that led to the development of modern international law.

At first glance, it would appear that these large territorial agglomerations formed empires and could reasonably be so labeled. The law that was emerging to provide a set of ground-rules for the relations among European governments might be better styled inter-imperial rather than inter-national law, because the major impetus for its creation were disputes about freedom of the seas and the right to trade with Asia and the Americas.[57] Yet, the terms empire and emperor were not employed officially, although the term imperial was used, at least by the English in official documents but with a particular meaning. What made these terms difficult to use in political discourse was the fact that they possessed several meanings, meanings freighted with historic connotations that aroused various feelings, often negative ones. In order to understand the difficulties, it is necessary to outline these various meanings, meanings that had developed during the Middle Ages and provided a basis for the political vocabulary of the early modern world.

(1) The *locus a quo* for any discussion of the medieval conception of empire was the imperial coronation of Charlemagne in 800. This act was linked to at least three conceptions of empire: Frankish, papal, East Roman. From the Frankish perspective, the coronation could reflect the importance of Charlemagne and the vastness of his conquests.

From the perspective of Pope Leo III (795–816), the coronation may have only meant that Charlemagne had become the protector of the papacy against its enemies in central Italy. From the perspective of the emperor who resided in Constantinople, the coronation raised the issue of whether there was one empire and one emperor or two empires and emperors. There was also the question of the relationship of Charlemagne's empire to that of Augustus and Constantine. Each of these issues emerged in subsequent discussions of the events of 800, with the different parties involved drawing different conclusions about the meaning of the coronation.

Subsequent discussion of the empire focused on the role of the papacy in the imperial coronation. Was the papal role constitutive, that is, did the pope's crowning of the candidate establish the emperor, or was the papal role only liturgical, like that, for example, of the archbishop of Canterbury in the coronation of the English king? Supporters of the papal conception argued that Leo III had transferred the empire from east to west because the function of the empire was the protection of the Church and its head. The theory of the *translatio imperii* defined the empire as an office within the Church with the emperor acting at the behest of the pope.

(2) The revival of Roman law in the eleventh and twelfth centuries provided yet another meaning for the term emperor because the Roman law contained the phrase 'the emperor is the lord of the world [*dominus mundi*]', a phrase that could be extended to justify a universal Roman imperial power without reference to the papacy or to Christianity. This definition of the emperor's role was obviously in stark contrast to the papacy's conception of the emperor as the pope's agent in administering the world.

(3) Along with the identification of the imperial office with the king of the Germans, beginning with Otto I (936–73) who received imperial coronation in 962 at the hands of Pope John XII (955–63), there gradually emerged a redefining of the nature of the empire. Frederick Barbarossa (1152–90) identified the empire as the *Sacrum Romanum Imperium*, the Sacred or Christian Roman Empire, clearly distinguishing it from the ancient pagan empire. During the fifteenth century a further specification appeared as the empire became the *Sacrum Romanum Imperium Nationis Teutonicae*, that is, the Holy Roman Empire of the German Nation.[58] This conception limited the empire to the territories ruled by the German monarch.

(4) Because the Romans had conquered various kingdoms in the course of their expansion, they employed the term *imperium* to mean rule over kingdoms, a usage that Isidore of Seville (c. 560–636) included in his *Etymologies*, making it thus available to medieval writers anxious to praise the rulers who employed them.[59] Various medieval rulers, kings in England and Spain for example, were occasionally referred to as emperors because they had conquered neighboring lands and brought them under their *imperium*.

(5) The notion of *imperium* also acquired a meaning approximating the modern term sovereignty. Kings were described as possessing within their kingdoms the kind of power that the emperor possessed in his empire, that is, a king was not subject to the jurisdiction of some higher secular ruler. This concept, interestingly enough, first appeared in a decretal of Pope Innocent III (1198–1216) when he explained why he would not interfere in a case that arose in France. Subsequently, this concept was extended to include exemption from papal jurisdiction as well. Henry VIII (1509–47) was to employ the term 'imperial' in this fashion when he explained why he and not the pope was the Supreme Head of the Church in England.

(6) One of the most famous of all discussions of the concept of empire appeared in Dante's (d. 1321) *Monarchia* where the poet offered the theory that a universal Christian empire was the logical

and necessary goal of humanity. In his view, however, it was the emperor and not the pope who stood at the apex of the Christian world, thus reversing the relationship between the spiritual and the temporal powers as popes and canon lawyers had defined them.

The conceptions of *imperium* and *imperator* outlined thus far were political in nature. That is, they dealt with various political structures and the relationship between spiritual and secular jurisdictions within Christian society. These terms could, however, be employed in other ways, ways that might be labeled moral or spiritual.

(7) In spiritual and theological circles, the term empire carried a significant eschatological meaning, referring to the series of four powerful empires that the Prophet Daniel described as agents of God's providential plan for mankind. It was possible to identify an emperor as the last in the line of world rulers whose reign would mark the beginning of the end of human history.

(8) Finally, the terms empire and emperor could have a moral connotation when used to refer to a tyrannical and corrupt form of government that destroyed the ancient Roman republican tradition. Many, although certainly not all, Renaissance humanists used these terms in this fashion, encouraging a conception of *imperium* and *imperator* that flourished in the modern world.[60]

All of these conceptions of empire flourished in the Middle Ages and were known to those involved in the development of early modern political thought. While no single medieval or early modern political thinker may have been conversant with all of these meanings of 'empire' and 'emperor', taken collectively these various meanings provided the basic vocabulary for early modern discussions of large-scale, even universal, governance. Like the term state, however, emperor and empire had several meanings that led to a great deal of confusion in early modern political thought.[61] The fact that state and empire represented the two political structures that were evolving in the period 1500–1800 made the confusion even worse.

One more factor shaped the early modern use of imperial language, the interest in the ancient world that characterized the Renaissance. This interest led to efforts to understand the Roman world in its historical context, an effort that eventually underscored the fact that the medieval understanding of the terms *imperium* and *imperator* was not identical with the Roman usage. When medieval writers used these terms, they did so in a context that was unlike that of the Roman world because medieval knowledge of the ancient world was limited. It is not even clear that medieval men realized the nature of the differences between their world and that of the ancients.[62] One anthropologist has argued that it was not until Renaissance humanists concluded that 'archaeological monuments could provide a more direct testimony of antiquity than the literary tradition' that Europeans became aware of the differences between themselves and their predecessors.[63] Only when Europeans could look at representations of ancient life did they realize that the ancients were different from themselves. Thus, when medieval writers discussed one of the various meanings attributed to *imperium* and related terms, they were doing so in ways that would not necessarily have been intelligible to the ancient Romans who first employed the term. In order to appreciate the medieval understanding of *imperium* and *imperator*, it is first necessary to understand what the Romans meant by these terms.

In the ancient Roman world, the term *imperium* meant power, specifically 'the legal power to enforce the law'.[64] The *fasces* that the lictors carried before the consuls on state occasions reminded all who saw them that the consuls bore the *imperium*, the power of life and death, over the citizens of the Republic. Thus, originally, *imperium* had no territorial connotation. The related term *imperator*, however, could include something of a territorial connotation because this title was granted to a successful general who had won a significant victory at a particular time and place.[65] That term obviously contained the possibility of a territorial identification as Roman generals conquered various peoples and brought their lands under Roman control.[66]

By the time of Augustus, as the Romans extended their sway over a wide array of peoples, *imperium* was coming to be understood in two ways. In the first place:

> The *imperium populi Romani* was the power Romans exercised over other peoples, viewed in its widest sense. What we call the Roman empire, that is the empire viewed as a political entity, was usually conceived by the Romans in terms of people, the *populus Romanus* and its *socii et amici*.[67]

By the time of Augustus, however, the Romans appear to have begun to understand *imperium* not only in terms of power over other people but also in a territorial sense to describe newly acquired lands, lands that had become 'subjected to the *imperium* of the Roman people'.[68]

Such use of *imperium* bridged the traditional use of the term and its modern use, that is, to describe specific territory or collection of territories. As Andrew Lintott has pointed out,

> the Romans also viewed their power as extended in space. The title of Augustus' official autobiography was *Res gestae divi Augusti quibus orbem terrarum imperio populi Romani subiecit* [The deeds of the Divine Augustus by means of which He Subjected the Entire World to the Power of the Roman People]. Thus for Augustus the Roman empire was not only the whole world controlled by Rome: it was equivalent to the world itself.[69]

This early development of the concept of *imperium* had to treat with care the sensibilities of the citizens of the Republic who despised the transformation of the Republic into the Augustan monarchy. These citizens, for whom Tacitus spoke, objected to the extension of Roman citizenship to provincials, thus blurring the distinction between the Romans and those whom they had conquered. The long-term result was the 'idea of an *Orbis Romanus* in which even this distinction of citizen and non-citizen is being effaced'.[70] They saw themselves as an imperial people whose collective *imperium* ruled over others in the sense of territorial conquest but who, themselves, were subject to the traditional republican conception of *imperium*. Only gradually did the descendants of the ancient Romans come to accept the notion that they too were subject to the *imperium* of an *imperator* in the modern sense, that is, to become a subjected people, not an imperial one.

The notion of *imperium* could, however, possess a positive meaning as well. For Virgil, although he did not employ the term *imperium* as such, the rule of the Romans over other peoples was an intrinsically good thing.

> Others, no doubt, will better mould the bronze
> To the semblance of soft breathing, draw, from marble,
> The living countenance; and others plead
> With greater eloquence, or learn to measure,
> Better than we, the pathways of the heaven,
> The rising of the stars: remember, Roman,
> To rule the people under law, to establish
> The way of peace, to battle down the haughty,
> To spare the meek. Our fine arts, these, forever.[71]

There is in these words a hint of what in the late nineteenth century would be called the 'White Man's Burden' defense of European expansion overseas, a moral or humanitarian justification for expansion and conquest. Thus, in the classical vocabulary, the term *imperium* contained several meanings that could then be employed according to the point that a writer wished to make. During the Renaissance, humanists who became fascinated with the work of Cicero, Livy, Tacitus, and so on revived these meanings of the term, often, but not always, following the lead of Livy and Tacitus in condemning empire and imperialism as sounding the death-knell of republicanism.[72] These classical Roman usages of *imperium* were not employed in Charlemagne's court where the praises of republican civic virtue would have been almost incomprehensible. Virgil's words in the *Aeneid*, however, were voiced occasionally by defenders of expansion in the early modern era and would not have been out of place at Charlemagne's court.[73]

The multiple meanings of *imperium* and *imperator* formed an important theme in the history of political thought from the eighth to the eighteenth centuries. The images of various emperors, from Augustus (27BC–AD14) to Charles V (1519–55), the conflicts between ecclesiastical and secular powers over the nature and role of the empire, the identification of imperial power with despotism and moral corruption, all these affected the ways in which early modern writers and officials understood what was meant by empire and emperor.

1 From the Carolingian Empire to the Holy Roman Empire of the German Nation

Charlemagne really came to Rome to restore the Church, which was in a very bad state indeed …. It was on this occasion that he received the title of Emperor and Augustus.[1]

The coronation of Charlemagne is not only the central event of the Middle Ages, it is also one of those very few events of which, taking them singly, it may be said that if they had not happened, the history of the world would have been different.[2]

Both the birth and the death dates of the medieval Empire are matters of unambiguous public record. From the day on which Pope Leo III (795–816) crowned Charlemagne (771–814), Christmas Day in the year 800, until 6 August 1806, when Napoleon's actions caused Charlemagne's final imperial successor, Francis II (1792–1806), to give up the imperial crown brought it to an end, there was a Roman Empire functioning in Western Europe.[3] The specificity with which we know its beginning and its end, however, is misleading. To say that Francis II surrendered Charlemagne's crown is to assume that his empire was the same as Charlemagne's.[4] Comparing maps showing the territorial extent of the two rulers' domains would quickly disabuse the observer of the belief that Charlemagne and Francis II ruled the same domain. While Charles's domains stretched south and west from their heartland along the Rhine, into Italy and Spain, Francis II's empire was centered on the Austrian lands that formed the base from which the Habsburgs pushed south and east. To the extent that Charlemagne had a capital, it was Aachen, Aix-la-Chapelle, in the Rhineland, while Prague and then Vienna served the Habsburgs as capitals as they pushed into southeastern Europe.

The shift of the medieval empire's center of territorial gravity from west to east in the course of its millennium of existence is only one of the problems involved in understanding the nature and significance of the concept of empire in medieval and early modern Europe. A second problem concerns the nature of its powers and jurisdiction. A third problem is the nature of the relationship between the emperor and the other rulers of Europe. A fourth problem, one rooted in the very act of creating the empire in 800, was the relationship between the emperor and the pope and, in a broad sense, the relationship of the emperor to the Christian Church and people as a whole. Finally, there was the problem of the relationship between the emperor in the West and the East Roman Emperor. Was the ruler at Constantinople the true Roman Emperor; or was he even an emperor at all, or, to use a term usually associated with the history of the papacy, was there an emperor and an anti-emperor?[5] In the final analysis, Charlemagne's coronation not only re-established the Empire in the West, it also raised a series of questions about the nature of empire and empires.

The events of 800 appear to have had different meanings for Charlemagne, Leo III, and their respective adherents as well as for the imperial court at Constantinople. Later observers, looking back at the coronation, understood it in different ways depending upon their political agendas. What to twentieth-century students appears to be the continuous evolution of imperial ideas and institutions from the ninth to the nineteenth centuries turns out, upon careful examination, to be much less coherent. Just as the crown that Francis II surrendered in 1806 was not actually that of Charlemagne, so too the empire he surrendered was not exactly that of Charlemagne or of Otto I (962–73) or of Charles V (1519–55), although it was clearly related to these earlier empires. To some extent, the imperial idea was a process that over the span of a thousand years became incarnated in a variety of institutional forms and that were understood in a variety of ways.

The territorial shifts that occurred in the course of the medieval empire's history were not, however, the first shifts of that sort. In fact, Charlemagne's empire could be said to have been the third Roman Empire, the first being the ancient *Imperium Romanum* and the second being the Empire whose head had resided at Constantinople since Constantine (311–37) moved his capital there in 330. Just as the nature of the medieval empire underwent a series of changes and transformations from 800 onward, so too it had already undergone a series of changes before Christmas Day 800. As Thomas Noble pointed out: 'It is wrong, certainly, to write and to interpret [the history of the empire] on the basis of a static, timeless conception of the imperial office. The imperial dignity assumed by the Carolingians was not exactly like any one that had preceded it and differed from all of those which followed.'[6] In order, therefore, to appreciate the history of the concept of empire after 800, it is first necessary to examine its development before 800.

At first glance, the coronation of Charlemagne in 800 was a simple and clear transaction, a scene carefully documented in contemporary sources. In fact, however, this clarity is misleading. Apparently, from the very moment of the coronation ceremony, the various participants interpreted it in different ways. If Einhard is to be believed, Charlemagne did not take the imperial coronation very seriously. Charlemagne, he wrote,

> made it clear that he would not have entered the cathedral that day at all ... if he had known in advance what the Pope was planning to do.[7]

On the other hand, there is also evidence to support the view that Charlemagne, Leo III (795–816), and the Roman people took it quite seriously, although understanding the situation in different ways.

Charlemagne's presence in Rome was the result of Leo III's request that the Frankish monarch resolve the dispute between the pope and a Roman faction that had imprisoned and tortured him.[8] When Pope Leo turned to the king of the Franks for assistance he was not initiating a new papal policy. From the mid-eighth century onward, the papacy was increasingly interested in seeking a rapprochement with the Carolingians, beginning with the first Carolingian monarch, Charlemagne's father, Pepin, who had ousted the last of the Merovingian kings around 750 with the assent of the pope.[9] Subsequently, Pepin intervened in Italian affairs on behalf of the papacy, serving as a protector against the Lombards.[10] Charlemagne followed in his father's footsteps, intervening in Italy to repress the enemies of the papacy before coming to Rome to settle the affairs of Leo III. During the last half of the eighth century, the King of the Franks was clearly becoming the recognized protector of the papacy.

According to the chronicler Notker, writing toward the end of the ninth century, Leo III had first asked the emperor at Constantinople, whom he identified as Michael I, to help him, but the emperor refused.[11] Only then did Leo turn to Charlemagne, 'the head of the world' according to Notker, for assistance.[12] Charlemagne came to Rome and settled the conflict between the pope and a faction of the Roman people in favor of Leo III. At mass on Christmas,

Pope Leo placed upon his head a crown and the whole Roman people acclaimed him: Life and victory to Charles, Augustus, crowned by God, the great and peaceful Emperor of the Romans! And after the laudation he was adored by the pope in the manner of ancient princes and instead of Patricius he was now titled Emperor and Augustus.[13]

The description of the events of 800 that the *Frankish Royal Annals* presented contained several puzzling elements.[14] In the first place, there was the role of the pope. As the annalist described the coronation, the pope placed a crown on Charlemagne's head and then prostrated himself before the emperor, a procedure that recalled the proskynesis that had became part of the imperial ritual in the reign of Diocletian and had remained part of the coronation ritual in Constantinople.[15] Furthermore, the pope appears to have acted only as an agent in the coronation, not as the possessor of a superior authority. A superior would not have prostrated himself before his inferior. Did the annalist believe that it was Charlemagne's great military achievements that justified his assumption of the imperial title? Was the pope only serving as the representative of the Roman people when he placed the crown on Charles's head? Indeed, the role of the Roman people as the annalist described it provided another puzzle. Were the people acclaiming Charles as a successful warrior in the manner of Roman warriors acclaiming their victorious general as *imperator*, or were they claiming the right to elect the emperor as their ruler?[16]

The picture of the pope representing the people who approved the act of coronation by acclamation suggests a scene from one of the older historians.[17] This version of the coronation in effect reversed at least one aspect of the later papal view of the right relationship between spiritual and temporal leaders, that is, who prostrates himself before whom, demonstrating who is the superior and who is the inferior. Earlier, in 754, at the beginning of the close relationship between the pope and the Frankish monarchs, Pepin, father of Charlemagne, met Pope Stephen II (752–57) at Ponthion. Describing the meeting, the pope's biographer in 'a symbolic detail … tells us that Pippin, after dismounting from his horse, threw himself on the ground and then performed the service of a "strator" to the pope' leading his horse a short distance.[18] While the term proskynesis was not employed, the writer would appear to have been suggesting it, a conclusion supported by the subsequent act of leading the pope's horse.[19] Both actions demonstrate the ruler's ceremonial deference to the pope.

From Charlemagne's perspective, the coronation in 800 may well have been only a recognition of his power in Italian affairs and in western Europe generally. By this time, however, his career as a conqueror was at its peak. He had extended Carolingian power further into central Europe with the conquest of the Saxons and Bavarians, successfully assaulted the great Avar camp on the Danube in 795 and 796, seized the massive treasure they had acquired over decades of war.[20] In addition, he had assumed the title of King of the Lombards to end the Lombard threat in central Italy.[21] By his involvement in Italian affairs, Charlemagne was also demonstrating his power in a region where, in theory at least, the emperor at Constantinople should have been active, but was not. The expansion of the Carolingians into Italy in the last half of the eighth century filled the vacuum created by the withdrawal of East Roman imperial power. In 751 the Lombards conquered the Exarchate of Ravenna, forcing the withdrawal of the last remnants of imperial government from Ravenna, thus all but ending any imperial role in Italy.[22] As a result of these successes, Carolingian chroniclers portrayed Charlemagne as a powerful, energetic ruler, very unlike his Merovingian predecessors. Einhard, for example, portrayed the Merovingians as weak rulers who deserved to have lost their throne to the Carolingians.[23] Subsequently the last Merovingian ruler, Childeric III, came to symbolize powerless rulers, those who bore a royal title but who did not exercise any real power.[24]

Charlemagne's actions after his imperial coronation do not clarify for us his understanding of that event. For example, he may well only have seen it as a sign of his power and extensive territorial possessions in western Europe. Even as emperor, he did not identify himself with Rome but with the traditional Frankish heartland, building a church and a palace at Aachen with materials brought from Italy, especially Ravenna, an act that in some ways reflected the *translatio imperii*, the transfer of the empire from Constantinople to the west.[25] Apparently, he also dressed in imperial fashion on two occasions. According to Einhard, although Charles 'hated the clothes of other countries', on two occasions, at the behest of popes, he 'put on a long tunic and a Greek mantle, and ... [wore] shoes made in the Roman fashion'.[26]

Charlemagne's official documents used imperial language but in such a way as to obscure what he – or the clerks who drew up the documents – meant by this language.[27] Beginning in 801, his official documents were headed 'Charles, crowned by God most serene, august, great, peaceful emperor, ruling the Roman Empire and who is by the mercy of God king of the Franks and Lombards'.[28] In the opinion of

Thomas Noble, this formula suggests that 'Charlemagne's empire, and his imperial office, were Christian and Frankish. Charlemagne did not see himself as a Roman emperor, and he in no way imagined himself to be a successor to or a replacement for the Byzantine emperors.'[29] Noble also pointed out that the terminology traced Charlemagne's title directly to God and made no mention of any papal role in the process. Indeed, the language placed the Roman empire and, therefore, its people under Charles's imperial rule, removing them from any role in his selection as emperor. He even appears to have equated the Romans with the Franks and Lombards over whom he reigned, suggesting that there was nothing special about ruling the Romans. Furthermore, it is also noteworthy that the title specifies no particular territories that Charlemagne ruled, only peoples. It may well be, as Folz has argued, that Charlemagne's conception of empire was far broader than any traditional Roman imperial vision because 'it was, above all, a religious vision of the world', the 'Christian Empire'.[30] That Charlemagne saw matters so clearly is, however, open to question.

It should also be mentioned, however, that Charlemagne may have downplayed the traditional imperial trappings because he realized that this role antagonized the emperors at Constantinople. Einhard and Notker claim that Charlemagne was aware of the antagonism of the East Roman rulers to his new title and was sensitive to it.[31]

To the extent that Charlemagne's empire was conceived of as a Christian empire, however, it posed a problem for the independence of the empire from the Church. To at least some learned clerics at the Frankish and at the papal court, the coronation of Charlemagne was of great significance, the final step in a process by which several popes identified the Frankish king with the Christian Roman Emperors in such a way as to bring the King of the Franks under some form of papal control and to have him serve as the papacy's protector.[32] The need for a protector had been apparent to the papacy for some centuries as the eastern emperors gradually withdrew their forces from western Europe.

Charlemagne's plans for providing thrones for each of his three legitimate sons offer some suggestions about how he understood the empire. The first plan, a capitulary of 806, divided up his domains in such a way as to give each son a kingdom. The capitulary referred in several places to the '*regnum*' and the '*imperium*', but in terms of the division specifically mentioned only the *regnum*. The *regnum* was a single unit, subdivided into three portions (*sed trina portione totum regni corpus dividentes*), and the three brothers were admonished to work together in 'peace and charity'.[33] Charlemagne made no special provision for the transmission of the imperial title and office.[34] The language of the capitulary suggests that when Charlemagne spoke of the totality of his possessions, he used the terms kingdom and empire, suggesting that taken together the lands of his sons formed a single unit, a kingdom and yet more than a kingdom, an empire.[35] When referring to the lands awarded to each of his sons, however, he always used the term *regnum* alone. Furthermore, Charlemagne did not distinguish the status of any one of sons in this division. The three sons were in a sense three royal co-rulers of the Carolingian empire.

The plan outlined in the capitulary of 806 echoed earlier Merovingian succession practice, at least to the extent that it provided for several heirs and several kingdoms working cooperatively within the framework of a single society. In acting as he did, Charlemagne was following the 'Frankish custom of dividing up the kingdom among the surviving throneworthy sons', a long-standing practice.[36] At this stage, Charlemagne seems to have had no hesitation in referring to the lands that he was passing on to his sons as an empire, yet he appears hesitant to identify an emperor. This may have been because he saw the imperial title he had been awarded in 800 as a personal one and not an office or title to be passed on to one of his sons. Furthermore, the plan of 806 did not assign responsibility for the protection of the papacy to any of his heirs. Timothy Reuter has suggested that he saw them acting jointly to protect the papacy, a view linked to the fact that each of the heirs 'had control of an Alpine pass into Italy', presumably to insure rapid response in the event of a crisis in Italy.[37]

The premature deaths of two of Charlemagne's three sons meant that all of his possessions would devolve to the survivor, Louis the Pious. In 813, 'when old age and illness were already weighing heavily upon him', Charlemagne convened the great men of his kingdom and, according to Einhard,

> with the agreement of all who attended … gave Lewis a half-share in his kingship and made him heir to the imperial title. He placed the crown on Lewis' head and ordered that he should be called Emperor and Augustus.[38]

This scene suggests that Charlemagne saw the imperial title as something associated with the rulership of the Franks. Furthermore, both of his actions regarding Louis the Pious required the 'agreement' of the great men of the kingdom, suggesting that the Franks and not the Romans were now the imperial people.[39]

One group that was clearly missing in Charlemagne's settlement of the succession in 806 and 813 was the clergy. Neither the papacy nor the Frankish clergy played any role in the disposition of the empire or in the selection of the emperor. While the empire was a Christian one in that it involved the protection of the Church, especially in Italy following the example of Charlemagne and his father, such intervention was to be done as the rulers saw fit, not as the pope ordered.[40] Charlemagne clearly did not see the imperial office as an office whose occupant acted at papal direction.

During the reign of Louis the Pious (814–40), the links between the papacy and the empire reappeared. In 816, Pope Stephen IV (816–17) traveled to Rheims where he recrowned and consecrated Louis the Pious as emperor, thus reasserting a papal role in the appointment of the emperor. Louis even prostrated himself before the pope in imitation of the proskynesis, the act of prostration before the emperor, and then led his horse as papal *strator*, suggesting some form of subordination to the pope.[41] The scene was a reflection of his grandfather Pepin's relation to the pope, not Charlemagne's. The pope was clearly seeking to clarify the role of the emperor in the government of the papal lands in central Italy.[42] Pope Stephen's actions, however, did not change Louis's status, although it 'enhanced the Christian characteristics of the office conferred upon him by his father)'.[43]

The re-coronation of Louis the Pious enhanced the Carolingian conception of empire. For the Carolingians, the imperial title identified a powerful ruler and could be claimed by any ruler who demonstrated unquestioned superiority over the other rulers around him. As Charlemagne emphasized in his documents, the title came from God (*per misericordiam Dei*), not from the Church or the pope. Furthermore, as he noted in the selection process that led to Louis the Pious being associated with him in imperial status, he sought the agreement of the Frankish nobles, not that of the Roman people. At the same time, the emperor possessed a Christian character with the responsibility of protecting the Church, especially the papacy, and thus the people of central Italy.

Subsequently, like Charlemagne, Louis the Pious issued two capitularies that assigned kingdoms to each of his sons, a process that eventually led to civil war as the three sons of his first marriage objected to Louis's attempt to provide a kingdom for his fourth son, the child of his second marriage.[44] The capitularies of 817 and 831 reflect Charlemagne's capitularies of 806 and 813. The most important element is that the Frankish ruler, in conjunction with the leading men of the kingdom, had the responsibility for determining the succession. In 813, Louis reaffirmed the fundamental unity of the Frankish lands, the empire, while providing for each of his sons a kingdom of his own. In addition, Louis named his oldest son, Lothair (840–55), as his co-emperor and successor.[45]

The revised succession plan of 831, necessitated by the birth of a son to Louis's second wife, Judith, led to a vicious civil war as the members of the Carolingian family battled for what each believed to be his rightful share of the inheritance.[46] From the perspective of the Carolingian concept of empire, however, the conflict only reinforced the view that the empire was theirs to dispose of as they saw fit. In 833 the rebels brought 'Pope Gregory IV from Italy to stiffen the faint-hearts' and finally deposed Louis 'in an episcopally staged ritual'.[47] Louis subsequently recouped his office, punished the rebels, and arranged for the succession. The important point here is that while churchmen, even the pope, were involved in the conflict and deposition, they played a role subordinate to the roles that Louis and his enemies played. They blessed the emperor, but they did not create – or depose – him. Furthermore, papal interest in the Carolingians lay in the ability of the Frankish rulers to protect the papal lands in Italy, not in their conquests elsewhere.

For the Carolingians, emperor was a title of honor that added nothing to their power or territories. At most, the imperial title provided some responsibilities, such as the protection of the papacy. The empire had no governmental infrastructure. It lacked any real institutional infrastructure to hold it together. Charlemagne may have had some conception of the need for such structure and instituted the *missi dominici* to audit the administration of justice, ecclesiastical affairs, royal revenues and so on.[48] Nevertheless, the vast extent of the territories involved precluded any centralized imperial government.

If Charlemagne and Leo III had intended to recreate in some fashion the ancient Roman Empire, they failed. A glance at the territories involved makes it quite clear that Charlemagne's empire had little relation to the empire of Augustus. It might be argued, however, that, from the papal perspective, the concept of *imperium* that undergirded the Carolingian empire was the Roman notion of *imperium* as power or jurisdiction in a non-territorial sense. This *imperium* was

now understood in a Christian sense, echoing Virgil's conception of
the mission of the original Roman *imperium*. Charlemagne's intellectual and cultural advisor, the Anglo-Saxon scholar Alcuin, once wrote
to his master, quoting Virgil by way of St Augustine's *City of God* that
it was the responsibility of the good ruler 'to spare the weak, to bring
down the proud'.[49] Werner Ohnsorge has pointed out that 'In the
hymns and the prayers of the West the "Imperium Christianum" took
the place of the "Imperium Romanum" after the fall of the Western
Roman Empire.'[50]

Although the imperial title survived among Charlemagne's descendants, it was an ever more limited one, a virtual ghost of the power
that the term was supposed to reflect. Furthermore, the descendants
of Charlemagne and Louis the Pious fought among themselves for
control of parts of the Carolingian inheritance as their ancestral lands
were confronting Viking, Muslim and Hungarian threats along the
borders of the Carolingian world. The several treaties, Strasbourg
(842), Verdun (843), Mersen (870), that proposed to define the relations among the descendants of Charlemagne and Louis the Pious
describe an empire that was fading rapidly into political irrelevance.[51]
Rosamund McKitterick summed up the situation of Louis the Pious's
sons this way: 'The position of Emperor became a nominal overlordship with real responsibilities in Italy and in relation to the papacy,
but with little power in the Frankish kingdoms apart from his own.'[52]
The empire of Charlemagne became less a political reality and more a
vision of political order. In the century following the death of Louis
the Pious, a series of weak Carolingian rulers bore the imperial title,
seeing it as a family inheritance.[53] The rulers of the Middle Kingdom
retained the imperial title and the mission of protecting the papacy
from its enemies in Italy.[54] In effect, the scope of the empire was
reduced from being coterminous with Christian society to being the
defender of a relatively small area of central Italy.

The notion of empire might have faded into disuse or acquired a
more limited meaning if a series of German emperors had not revived
it in the tenth century. It is important to realize that although the
history of the empire from 800 to 1806 appears to be a relatively
straightforward, indeed linear, development, in fact it was not. The
empire was revived – or reinvented – several times in its career. Each
of these imperial revivals, although rooted in an imperial tradition,
created a somewhat different concept of empire than had existed previously. Rather than being linear, the concept of empire is a series of
interrelated layers, like geological strata.[55]

In the mid-tenth century, the Ottonian kings of Germany acquired the imperial crown and title that the Carolingians had worn, beginning the identification of the imperial title with the king of the Germans, a connection that lasted until 1806. For Otto of Freising (c. 1114–58), member of the Hohenstaufen family of emperors and chronicler of the Christian empire of the twelfth century, the decline and fall of the Carolingians was only another sign that 'it is clear that no trust is ever to be reposed in powers that are doomed to perish .... Accordingly, since all the kingdoms of the earth have suffered overthrow, and since even the kingdom of the Franks, who were the last that were privileged to possess Rome, was, as we shall see, diminished from the time it was divided ...'.[56] Otto's elegy suggests that the *translatio imperii* was a continuing process as one empire succeeded another in a continuing series of imperial risings and fallings.[57]

At the death of Louis the Child (900–11), the last Carolingian ruler of the German kingdom that Charlemagne's grandsons had created in 843, the German nobles elected a king who was not a Carolingian, Conrad I (911–18). Conrad in turn designated the Duke of Saxony as his successor, an action that led to his coronation as Henry I (918–36). Although the names of both rulers are often given in textbook lists of medieval emperors and Henry I was termed emperor by some chroniclers, neither Conrad nor Henry ever went to Rome to be crowned emperor by the pope, nor did they play any role in papal politics.[58] In these years, up until 962, a series of Italian nobles acquired the imperial title from the hands of various popes anxious about the security of their lands.

The imperial status attributed to Henry I stemmed from his military role, as the leader of the Germans against their enemies, not from any ecclesiastical ceremony. Henry was the leader of the Germans, ruler over lesser kingdoms, successful in battle, so that he became identified with the *imperator* of the Roman tradition, the successful general acclaimed by his troops. If this practice had continued, the imperial title might have drifted out of use or been used in a generic sense, that is to identify rulers of large kingdoms that contained a multitude of lesser principalities and even smaller kingdoms.[59] This did not happen, however, because a line of tenth-century German kings chose to play an imperial role modeled on Charlemagne.

The key figure in the revival of the imperial title and the kind of mission that Charlemagne's use of the term implied was Otto I (936–73; emperor 962). The first significant use of the term *imperator* in his reign came with his victory over the Magyars at Lechfeld in 955. A contemporary chronicler, Widukind (b. c. 925), who reported on this victory, declared that at the end of the battle, Otto's troops acclaimed him. 'Honored in a great triumph, the King was hailed by his army as emperor and father of his country.'[60] Here again, the term *imperator* appears in the ancient Roman sense of the word, perhaps saying more about the chronicler's education than it does about that of Otto's troops. The acclamation by the soldiers also echoes the Roman people's acclamation of Charlemagne. Nevertheless the chronicler reflects the Ottonian view of their role in the political world of tenth-century Europe.

Perhaps linked to Widukind's identification of Otto I as an *imperator* acclaimed by his troops, was an occasional reference to the Ottonians as emperors by virtue of ruling three kingdoms, Germany, Italy and Burgundy.[61] This use of the imperial title was also found elsewhere in the tenth to the twelfth centuries as chroniclers and officials struggled to develop a vocabulary to describe the kinds of political units that were emerging in western Europe.[62]

Even before Otto I had defeated the Magyars at Lechfeld, he had intervened in Italian affairs in a fashion similar to that of Charlemagne. In 951–2 he attempted to stabilize the chaotic political situation in Italy, married Adelaide of Burgundy, widow of Lothar II, the King of Italy, and declared himself King of Italy. He also desired imperial coronation, but the pope, Agapetus II (946–55), refused the request.[63] Then, in a series of events that was to be repeated throughout the Middle Ages and on into the sixteenth century, Otto was forced from Italy. Although his intervention was initially welcome to many of the higher clergy and nobles of Italy, his continued presence was not. In addition, while Otto was in Italy, his son Liudolf plotted against him, necessitating his return to Germany. Only in 962, after another expedition to Italy, did Otto receive imperial coronation.[64]

In many ways, when later observers discussed the medieval empire, while they may have identified it with Charlemagne's empire, in fact they usually described the Ottonian empire. There are at least two fundamental differences between the Carolingian and the Ottonian conceptions of empire. In the first place, although Charlemagne himself received the imperial title from the hands of the pope in Rome, he crowned Louis the Pious as his successor, indicating that in his opinion there was no need for the pope to officiate at an imperial coronation.[65] From Otto I until the sixteenth century, however, papal coronation was considered essential to possession of the imperial title.[66] The emperor was only emperor-elect until the pope placed the crown on his head.[67]

In the second place, the Ottonian empire differed from that of Charlemagne in that the Ottonians were far more concerned with Italy than the Frankish emperor had been. As Geoffrey Barraclough pointed out many years ago, rather than following the example of Charlemagne, Otto I appears to have followed that of Lothar I (840–55) 'who combined the imperial title with rule over the Middle kingdom', that is, the land that stretched from the North Sea to Central Italy, the least viable of the three kingdoms that Louis the Pious had created for his sons.[68] Subsequently, historians, especially German nationalist historians, were to condemn the imperial policy of the medieval German monarchs for blocking what they perceived to be the natural course of German political development toward the creation of a German state [in the modern use of that term]. From that perspective, the victory of the imperial idea over the idea of the state in Germany in the sixteenth and seventeenth centuries delayed the creation of a German state until 1871.[69] Such opinions, however, reflect modern conceptions of government and politics, not medieval ones.

Like the empire under Charlemagne, the Ottonian empire was expansionist, but not in the same directions. It aimed east and south, into the Slavic lands and toward Constantinople. The creation of the archdiocese of Magdeburg in 962 was a symbol of Otto's eastward push. All dioceses subsequently created in the east would be subject to Magdeburg, with the corollary that the lands involved would be subject to German imperial overlordship.[70]

Otto also sought a rapprochement with the emperor at Constantinople by marrying his son and heir, the future Otto II (973–83), to Theophano, a member of the East Roman imperial family.[71] What might have eventuated from this marriage, perhaps a joint empire of some sort, is unknown because of the early deaths of Otto II and of his son, Otto III (983–1002). The brief career of Otto III suggests that the Ottonians might have emulated Carolingian practice, that is subordinating the papacy, and the Church, to the empire. Friedrich Heer has argued that:

Otto III saw Rome as the *urbs regia*, the city of the emperors, and not as the city of the popes .... The popes, he declared, had first squandered the property of the Roman Church and then tried to replenish it by robbing the Emperor.[72]

Otto III's vision of the future may be contained in the motto he chose to adorn his official seal: *Renovatio imperii Romanorum*.

Some scholars have argued that these words contain a vision of a great empire.

> Otto III realized that a Europe conceived as a religious-political union of peoples and as a zone wide open to movements of intellectual and spiritual reform needed a staunch and trustworthy head. This could be none other than the Roman pontiff .... The Ottonian conception of the imperial office entailed raising the papacy from its provincial narrowness and corruption to a position of European esteem.[73]

Even if this was true, and even if Otto III could have overcome the numerous obstacles to the achievement of such a vision, he would not have recreated the Roman Empire, that is, he would not have recreated the essentially Mediterranean empire of the Romans. Furthermore, the goal suggested here was not an empire based solely on conquest and maintained by force but, ultimately, a federation of Christian societies under the leadership of the Emperor. There is, however, no evidence that anyone but some German officials and intellectuals ever supported such a program. The rulers of the emerging kingdoms of Europe did not see themselves in such terms.

The deaths of Otto II and Otto III prevented any extended development of a concept of empire that was specifically Ottonian. It is also clear that by the death of Otto III, a single concept of empire had not emerged. Instead, the Carolingian and Ottonian eras had contributed to the development of several themes that could contribute to a general theory of empire.

In the Ottonian era, like the Carolingian, the concept of empire had several meanings. In the first place, the Ottonians were Roman emperors because they claimed rule over the city of Rome, the seat of the ancient emperor. In the second place, they were emperors because they were kings 'over many peoples', a role that 'called for some visible expression and recognition', as Karl Leyser phrased it.[74] They were also emperors because of their heroic victories over the enemies of Christendom. Finally, they led the *Imperium Romanum* in some vague association with Christian society as a whole or, as Friedrich Heer has phrased it, '*Imperium Romanum* = *Imperium Christianum*, that is to say European Christendom.'[75] This last was especially identified with their role as the protectors of the papacy. In practice, however, the real power base of the Ottonians lay in their family lands and in the German kingship.

Had Otto II and Otto III lived and reigned for a longer span of time, it is possible that the Ottonians would have been able to achieve at least some of their imperial goals, although not the grandiose one of a universal Christian empire attributed to them. The Ottonian conception of empire was a narrower one than the Carolingian, large territorially perhaps but not universal, not co-terminous with Latin Christendom.[76]

The Carolingian and Ottonian concepts of empire involved a recognition that certain rulers were unusually powerful and played a dominant – or hegemonic – role in the Latin West. These conceptions of empire, however, were also associated with possession of or jurisdiction over Italy, especially the city of Rome. To that extent, these conceptions of empire were also linked to a weak papacy that depended upon strong secular rulers to protect it from predatory neighbors. Given the condition of Rome in the times of Charlemagne and Otto I, it is also easy to see how the secular protectors of the papacy became its masters in the eleventh century, as a series of German king-emperors imposed a line of reforming popes on the people of Rome, this time not saving the papacy from enemies from without but from those within. In the first half of the eleventh century, most dramatically in the reign of Henry III (1039–56), Church reform was imposed upon the Roman pontiffs. In forcing the removal of bad popes and the election of reforming ones, the Salian emperors were extending the role that Charlemagne and Otto I had played in the leadership of the Church.

One unforeseen consequence of the German-sponsored reform movement was that the reformed popes and their supporters came to conclude that secular involvement in ecclesiastical matters, especially in the appointment of the higher clergy, was itself a major cause of ecclesiastical corruption.This in turn led to the investiture controversy in which, from about 1050 to 1215, popes, emperors, and their advisors and partisans battled over the nature of the relationship between the spiritual and the temporal powers in Christian society.[77] The conflict was one of the first political struggles to generate an extensive polemical literature as each party sought to explain its position and to win support for it from among the those who were undecided.

As a result of this conflict there emerged two conflicting concepts of empire, one associated with the German emperors, the other developed by the papacy and the canon lawyers. From the German perspective, following loosely in the steps of Charlemagne and Otto I, the papacy was under the protection of the emperor. While the pope might crown the emperor, this coronation did not constitute the emperor, because his status was derived from God and from the German princes who elected him king of the Germans. Indeed, it was the emperor who was in the final analysis God's chosen leader of Christian society, judge even of the pope.

Perhaps the most forceful statement of the emperor's superior role in Christian society appeared in 1076 when the emperor-elect, Henry IV (1056–1106), responded to a letter in which Pope Gregory VII (1073–85) criticized him for his treatment of the church in his lands. Henry's answer was an attack on Gregory and on his conception of the relationship of the pope to secular rulers. He began by contrasting the ways in which he and Gregory obtained the offices they occupied. Henry was 'King ... by the pious ordination of God', while Gregory had become pope 'by usurpation' and was a 'false monk'. Gregory had 'dared to threaten to take the kingship away from us – as though we had received the kingship from you, as though kingship and empire were in your hand and not in the hand of God'. In Henry's view, he had 'been anointed to kingship among the anointed' and 'am to be judged by God alone unless ... I should deviate from the Faith'. Furthermore, Gregory's actions were upsetting the social order, because he had 'armed subjects against their prelates'. In effect, Henry was accusing Gregory of turning the world upside down, seeking to place himself at the head of Christian society in the place of God's chosen agent. The concluding words of the king's letter demonstrated his seriousness of purpose and his conception of his role in Christian society: 'I, Henry, King by the grace of God, together with all our bishops, say to you: Descend! Descend!'[78]

As we will see in Chapter 3, Henry IV was correct in seeing Gregory VII's position as a threat to one traditional view of the relationship between the pope and the emperor. During the investiture controversy a line of popes, lawyers, and polemicists developed a theory of papal–imperial relations that would in fact reverse the nature of the relationship, placing the pope in the superior position. When Gregory ordered Henry deposed in February 1076, he was asserting a kind of power over secular rulers that Henry III had exercised over popes a generation earlier.

At this point, however, the nature of the papal–imperial relationship was not fully clarified. Gregory had ordered Henry deposed from his German kingship but not from the imperial office, because at that point he had not been consecrated by the pope.[79] Henry's position did not make an absolute distinction between the royal and the imperial offices. He appears to have taken for granted that as the elected king of the Germans he would also become emperor whether or not Gregory VII approved. Furthermore, according to Henry's argument, Gregory had no constitutive role in the selection of a king or emperor and therefore no power to depose him unless he embraced heresy.[80]

Although some aspects of the Investiture Controversy were resolved by the Concordat of Worms in 1122, the question of the nature of the relation of the pope to the emperor, particularly with regard to the significance of the imperial coronation ceremony, was not resolved. The emperors of the twelfth century continued to see their election as king as the basis for their assuming the imperial office and that the papal role was liturgical, not constitutive. Furthermore, as the papacy continued to develop its theory of empire, so too supporters of the German monarchs continued to counter with their own theories.

The reigns of three Hohenstaufen emperors, Frederick I Barbarossa (1152–90), Henry VI (1190–97), and Frederick II (1212–50) brought the medieval imperial ideal to its fullest development. Here again, however, while the language and images of empire that the Hohenstaufen employed were traditional, they not only added to the vocabulary of empire, they reasserted the German presence in Italy, and they also reasserted the universal imperial claims. The imperial vision of the Hohenstaufen was much larger than that of the Salians or even the Ottonians.

The most important symbolic gesture of the Hohenstaufen era was the use of the phrase 'The Holy Empire (*sacrum imperium*)' to identify the Empire, a phrase that became 'a standard formula' in the reign of Barbarossa.[81] This term identified the empire as a sacral institution parallel with the Holy Church, reinforcing its independence from the kind of ecclesiastical jurisdiction that papal claims to judge kings and emperors asserted: the Holy Roman Empire and the Holy Roman Church were jointly at the head of Christian society.

Furthermore, Barbarossa and those in his circle also asserted imperial superiority over the kings of Europe. 'The writings of the period occasionally use the words "petty kings" (*reguli*) and "kings of the provinces (*reges provinciarum*)" for the other rulers of Europe.'[82] The hegemonic claims contained in these words, while generally ignored by those to whom they were directed, nevertheless do reflect the outlook of Barbarossa.

One arena in which the Hohenstaufen might have implemented a policy of hegemony over the kings of Europe, or at least some kind of leadership, was in the crusade. What better way to demonstrate the emperor's role as defender of the Church and of Christendom than to lead the assembled armies of Europe under the command of their respective rulers, the lesser monarchs, the kings of the various provinces of Christian Europe? In fact, of course, the 'older western idea of a Christian *imperium* under an emperor gave way to a system of international politics in which the individual countries simply pursued their own egotistical ends'.[83] Frederick I and his grandson, Frederick II, led crusades but did not do so in their capacity as the unchallenged leaders of Christian Europe, but as leaders of their own lands.

In terms of their relationship with the papacy, the Hohenstaufen, like Charlemagne and like the Ottonians, saw their possession of the empire as being independent of the papacy. This did not mean that the emperor was not to receive the imperial crown at the pope's hands, but it did mean that the papal action did not create the emperor but only confirmed in office the candidate for the imperial throne whom the German princes, representing the new imperial people, had selected. The Hohenstaufen conception of empire was clearly illustrated in the name originally selected for the future Frederick II, Constantine, 'a programmatic name that would have proclaimed to all the world both his father's Norman aspirations and his imperial Roman belief and general intentions'.[84]

Barbarossa had more dramatically stated his view of the nature of the empire when meeting with representatives of the pope, Adrian IV, at Besançon in 1157. In a famous scene that Frederick's uncle, Otto of Freising, described at length, Barbarossa took great offence at a letter from the pope that seemed to suggest that Barbarossa held the Kingdom of Italy and the imperial title as fiefs from the pope. The significance of the letter lay in the meaning of the term *beneficium* that the pope used to describe 'what great dignity and honor she [the Church] bestowed upon you, and with how much pleasure she conferred the emblem of the imperial crown' upon Barbarossa in 1155.[85] The term was ambiguous, and while the pope later claimed that he only meant to say that the papacy had performed a good deed in crowning Frederick, the German nobles assembled there understood the term in a different sense.[86]

To the German nobles, however, the term *beneficium* meant fief, so that they understood Adrian IV to have labeled the empire a fief of the papacy. According to Otto of Freising, they shouted their anger and dismay at such a conception of the empire. Their wrath reached its height when 'one of the [papal] ambassadors ... inquired: "From whom then does he have the empire, if not from our lord the pope?"', a response that nearly caused the ambassador's death.[87]

Barbarossa took advantage of the opportunity that the tumult raised to circularize the German bishops in two letters, outlining his conception of the empire, a conception that echoed Carolingian and Ottonian conceptions of empire but not the papal. The first letter began with a forthright statement of the divine origin of his imperial title: 'the Divine Sovereignty ... has entrusted unto us, His anointed, the kingdom and the empire to rule over ...'. Frederick asserted that 'through election by the princes, the kingdom and the empire are ours from God alone'. Barbarossa even pointed to the great age of the empire 'which has stood, glorious and undiminished, from the founding of the City [Rome] and the establishment of the Christian religion' and was therefore older than the Church itself.[88]

In the second letter, of October 1158, several months later, Barbarossa restated his earlier position on the source of his power, royal and imperial. 'The free crown of the empire we ascribe solely to the divine beneficence [*beneficium*].' This 'beneficence' came to him through election by the nobles. The papal role, 'the final anointing, as emperor, indeed pertains to the supreme pontiff', but this comes only after his election as king and his royal anointing which is 'the prerogative of the archbishop of Cologne'. The implication of Barbarossa's discussion of the papal role in the imperial coronation was that his role was not constitutive any more than the archbishop of Cologne's role in the royal coronation was constitutive.[89]

The controversy at Besançon provided an opportunity for both Adrian IV and Barbarossa to define the nature of the empire and the relationship between the empire and the papacy. In the face of the emperor's forceful assertion of the autonomy of the imperial office, the pope had little choice other than to retreat from any suggestion that the empire was a papal fief. At the same time, the emperor did not reject outright any papal role in the imperial coronation, something he had done when some of the Roman people, claiming to be the Roman Senate, asserted their right to elect the emperor. He did not claim, for example, that he, like Charlemagne, could crown an emperor. The events at Besançon and the series of letters that followed were stages in the development of theories of empire, German and papal, but these letters indicate that neither party as yet possessed a fully developed theory of empire.

The reign of Barbarossa did see the emergence of a basis for a fuller theory of empire, one that did not rest on divine or ecclesiastical origins. The revival of Roman law in the eleventh and twelfth centuries, part of the classical revival of the twelfth century, enabled Roman lawyers in the service of the German monarchs to develop a concept of empire that could stand against the ecclesiastical model.[90] The Hohenstaufen use of ancient Roman language and law was part of a trend toward reviving ancient political and legal forms in the twelfth century. In Italy, for example, a number of cities overthrew ecclesiastical rulers and created – or claimed to recreate – the ancient city-state form of government.

In 1155 the leaders of the rebel government of Rome, styling themselves the *Senatus populusque Romanus*, asserted two goals, "'renewal of the holy Senate'" and "'restoration of the Roman Empire'".[91] The latter aim led to the assertion that they had the right to crown the Roman emperor, a claim that generated an insulting letter from Barbarossa. Frederick poured scorn on a small group of people who called upon the Germans to protect them from their enemies and who then had the presumption to insist that they and they alone elected the emperor. The people who made this claim were characterized by 'misery ... frailty ... weakness ... anxiety', hardly the qualities of an imperial people. Frederick went on to justify his possession of the imperial title in the bluntest of terms: 'I am the lawful possessor. Let him who can, snatch the club from the hand of Hercules ...'.[92] Frederick's title needed no senatorial or, presumably, ecclesiastical blessing. It was his by right of conquest as had been the case for the ancient emperors.

At the same time, however, Frederick's court circle contained lawyers trained in the revived Roman law, a law that contained language out of which they could construct a theory of empire to counter the ecclesiastical concept of empire that placed the empire and the emperor under papal jurisdiction. The key phrase in Roman law on the imperial office was the *lex regia*, the law that traced the imperial office to the transfer of *imperium* from the people to the emperor. 'Within the corpus of Roman law, the *lex regia* referred only to the emperor's legislative authority ... but ... twelfth-century thinkers readily interpreted *lex regia* as a general statement on the emperor's entire prerogative.'[93] The attempt by the rebellious Romans to use this principle of Roman law as a basis for asserting a claim to select the emperor was, at best, naive, but the employment of Roman law in defense of the imperial title and power was to have a long life.

One of the most famous scenes in the intellectual history of the twelfth century was the meeting between Frederick Barbarossa and the four leading professors of Roman law, a meeting that took place as he was on his way to Rome to receive imperial coronation in 1155. This meeting suggests that he planned to have 'close links to the chief representatives of the new jurisprudence'.[94] In 1158 he followed up this meeting with an assembly at Roncaglia where he and his imperial office were described in terms from Roman law, terms that included references to the *lex regia* and to the emperor as '"the living law"', and political claims such as 'all jurisdiction derives from the emperor'.[95]

The Roman lawyers who served Barbarossa also knew well that Roman law termed the emperor 'the Lord of the World (*dominus mundi*)', a phrase that gave rise to another famous scene, one in which Frederick asked two of the famous lawyers he met at Roncaglia whether he was indeed universal lord.[96] Although one of the lawyers agreed that Frederick was 'lord of the world' with regard to property, the answer that Frederick preferred, even the other lawyer, who denied this power, assumed that there was 'a sovereign with universal jurisdiction based on a universal system of law'.[97]

Barbarossa's long reign might have made it possible to create a powerful imperial presence in western Europe combining as he did, military strength and an intellectual rationale for the empire. Furthermore, by arranging for the marriage of his son, the future Henry VI, to Constance, the heiress to the Norman throne of Sicily, Barbarossa prepared the way for the creation of a richer base for Hohenstaufen power. Henry VI in turn arranged for the marriage of his brother, Philip, Duke of Tuscany, to a daughter of the East Roman emperor, suggesting the reunion of eastern and western empires.[98]

The efforts that Barbarossa and Henry VI made in connection with the empire have intrigued historians. How did the Hohenstaufen envision the empire? Did Barbarossa and Henry VI envision a restoration of a universal Christian empire, one that would bring the kingdoms of Europe under the imperial umbrella? Barbarossa did refer to the kings of Europe as *sub reguli*, rulers of provinces within the empire, and Henry VI was able to extort from Richard the Lion Heart (1189–99) a recognition of 'German suzerainty' suggesting that he wished to employ feudal bonds to reinforce imperial claims to jurisdiction.[99]

In fact, it is not entirely clear what the Hohenstaufen intended with regard to the empire and how they conceived of it. The Hohenstaufen conception of empire is one of the great 'what ifs' of medieval history, because, while the letters and actions of Barbarossa and Henry VI contain hints at a universal empire, an unfortunate event, the early

death of Henry VI, prevented the fulfillment of a coherent conception of empire. If he had reigned for 38 years as his father had done
and had succeeded in implementing the policies he pursued in the
seven years of his reign, Henry VI might have created a formidable
empire. His early death, however, 'a catastrophe for Germany', was
also a catastrophe for the empire.[100] His heir, the future Frederick II,
was an infant, a situation that led to a civil war between two claimants
for the German throne and the imperial title. Furthermore, as we
shall see, Henry VI's premature death also led to the fullest exposition
of the papal conception of the empire, Pope Innocent III's
(1198–1216) decretal *Venerabilem* (1202). In addition, although
Frederick II's lengthy reign contained echoes of the imperial vision of
his father and grandfather, he was not successful in renewing their
vision and, with his death in 1250, the Hohenstaufen imperial reign
for all practical purposes came to an end, although it lingered on in
the brief reign of Frederick's son Conrad IV (1250–54). The two
decades of interregnum that followed Conrad's death, ended only with
the election of Rudolph of Habsburg as King of the Germans in 1273.
Rudolf did not, however, receive imperial coronation from the pope, a
situation that continued until 1312 when Henry VII was crowned
emperor by the pope.[101]

The death of Frederick II and the failure of his efforts to create an
empire that consisted of more than his hereditary possessions marked
the end of the great days of the medieval empire.[102] For the rest of the
Middle Ages, no king of Germany and Holy Roman Emperor possessed the might of an Otto I or of a Barbarossa. In the fifteenth
century, the weakness and limited extent of the empire led to its being
labeled the Holy Roman Empire of the German Nation, a title that
limited its scope to the territory that the German kings actually
ruled.[103]

The imperial visions of the Carolingians, the Ottonians, and the
Hohenstaufen were not identical. Their differences reflect some of
the various ways in which the notion of empire was understood in the
earlier Middle Ages. Above all, the notion of the empire as universal
or, at the least coterminous with Christendom, was fading though it
had not disappeared. The existence of the Eastern Empire alone suggested that at the very least the identification of the western empire
with Christendom was not unchallenged. On the other hand, it was
also possible to restrict Christendom to the Latin West.[104]

The decline in the significance of the empire for the Carolingians
reflects the decline of real Carolingian power. If Charlemagne's

imperial title rested on the fact of his power in Francia and in Italy, and on his conquests in the north and east, then the subsequent weakness of his heirs meant that the imperial title was improperly applied to them.

Only the papacy appears to have retained a strong interest in the imperial title, but this interest was rooted in its need to find a protector in the constant struggle for control of central Italy. The ceremonies that attended the relations of the popes with the various Frankish rulers tended to emphasize the papal origin of the imperial title and of the function of the emperor as the papacy's protector. The revival of the imperial title in the Ottonian era reflected both the functional role of the emperor in central Italy and the source of the title in the recognition of the power of the monarchs who bore it. The continuing interest of emperors and would-be emperors in Italy served as a reminder that to the papacy at least the empire was inextricably linked to the city of Rome.

The conception of empire that a series of emperors from Charlemagne to Frederick II developed over 450 years was not a single, consistent vision of empire, the linear development of a coherent vision. There was a core of imperial ideas, a kind of intellectual storehouse that emperors, propagandists, and lawyers could draw upon as various rulers and dynasties attempted to develop their own imperial visions. Each of these visions, however, was different, reflecting the different ways in which various rulers employed the available materials to construct concepts of empire. These different conceptions of empire bore many resemblances to one another, yet each had its own character.

There were several constants that characterized the imperial vision. In the first place, the empire was associated with control of central Italy and the city of Rome. From Charlemagne to Frederick II and beyond, as late as the sixteenth century, the imperial office was linked to jurisdiction over the imperial city. This did not necessary mean that the bearer of the imperial title saw himself as obtaining that title from the Roman people, only that the bearer of the title had jurisdiction over them. Charlemagne, for example, asserted his rule over the Roman Empire and Barbarossa scorned the Romans' claim to elect the emperor.

A second constant was the link between the papacy and the empire, a link that various emperors and popes understood in different ways. Charlemagne could act as a judge in a case involving the pope, and Henry III could depose popes and secure the election of his own

choices. Other German emperors could support anti-popes, suggesting that they, and not the electors in Rome, after 1059 the cardinals,
could select the pope. Although Charlemagne's coronation of Louis
the Pious suggested that he did not believe that papal coronation was
essential to becoming emperor, later emperors came to accept the
papal anointing as essential to full possession of the office. Until
papally crowned, the King of the Romans was also King of the
Romans but not emperor. There were great differences of opinion,
however, about the effects of papal coronation: did it create the
emperor or did it simply ratify the choice of the German princes?
Nevertheless, after Louis the Pious's coronation at the hands of his
father, all subsequent emperors, as opposed to emperor-elect,
received the imperial crown at papal, or anti-papal, hands until the
sixteenth century.

Another common characteristic of the theories of empire concerned the selection of the candidate for imperial coronation.
Charlemagne's coronation at the hands of Leo III appears to have
included at least the approval of the Roman people who acclaimed
him. His subsequent coronation of his successor included the agreement of the great nobles of his kingdom. By the twelfth century,
however, the Germany nobility had become the body that elected the
King of the Germans who in turn would be raised to the imperial
office. They could elect any Christian to that office, as the occasional
attempts of English and Spanish princes to acquire the imperial title
demonstrated, but generally they elected a German noble.

Another constant was the problem of the relationship between the
western emperor and the emperor at Constantinople. From the pro-
posal that Charlemagne wed the Empress Irene to the Hohenstaufen
marriage with a member of the eastern imperial family, there were
attempts to unite the two empires in some sort of a dynastic alliance,
but none achieved any success.[105] Nevertheless, the repeated efforts at
a dynastic connection suggests that the western emperors, if not the
eastern, believed that the two empires ought to be linked in some way,
even if they were not reunited into a single imperial structure.

Finally, all of the families that acquired the imperial title wrestled
with the extent of their jurisdiction, if any, over the emerging kingdoms of Europe. Charlemagne could assume that all of the lands that
he ruled would remain an *imperium* even though there would be kings
within it, but would these kingdoms remain subject to later emperors?
The fact was that as the empire became identified with the German
monarchs, the kings of France, part of the Carolingian *imperium*, were

clearly exempted from imperial jurisdiction. As we shall see, by the thirteenth century, lawyers in various European kingdoms were asserting the independence of their kingdoms from imperial jurisdiction.

The German emperors themselves were cautious about asserting their jurisdiction over other rulers. Even though Frederick Barbarossa referred to the kings of France and England as 'kings of provinces', he 'never envisioned either the reconquest of the provinces subject to the ancient Empire, or the exercise of lordship over the Western monarchies. ... But he undoubtedly perceived the imperial dignity as, in some sense, preeminent among the kings of Europe.'[106] In other words, the emperor did not possess universal jurisdiction, but he did possess a status superior to that of any other ruler, a status that included some kind of general responsibility for Christendom.

What the German vision of empire lacked was a single unifying conception of what the empire was and what it stood for. The German emperors, lawyers, and polemicists possessed several imperial visions, not a single one. Or, perhaps, it would be better to say that for the Germans the concept of empire was a concept in process of development, the various imperial visions produced from Charlemagne to Frederick II being stages in a process that would, one day, end with the development of a complete theory. In fact, however, it was not the Germans who produced the most complete conception of the empire and its role and functions within Christian society, but the papacy.

2 Other Medieval Empires

It is obvious that the empire is not with the Greeks although [their ruler] is termed emperor ... as piece on a chess board is called a king ....[1]

There is no contemporary evidence to support the charge, brought many years later by Gerald of Wales, that Henry II's ambitions extended even *ad Romanum imperium*. The fact is that there never was an Angevin Emperor either Holy or (in view of the Angevin legend of their descent from the devil) unholy.[2]

The imperial coronation of Charlemagne was of course a challenge to the imperial status of the East Roman or Byzantine ruler. Were there now two empires? The implication of the papal theory of the *translatio imperii* was that there was only one unity that could be called empire, the one designated as the defender and protector of the papacy. A contemporary observer might have expected that the East Roman emperor would have issued a condemnation of Charlemagne's imperial coronation. The East Roman Empire, however, seems not to have paid any attention to the events of 800 except for the observation of one chronicler: 'In this year in the month of December, Charles, the king of the Franks, was crowned by Pope Leo.'[3] The chronicler provided no explanation for the coronation. His words suggest, however, that he saw the papal coronation only as some form of royal ceremony, not an imperial one, perhaps only providing papal approbation for Charlemagne's activities and certainly no threat to the East Roman imperial title.[4] On the other hand, Einhard declared that Charlemagne 'endured with great patience the jealousy of the so-called Roman Emperors, who were most indignant at what had happened', an observation that suggested significant East Roman interest in the events taking place in the West. Both observations also suggest that there was only one empire, although there was obviously disagreement about what and where it was and who actually ruled it.

In an entry for the year 801, the Annals of Lorsch provided some additional details about why Pope Leo transferred the seat of the empire to the West and awarded the imperial crown to Charlemagne. The annalist argued that 'the name of emperor had now ceased to exist in the land of the Greeks and because they had a woman as emperor...'. Furthermore, Charlemagne 'now held Rome itself, where the Caesars were always accustomed to have their residence, and the rest of the places which they held in Italy, Gaul, and Germany'.[5] Apparently, the annalist could not conceive of a female ruling the empire, so that Irene could only have been a pretender to a throne that was effectively vacant. Furthermore, he was making the practical argument that Charlemagne's domains comprised the heartland of the original Roman Empire. The eastern emperor had deserted these lands and now Charlemagne had emerged to restore them to imperial control. Charlemagne was acting as the true emperor in the lands that belonged to the empire, so, therefore, he deserved to be called emperor.

It was, of course, possible to argue that there were now two emperors and two empires, both Roman in origin, one in the east and one in the west. This had been the situation from 364 to 476.[6] Such a position would mean a new understanding of what the (or an) empire was, a meaning that would deny the essential unity of the empire. On the other hand, as Robert Folz has pointed out, it would have been possible to see one of the claimants to the imperial title as an 'anti-emperor', thus explaining the presence of two emperors within the one empire.[7] Folz's language here echoes the problem that the Church had periodically faced in the wake of a disputed papal election. The essential unity of the Church remained even when there was a dispute about who was the rightful occupant of the papal office. Pope and anti-pope could exist at the same time.

The desire in at least some quarters to eliminate the appearance of division might underlie an East Roman chronicler's report of a rumor that Charlemagne would marry Irene and so end any doubt about the unity of the empire.[8] This suggests that in at least some East Roman circles the unity of the empire would be reaffirmed by the union of emperor and anti-emperor without necessarily deciding which was which.[9]

Charlemagne himself seems to have been uninterested in a direct confrontation with the East Roman Emperor over which of them was the true emperor of the one empire. In 813, for example, writing to his counterpart at Constantinople, Charlemagne identified himself as 'Emperor and Augustus and also King of the Franks and of the Lombards', a formula that could be interpreted in such a way as to suggest that there was no conflict between the roles of the two rulers.[10] Charlemagne's identification of himself as ruler of the Franks and Lombards suggests that his imperial title stemmed from his possession of more than one kingdom, that is an emperor was a king of kings. Elsewhere Charlemagne defined his imperial role as 'The emperor who now directs the Roman empire, not as emperor of the Romans'.[11] These usages allow for the fundamental unity of the empire but also for functional administrative divisions within it. They also avoided the issue of who is the true emperor.[12]

Later in the ninth century, however, as a result of the continued Carolingian use of the imperial title, the eastern ruler, Basil I (867–86), wrote to the western holder of the imperial title, Louis II (855–75), king of Italy, complaining that Louis II had no right to the imperial title. In a letter now generally accepted as authentic, Louis II responded to Basil's criticism, asserting very forcefully the right of the Franks to hold the imperial office and title.[13] In fact, his assertion of the Franks' right to the title provided a direct challenge to the East Romans.

In the first place, Louis II denied that there was anything wrong with a Frankish ruler inheriting the imperial title. After all, the soldier-emperors had come from a variety of ethnic backgrounds, including 'Spaniards, Isaurians, and Kazars'.[14] If these peoples could be legitimate emperors, why not the Franks? Furthermore, Louis rejected Basil's argument that the imperial title could not be inherited. In the Carolingian's opinion, the qualities that his people possessed were the equal of those possessed by other peoples who had provided emperors in the past. Presumably, the family of Charlemagne possessed the moral, martial and other qualities of their people and so their hereditary succession to the imperial throne was perfectly justified, just as it had been for the families of the earlier soldier-emperors. Indeed, Basil himself was to initiate an imperial dynasty, the Macedonian emperors, who would rule by hereditary succession until 1056.[15]

Louis II went on to explain that Basil should not be surprised that the Carolingians called themselves not 'Emperors of the Franks but Emperors of the Romans'. In saying this, Louis II was overlooking the fact that Charlemagne and his immediate successor, Louis the Pious (814–40), had identified themselves as Emperors of the Franks and of the Lombards, not as Emperors of the Romans.[16] Louis II argued that 'if we had not been emperors of the Romans, we would not be [emperors] of the French either'. He then went on to explain that the Roman people themselves gave the imperial title to his ancestors because God willed that the Carolingians take responsibility for 'the governance of the city and of the people, as well as the protection and exaltation of the mother of all the churches...'. Finally, Louis II pointed to the coronation of Charlemagne in 800 as ultimate proof of the legitimate imperial status of the Frankish emperors.[17]

Turning to the situation at Constantinople, Louis pointed out that those who ruled there were usurpers who lacked ecclesiastical blessing and whose possession of the imperial title rested on, at most, the approval of the senate. Some East Roman rulers even lacked that element of legitimacy, basing their claim to the office on 'acclamation by the army'. Louis and his curia either did not realize or chose to overlook the fact that acclamation was indeed the original source of the title of *imperator*. Even more damning was the fact that some emperors reached the imperial office as a result of the machinations of women (*a feminis*), probably a reference to the Empress Irene, and others by some even baser means.[18] As Steven Fanning recently observed, the letter 'contrasted Louis' honorable imperial title with Basil's own title gained with sullied hands'.[19]

Furthermore, Louis II pointed out that God granted the imperial office and title to the Franks because they were a 'rugged people' (*de Francorum duritia*), presumably in contrast to the decadent Easterners and Romans. In addition, the Franks were spiritually rugged, so to speak, remaining true to the Christian faith (*propter bonam opinionem, orthodosiam*) in contrast to the heretical teachings held by those in the East. Finally, in an interesting twist on the establishment of Constantinople, Louis II pointed out that the East Romans 'not only deserted the city and the seat of the empire, but, losing the Roman way of life and even the Latin language, they established their capital in another city and utterly transformed the language and way of life of the empire'.[20] Thus, in Louis II's eyes, Constantinople signified not the survival of the empire but rather the flight of the East Romans from the responsibilities of empire.

Some scholars, J.B. Bury, for example, concluded from their analysis of the evidence that during the Carolingian era there emerged a theory of two empires, joined perhaps in some kind of fraternal relationship but in any event breaking the tradition of a single empire.[21] Robert Folz has argued that Louis II recognized the existence of two empires when he identified himself as 'Louis, by command of Divine Providence, August Emperor of the Romans' and Basil as 'our well-beloved spiritual brother Basil, the very glorious and pious emperor of the New Rome'.[22] The difficulty with this view is that the Franks generally denied the legitimacy of their eastern counterparts, pointing out in particular their lack of papal consecration. The letter of Louis II does not seem in fact to suggest two emperors (and two empires) but an emperor and an anti-emperor, one empire with two claimants to the throne. To reject the notion of a single empire was something that neither the Carolingians not their eastern counterparts could have accepted. When these rulers addressed one another, they employed the titles that the other conventionally employed. This did not necessarily mean accepting the legitimacy of the claim that the imperial title implied.[23]

As if to counter the claim that the empire had been transferred to the West by the action of Leo III, the East Romans developed their own theory of *translatio imperii* that justified the Byzantine possession of the imperial office.[24] When Liutprand of Cremona went to Constantinople in 968 as the representative of Otto I, he criticized the weakness of the Byzantine emperors who had lost control of the west and so had caused the pope to lose possession of those lands that were rightfully his.[25] After all, those possessions were the gift of 'Constantine, the august emperor who founded this city and called it after his name, as world-ruler gave many gifts to the holy apostolic Roman church, not only in Italy but in almost all the western kingdoms...'. These lands, lost to the pope because of the incapacity of the eastern emperors, Otto I restored to the papacy, retaining from all of these lands not a single 'city, an estate, a vassal or a serf'. Liutprand challenged the East Roman emperor to do the same thing, to 'restore to the church of the apostles what lies in his kingdom...'.[26] In Liutprand's opinion, the fact that Otto had restored the lands included in Constantine's gift to the papacy demonstrated that he, not the weak eastern ruler who was unable to prevent the loss of these lands to the invading barbarians, was the true emperor.

To this assertion of the theory of the *translatio imperii*, the Byzantines had an answer that Liutprand reported in a subsequent discussion. According to the representatives of the East Roman emperor, the pope, John XIII (965–72), under pressure from Otto I, had sent an offensive letter to Constantinople 'calling him the emperor of the "Greeks", not "of the Romans".' This mode of address effectively denied the true imperial status of the eastern ruler. The East Roman response was a forceful statement of their conception of the *translatio imperii*.

Hear then! The silly pope does not know that the holy Constantine transferred hither the imperial sceptre, the senate, and all the Roman knighthood, and left in Rome nothing but vile minions — fishers, namely, pedlars, bird catchers, bastards, plebeians, slaves.[27]

Recognizing the precariousness of his situation, Liutprand prudently responded that he "'was writing this to the honour of the emperor not his shame'". Then, in language similar to that of Louis II, Liutprand went on to say:

> We know, of course, that Constantine, the Roman emperor, came hither with the Roman knighthood, and founded this city in his name; but because you changed your language, your customs, and your dress, the most holy pope thought that the name of the Romans as well as their dress would displease you.

In the future, according to Liutprand, papal letters to the East Roman ruler would be headed: "'John, the Roman pope, to Nicephorus, Constantine, Basilius, the great and august emperors of the Romans!'" The East Romans apparently accepted Liutprand's explanation and praised him for resolving the matter.[28]

Liutprand clearly theoretically viewed the East Romans as degenerate, weak, and unable to perform the basic function of the imperial office, the protection of the Church, especially the papacy.[29] At the same time, he does not appear to have believed that there were two empires, one in the east, the other in the west. Clearly he saw the empire as a unity and Otto I as the true emperor because he functioned in the manner of a true emperor, protecting the Church and restoring the lands of central Italy to papal control.

The East Roman rulers seem not to have accorded real imperial status, at least not Roman imperial status, to their western counterparts. The title they did use for the western challengers was *basileus*, a title that Emperor Michael I (811–13) employed when referring to Charlemagne in 812. This title was, however, 'far from equality of status with the East Roman Emperor'.[30] After all, from the time that Constantine established his capital on the Bosphorus in 330 until May 1453, when the Turks finally captured Constantinople, the inhabitants of the city referred to themselves as Romans.[31] From at least the early ninth century, perhaps in response to Charlemagne's coronation, the eastern rulers identified themselves as 'Emperors of the Romans'.[32] For example, when Anna Comnena (d. after 1148) wrote her history of the reign of her father, Alexius I (1081–1118), she always referred to him as Alexius, Emperor of the Romans, and she did not use the imperial title for any other ruler.[33] The Roman Emperor Henry IV (1056–1106) was, for her, 'Henry, King of Germany', not emperor.[34]

Furthermore, the East Romans continued to develop their own theory of *the translatio imperii* in order to justify their possession of the imperial title and office. Anna Comnena argued that not only did the leadership of the Roman imperial world move to Constantinople in 330, the headship of the Church did so as well.

> For when the imperial seat was transferred from Rome hither to our native Queen of Cities, and the senate and the whole administration, there was also transferred the arch-hieratical primacy. And the Emperors from the very beginning have given the supreme right to the episcopacy of Constantinople, and the Council of Chalcedon emphatically raised the Bishop of Constantinople to the highest position, and placed all the dioceses of the inhabited world under his jurisdiction.[35]

In effect, Anna Comnena's position was that the *translatio* not only moved the imperial capital to the East but the spiritual capital as well.[36] In an interesting reversal of the relationship between the papacy and the emperors as described in the Donation of Constantine, she argued that by moving the capital to the east, Constantine had reduced the city of Rome's status and replaced it with Constantinople, thus making the bishop of Constantinople the senior ecclesiastical official. In making this argument she was reasserting the position taken at the Council of Chalcedon (451) that the ecclesiastical status of a city followed from its political status, so that the patriarch of New Rome, Constantinople, was superior to the pope, the bishop of Old Rome.[37]

By the early thirteenth century, half a century after Anna Comnena's death, in part at least as a reaction to the inability of the East Roman emperors to halt the Muslim advance, it became a cliché among canonists that the Byzantine emperor was no more a true emperor than the king in a chess-set was a real king.[38] The same might be said of the imperial title when the Carolingians applied it to their Byzantine counterparts, or the reverse. The use of the title was conventional, not a recognition of the legitimacy of the claim involved.

The use of the terms *imperium* and *imperator* in the correspondence between Frankish and East Roman monarchs was a reflection of the difficulties involved in the use of these terms. The terms were acquiring multiple meanings and being employed in circumstances that the ancient and recent Romans had not envisioned. Furthermore, these rulers were not the only ones in these centuries who employed the language of empire in their titles. They also appeared in the list of titles that other monarchs, especially in Anglo-Saxon England and in Spain, claimed and in the chronicles and other literature that discussed the rulers of several kingdoms. It may be the case that those rulers who claimed imperial status after Charlemagne's reign did not do so in imitation of Augustus and Constantine but 'to assert their independence from and parity with the Carolingians'.[39]

Even before the Carolingians first used the terms *imperium*, it was being used in Anglo-Saxon England. Indeed, the Carolingian use of the term may even have emerged from Alcuin, the Anglo-Saxon scholar who guided Charlemagne's educational program.[40] In the *Ecclesiastical History*, when discussing the coming of the Roman monk Augustine to England in 597, Bede (d. 735) had pointed out that the *imperium* of Ethelbert of Kent extended all the way to the Humber. Bede placed Ethelbert in a line of seven powerful rulers who dominated Britain south of the Humber River. He described these rulers as having *imperium* over various peoples outside their own kingdoms and the kings ruled (*imperavit*) these peoples.[41] When the compilers of the *Anglo-Saxon Chronicle*, following Bede, mentioned the line of seven rulers who possessed *imperium* over southern England, they identified these rulers as *Bretwaldas*.[42]

Here Bede was obviously employing the term *imperium* in the loose sense of some kind of jurisdiction or, as Wilhelm Levison has said, hegemony, over the lands outside of his own kingdom of Kent. Subsequently Bede referred to Canterbury as the 'capital of his [Ethelbert's] entire empire'.[43] Although this use of the term does suggest a territorial state, Bede may only have been employing it as a synonym for *regnum*, kingdom. Levison also suggested that Bede was inclined to employ 'the terms "*regnum*" and "*imperium*" indifferently'.[44] Bede may also have employed the term *imperium* to describe Ethelbert of Kent's power in order to emphasize the importance of the kingdom that was the starting point for the Christianization of England. There is perhaps even a faint echo of Constantine and Clovis in Bede's Ethelbert. The King of Kent was to be the founder of a Christian *imperium* in Britain.[45]

Throughout the eighth century other Anglo-Saxon writers also employed the terms *imperium* and *imperator*, usually to describe 'those of their kings (though not to them alone) who had authority also outside of their own territory'. Levison noted that Alcuin was already referring to Charlemagne's possessions as an *imperium* before the coronation of 800. Like some Anglo-Saxon rulers, Charlemagne 'had authority' over peoples whom he had conquered in the course of his career.[46] It has even been suggested that Alcuin was one of the voices that paved the way for the revival of the imperial title in an official way.

What was missing in any of these uses of the imperial language by the Anglo-Saxons was the source of the usage. Bede did not describe an Anglo-Saxon ruler as being acclaimed by his troops after a significant victory, nor did he describe any ecclesiastical ceremony in which a ruler received from the Church the imperial title. Instead, the use of imperial language to describe unusually powerful rulers, kings of kings, may have been due simply to the lack of a suitable term for such a ruler. This is especially true for Bede who wrote in Latin. What other words could he have used?

At the same time, the Anglo-Saxon use of the term *imperium* was not in itself enough to make its use by Charlemagne as important as it was to become. The Catholic liturgy also contained prayers that mentioned the *imperium Romanum*, thus sacralizing the notion of *imperium*.[47] In the long run, it was the papal adoption and employment of the imperial title, not simply the Anglo-Saxon usage, that gave it its significance in medieval Europe. Without that papal sanction, 'nobody would probably have paid much attention to the words of Alcuin. It [*imperium*] would have appeared to most a mere matter of terminology.'[48]

The imperial language appears to have gone out of use in Anglo-Saxon England in the ninth century. It is curious that the terms *imperator*, *imperium* and *impero* were not employed in discussions of Alfred's 18-year reign (871–99). Given the picture of Alfred in history books as the creator of the kingdom of England, especially after his victory over the Danes who had settled in eastern England, it is not difficult to imagine him being acclaimed as an *imperator* or being described as one by a chronicler. One reason for the lack of the imperial title in contemporary literature may have been that contemporaries recognized that in spite of his achievements, Alfred was less powerful than the Bretwaldas found in the *Anglo-Saxon Chronicle*.[49]

The imperial title reappeared in the tenth century, however, during the reign of Athelstan (924–39), Alfred's grandson. Two factors seem to have been involved. In the first place, Athelstan gained control over virtually all of the territory that modern England encompasses. In effect, he ruled 'over the western as well as the northern kings of Britain'.[50] As a king over kings, he fitted one of the definitions of an emperor. In the second place, Athelstan had extensive contacts with the powerful rulers of the continental kingdoms.[51] His three sisters married into the major families of the continent. One married Otto I, another wed Hugh Capet, and the third married Charles the Simple (emp. 893–923;d. 929).[52] In other words, the children of Alfred could legitimately see themselves as the equals of the great ruling families of the continent, one of which could claim an imperial past and another, the Ottonian, that was to claim an imperial future. Athelstan was confident enough in his own status as to title himself 'basileos of the English and king of all Britain'.[53] He or his clerical officials must certainly have been aware of the current use of the imperial title on the continent. The term *imperator* continued to appear in the official documents of subsequent Anglo-Saxon rulers. Its last appearance was in a document of Canute (1016–35) who was identified as an emperor who ruled five kingdoms.[54]

Scholars have disputed the importance of the use of the imperial title by the later Anglo-Saxon rulers. Sir Frank Stenton judged the use of imperial language as little more than a clerk's desire to give 'full scope to his ingenuity' that only led to the production of 'eccentric styles into which many historians have read an assertion of imperial dignity by tenth-century English kings'.[55] Folz, however, judged that the use of the term reflected the extent of the power that Athelstan and his successors possessed in England.[56] At the very least, the identification of Anglo-Saxon rulers as emperors reflects a belief among the learned clerks who staffed the chanceries of these monarchs that rulership over more than one kingdom deserved a superior title and that *imperator* served that purpose. At the same time, however, there was no ecclesiastical role or significance in the acquisition of imperial status. The actions of the rulers alone caused them to be recognized as emperors.

The use of imperial language in Spain in the early Middle Ages followed a course similar to that of such language in England in the same period. Some writers termed the late sixth-century Visigothic monarch, Reccared (586–601), an emperor.[57] In the tenth century, the term *imperator* reappeared in connection with the kings of León, although at first the title was not employed in official documents. It was, however, linked to the *reconquista*, thus suggesting that empire could mean rule over conquered lands. According to Joseph O'Callaghan:

> The title *imperator*, meaning 'king of kings,' expressed a claim to political supremacy over the whole of Spain, whether Christian or Muslim, and proclaimed the responsibility of the kings of León to

recover their heritage, to reconquer the ancient territory of
Hispania, and to expel the Muslims from the peninsula.[58]

In the eleventh century, the Castilian monarchs, heirs of the
Leónese tradition, employed the title *'imperator totius Hispaniae'* to
restate the 'traditional Leónese aspirations to hegemony throughout
the peninsula'.[59] In this case, however, the term *imperator* was used
not only to declare Leónese–Castilian domination of Spain itself but
also to assert independence of the papacy which was claiming some
form of domination over the peninsula. As part of the papal reforming
movement, Pope Gregory VII (1073–85) had requested that the
Spanish monarchs impose the Roman liturgy on the churches in their
lands. Alfonso VI (1072–1109) was willing to adopt the Roman
liturgy, even though there was strong resistance from those who
wished to retain the Mozarabic liturgy.[60]
What Alfonso VI would not accept, however, was Gregory VII's
claim that Spain, apparently as part of the Donation of Constantine,
was subject to papal jurisdiction in secular matters. What the pope
probably intended was to have Alfonso surrender his kingdom to
the pope and receive it back again as a fief, a relationship that
popes from Leo IX (1049–54) on had encouraged and later
accomplished.[61]
Under Alfonso VII (1126–57) 'the concept of a Leonese empire ...
reached its culmination and briefly acquired a juridical existence'.[62]
The possibility of Leónese domination of all of Christian Spain in the
twelfth century failed, however, and with the death of Alfonso VII in
1157 the use of the imperial title ended, as, instead of a unified empire
under Leónese–Castilian leadership, Christian Spain became five
independent kingdoms.[63]
Interest in an imperial title for the Castilian royal family did not die
out completely, however. A century after Alfonso VII's death, Alfonso
X (1252–84) sought to obtain the vacant imperial throne from the
pope. The confrontation between the papacy and Emperor Frederick
II (1220–50) that led to Frederick's deposition in 1245, coupled with
the papacy's interest in preventing another Hohenstaufen from
obtaining the imperial office, had encouraged candidates for the
imperial throne from outside Germany. Alfonso X spent a good deal
of money in pursuit of the title, a situation that generated problems
for him with the Castilians. Furthermore, his Aragonese counterpart,
James I (1213–76), stated strong objections to Alfonso's imperial
pretensions. The Aragonese ruler,

recalling traditional Leonese imperialist pretensions in Spain ...
rejected the notion that Alfonso X might be regarded as 'an
Hispanic emperor or that our realms and dominions are in any
subjection to him, by reason of empire.'[64]

In rejecting any kind of claim to jurisdiction over Aragon that
Alfonso X might claim as a result of election to the imperial throne,
James I was echoing the comments of a Spanish canon lawyer,
Vincentius Hispanus (d. 1248), who denied that the Roman Empire
had any jurisdiction over Spain. Vincentius had rejected imperial
jurisdiction for two reasons. In the first place, the Spanish had
regained control of Spain from the Muslims without imperial
assistance. Furthermore, the stupidity (*busnardiam*) of the German
emperors caused them to lose their empire.[65]

The use of the terms *imperium* and *imperator* in Spain both reflects
their use in the Carolingian world and differs from it. The obvious
similarity is that the Leónese writers and rulers who used this term
saw León's king as a conqueror, a ruler over defeated peoples and
kingdoms. Like the Carolingians, the Leónese rulers saw themselves
as having a religious mission to drive out the Muslims and to unite the
peoples of Spain. To the extent that León's rulers saw themselves as
having a divinely ordained mission to drive the Muslims out of Spain,
they were Christian emperors like Charlemagne who subdued the
Lombards at the behest of the pope. A poet even compared Alfonso
VII to Charlemagne, describing him as a 'worthy rival of Charlemagne
... his equal in lineage, bravery, and deeds of war'.[66]

Where the Leónese conception of empire appears to have differed
from the concept as employed elsewhere, however, is that it rejected
any notion that the imperial title was linked to a grant from the pope.
The Leónese monarchs awarded themselves, so to speak, the imperial
title to recognize their achievements and to identify their long-term
agenda. There is also one other way in which the Leónese use of the
imperial title differed from contemporary usage. They used it in such
a way as to reject any claim by other rulers to possess some form of
jurisdiction over Spain. That is, they denied the pope any power in
secular affairs on the basis of a Roman imperial grant and responded
in the same fashion to the threat that Alfonso X's claim to the
Roman empire might lead to a claim to jurisdiction over Spain. It
may well be no coincidence that one of the first canon lawyers to
assert the independence of a kingdom from imperial jurisdiction was
from Spain. In Anglo-Saxon England and in Spain during the

eleventh, twelfth, and thirteenth centuries a new concept of empire was emerging, a limited one that rejected any conception of universal jurisdiction and any ecclesiastical involvement. Instead, this *imperium* identified a powerful ruler, one who conquered other rulers and who was unchallenged within his kingdom. It reflected the legal theory that the king within his kingdom possessed the powers of the emperor within the empire.

By the beginning of the tenth century, even in the Frankish lands, the conception of empire associated with Charlemagne had died out as a serious form of government. The imperial title remained in the Carolingian family but had little practical significance. The use of the terms empire and emperor by other monarchs suggested that this language was losing its connection with ecclesiastical power and with some form of universal jurisdiction and was becoming identified with powerful rulers who claimed extensive but not unlimited territories and had conquered kings. In the case of Leónese rulers, it may even have been the case that they, or their courtiers, saw the Leónese as possessing a divinely ordained mission, one that came directly from God, not from the papacy.

Although the terms *imperator* and *imperium* appear to have gone out of general use in western Europe except for the Roman Empire and the East Roman Empire by the early thirteenth century, institutionally, if not semantically, other empires continued to exist. Some medieval historians, looking at the actual institutional structures that existed in medieval Europe rather than at the theoretical debates about universal imperial jurisdiction, have argued that the kingdoms that were emerging out of the collapse of the Carolingian world were in fact empires. Frank Barlow, for example, described the dynastic lands and claims of the new monarchies as 'the private empires of new dynasties'.[67] The result is that while the terms emperor and empire went out of general use, structures existed that did in fact fit the definition of an empire. If, as Maitland once wrote, 'the medieval church was a state' that is, in practice the medieval Church possessed all the characteristics of a state as defined in the modern world, something similar can be said of medieval empires.[68] They may not have been so labeled but nevertheless they possessed all of the characteristics usually found in the formal definition of empires. Aggressive families struggling to enhance their power and status over several generations came to dominate their rivals among the powerful noble families and to govern quite disparate territories, if not necessarily kingdoms, other 'nations', in fact.[69]

Furthermore, as John le Patourel has pointed out, 'historians tend to project the present into the past' so that the history of England or France or Germany is seen as always having been 'something fundamentally identical' with the England or the France or the Germany of today.[70] He argued that 'the effective political units from 1066 until sometime in the fourteenth century were not England and France as we ordinarily think of them, but a Norman empire and an Angevin empire and a kingdom of France (the 'Capetian'), overlapping and interpenetrating ...'.[71] To extend this a bit further, we should picture medieval Europe as a series of competing empires as various royal families attempt to extend their power over neighboring territories. What they labeled themselves as is less important than what they did.[72] Accepting the dictionary definition of an empire 'as a major political unit having a territory of great extent or a number of territories or peoples under a single sovereign authority', we would have to recognize the extensive and varied territories of, for example, Henry II as an empire, at least as much of an empire as the one ruled by the Roman Emperor.[73] He was, after all, King of England, Duke of Normandy, Duke of Aquitaine, Count of Anjou, and so on. In addition, he was the feudal overlord of both the King of Scotland and of the High King of Ireland.[74]

Some scholars have questioned whether this assemblage of territories was in fact part of a conscious plan of imperial development.[75] If there was not a conscious plan then, so it is argued, there could not have been an empire, only a collection of lands held together temporarily. As La Patourel phrased it, it is possible to conclude that

> the Angevin Empire was consciously formed by continuous policy, but that more than the rules of inheritance were involved, and that the rulers concerned took every opportunity to add to their possessions, to hold on to what they had, and to pass it all on, substantially intact, to their successors. Integration was therefore possible.[76]

The fundamental problem with regard to conceiving the Angevin family's various possessions as an empire with that term's emphasis on a conscious program of central rule lies not so much in the question of conscious policy but of institutional means to achieve some form of what le Patourel termed 'integration'. The goal of integration, however, was not the same as the goal that the ancient Romans faced. The Romans had conquered their empire and ruled it to a large extent by force of arms. They also relied on the cooperation of the leaders of the conquered societies to make common cause with the conquerors by granting them Roman citizenship and allowing the local elites to continue to govern in traditional ways.[77] Medieval empires, such as Henry II's, did include conquered territories, such as Ireland, but they also included lands acquired by inheritance, such as Anjou, and others obtained through marriage, as in the case of Aquitaine. The famous words applied to the Habsburgs, that where others conquered they wed and acquired an empire, applied to some degree to most other medieval empires.[78] At the same time, clever rulers of these disparate lands did seek to win and hold the support of the nobles by emphasizing bonds of feudal loyalty and by buying their support.

The way in which the English operated in Ireland reflects the way in which a conqueror sought to win the support of local powers. Shortly after entering Ireland, an action justified by the papal bull *Laudabiliter*, Henry II ordered the holding of a Church Council at Cashel (1172). The purpose of this council was to bring the Church in Ireland into conformity with the Gregorian reform of the Church, one of the reasons Pope Adrian IV (1154–59) issued *Laudabiliter*. The opening words of the constitutions of the council also serve to remind the reader who was responsible for calling the council. The council was called 'In the year of our Lord 1172, being the first year in which Henry, king of England and conqueror of Ireland, obtained the dominion of that island ...'.[79] It is clear that reform-minded Irish clerics saw English intervention in Ireland as helpful to their cause.[80] They may have even seen Henry II as acting on behalf of the papacy as the Carolingians had done.[81]

Throughout the Middle Ages, English rulers attempted to win over the native Irish by a variety of means. In 1175, for example, there was a treaty 'between Henry, king of England, and Roderic [Rory], king of Connaught', who also claimed to be the High King of Ireland, outlining the relationship between the two kings. 'The king of England has granted to Roderic ..., his liegeman, king of Connaught, as long as he shall faithfully serve him, that he shall be king under him, ready to his service, as his man'.[82] To the extent that an emperor was a ruler over kings, whether or not he was officially labeled as such, Henry II was an emperor over the king of Connaught and thus over the lesser Irish kings who were subject to the High King.[83] Henry was also the superior of King William of Scotland after defeating him in 1174.[84]

Henry II's policy of seeking oaths of fealty from the kings of the Irish did not lead to meaningful consequences, because the king of Connaught 'could scarcely exact obedience from his own subject-chieftains in Connaught, let alone those of Ulster or Munster...'.[85] Designating his youngest son, John (1199–1216) as Lord of Ireland in 1177 was an attempt at creating a more effective form of English rule in Ireland, but when John actually went to Ireland in 1185 the result 'was a fiasco'.[86]

One of the more significant aspects of this policy was to extend the advantages of English law to the Irish. This was only done on an individual basis, however, although as early as 1277, the leaders of the Irish, 'the community of Ireland', proposed paying 8000 marks in order to extend the Common Law to all of the Irish. As a result, two legal systems remained in Ireland, marking a fundamental division between the conquerors and the conquered, even though, to the English, 'the laws which the Irish use are detestable to God and contrary to all law'.[87] In a loose sense, the proposed extension of English Common Law to Ireland recalled the extension of Roman law to the conquered as a means of Romanizing the conquered and securing their loyalty.

The fact that medieval rulers ruled various lands acquired in a variety of ways did provide an obstacle to the formation of a real imperial government separate and apart from the governments of the constituent elements of those empires. Each had its own laws, customs, and practices, and the local leaders of each component of a 'dynastic empire' expected that the ruler they shared with other territories would respect their law and customs, some of which affected inheritance and could inhibit what a ruler could do with his territories. On the one hand, there 'can be no doubt that the rulers of kingdoms, duchies and counties long before 1087 regarded their dominions as impartible and hereditary possessions, that they formed dynasties and had typical dynastic ambitions'.[88] On the other hand, the territories that a dynasty acquired lacked the sense of coherence that the Carolingian *imperium* possessed so that the properties might be divided among several heirs without there being a sense that all of the parts belonged to some whole, some larger *imperium*. William the Conqueror's disposition of his various lands illustrates some of the problems. Normandy was left to his eldest son Robert, while England was left to his second son, William II (Rufus) (1087–1100). The third son, the future Henry I (1100–35) received his mother's lands and 5000 pounds of silver.[89] Subsequently, after a series of conflicts between Robert of Normandy and his royal brothers, aided perhaps by the fact that William Rufus had no offspring to provide for, the properties of the Conqueror were reunited under a single ruler, Henry I.[90]

The Norman and Plantagenet rulers wrestled with the problem of permanently linking disparate possessions into a single whole just as their successors in the sixteenth, seventeenth, and eighteenth centuries were to do. The disparate nature of their possessions was not, however, the sole problem the dynasties faced. The other problem was to insure the status of all of their sons. Le Patourel phrased the problem as one of attempting 'to preserve the essential unity of an "empire" while providing for younger sons according to their rank'.[91] These were, after all, 'dynastic empires', with all of the complications that dynasties face along with the problems of imperial governance itself. At the same time, it is clear that by the twelfth century, European rulers had moved away from the Merovingian and Carolingian pattern of dividing their territories among their sons as if they were personal possessions that could be divided at will.

Questions about the relationship between a ruling family and its various possessions continued to haunt royal families throughout the Middle Ages and on into the modern world.[92] A glance at the history of European dynasties demonstrates the capacity of the members of dynasties to fight for what they considered their proper share of the families' possessions. King Lear was not the only medieval ruler to face conflict with his children. Henry II's battles with his sons could have been the basis for a Shakespearean tragedy, as could Philip II's with his son that led to the son's death.

One solution to the problem of keeping disparate imperial territories united and meeting the status needs of members of the royal family was the appanage system that Louis IX developed in France. This practice resolved the problem of conflict within the royal family by granting lands to younger sons who might otherwise engage in conspiracies against the monarch. Younger sons then became rulers of significant areas within the kingdom, serving 'the king more or less as provincial viceroys'.[93] The lands of the appanage could not be alienated permanently because the land remained part of the royal domain.

A long-term, unforeseen consequence of the use of the appanage to resolve the problem of imperial unity was the freezing of local and regional laws, institutions, and cultural practices into permanent conditions. Rather than engage in a policy of consolidation and standardization that would create a uniform French nation and, eventually, a state, the French had to settle for what Joseph Strayer termed a mosaic state with all of the rigidity that image implies.[94] While the French monarchy, especially under Louis XIV, is generally described as absolutist, in reality even Louis XIV's freedom of action was limited by numerous restrictions and obstacles rooted in the multiplicity of customary rights, legal systems, and so on, that the mosaic nature of his dominions had kept in place for centuries.[95]

If we accept as a definition of empire, rule by force over several distinct peoples, it becomes clear that institutionally medieval Europe was a period in which virtually all attempts at large-scale governments were imperial in nature. The sixteenth-century states that scholars routinely identify as the basis of modern political thought and practice were the winners in a series of imperial wars that roiled Europe for centuries. It would be more accurate to say that the great theme of early modern political thought was the problem of converting these empires into states as we now define them. At the same time, however, there was also discussion of the possibility of retaining imperial government. In London and Madrid, to use only the most obvious examples, the desire to create states in the modern sense collided in the sixteenth century with the overseas empires that were being created. Could Castile or England be both a state and an empire? This problem faced governments from the sixteenth to the eighteenth centuries.

By almost any standard, medieval kingdoms were empires, as the territorial acquisitions of European dynasties in the early modern world were empires in fact, even if the term empire was not employed to describe them. By the thirteenth century, the only European powers that were described by the terms *imperium* and *imperator* were the Roman Empire and the East Roman Empire, the Empire of the Greeks. This lack of a term that defined the structure of the emerging European governments, more than kingdoms but not labeled empires, reflects a serious problem for both officials and intellectual theorists who attempted to grasp the nature of the new forms of government.

3 The Papal Conception of Empire

As the Papal revolution gave birth to the modern Western state, so it gave birth also to modern Western legal systems, the first of which was the modern system of canon law.[1]

In the twelfth century, the Roman and canon lawyers, the most important political theorists of the time, confronted an uncharted terrain: the relationship of the prince and the law.[2]

Only in recent years have scholars become aware of the importance of the medieval canon lawyers in the development of the concept of empire.[3] In a number of areas of what can be broadly construed as political thought, the canonists made important contributions. While philosophers in the Middle Ages tended to be restricted in their analysis of politics by the Greek, Roman and patristic traditions of political thought, the canonists were not. The canonists who emerged in the late twelfth century following the publication of Gratian's *Decretum* were legal practitioners who came to play a major role in the ecclesiastical bureaucracies, on occasion rising to the papal office itself.[4] In carrying out these roles, the canonists faced problems that did not exist in classical political thought. As they did so, they shaped the legal tradition, causing what Harold Berman has termed the 'legal revolution' of the twelfth century that in turn created modern European legal systems.[5]

As Walter Ullmann pointed out, however, the canon law differed from other legal systems in that it 'was nothing but the transformation of pure (theological) doctrine into an enforceable rule of action'.[6] Looked at from a slightly different perspective, canon law was the vehicle by means of which abstract moral principles would be transformed into the basic rules according to which an entire society would operate. Within that context, the most original and most complex problem facing the canonists was the relationship between spiritual power and secular power. The conception of a church that was not only independent of secular government but also possessed an institutional structure paralleling secular governments as well was completely unknown before the Middle Ages. Indeed, as J.N. Figgis noted long ago with, perhaps some exaggeration: 'In the Middle Ages the Church was not a State, it was the State; the State or rather the civil authority (for a separate society was not recognized) was merely the police department of the Church.'[7] The medieval empire, indeed all secular power, was, in the view of many popes and canonists, an agent of papal policy, the executor of papal policy.

The first volume of the universal canon law, Gratian's *Decretum*, appeared around 1140 and reflected the contemporary problems facing the Church. One of the most important of those problems was the problem of the relation of the papacy to the empire. That in turn was a specialized aspect of the overall problem of the relationship between the spiritual and the secular powers. The *Decretum* was not, however, a law book in the sense of being a set of statutes. It was a collection of statements on legal topics arranged in the *sic et non* fashion and organized as *distinctiones* or *causae*. As a result, it contained a wide range of materials that bore on the papal–imperial relationship, not all of which reflected the papal position.[8] Looked at from one perspective, these *distinctiones*, like many other sections of the *Decretum*, form an historical archive containing the fundamental documents of papal history. In effect, when Gratian compiled the *Decretum*, he provided the basic materials for a history of papal–imperial relations.

The fundamental premise of the canonistic conception of the relationship between the two powers was the existence of a shared, though not necessarily co-equal, responsibility for mankind. The fullest statement of this joint effort occurred in a letter from Pope Gelasius I (492–96) to the emperor Anastasius (491–518),

> Two there are, august emperor, by which this world is chiefly ruled, the sacred authority [*auctoritas*] of the priesthood and the royal power [*potestas*]. Of these the responsibility of the priests is more weighty in so far as they will answer for the kings of men themselves at the divine judgment. You know, most clement son, that, although you take precedence over all mankind in dignity, nevertheless you piously bow the neck to those who have charge of divine affairs and seek from them the means of your salvation ....[9]

The theme of dual powers governing mankind thus ran through the early medieval legal literature about the order of society.[10] This theme in turn echoed another duality with which Gratian opened the *Decretum*. The first *distinctio* began with the words 'The human race is ruled by two laws, that is natural law and customs.'[11] Both statements reflect the theme that there existed a single universal society function-ally divided into spiritual and temporal spheres of responsibility. At the same time, the clear implication of Gelasius's letter was that the pope as representative of the higher power has jurisdiction over all secular officials, even the emperor.

As the early development of the Church came within the framework of the Roman Empire, it was only logical that the popes and their advisors discussed the relationship between spiritual and temporal powers in terms of the Roman Empire. The gradual decline of imper-ial power in western Europe enabled the papacy to become indepen-dent of the eastern emperor's jurisdiction during the eighth century.[12] The political realities of Italy, however, forced the papacy to find a new protector against the Lombards who were filling the vacuum created by the imperial withdrawal from northern and central Italy. Increasingly through the eighth century the papacy looked to the Carolingians for that protection.

The coronation of Charlemagne in 800 marked the beginning of a new stage in papal–imperial relations. For the first time, a pope asserted that he had a role to play in the selection of the emperor. The *translatio imperii*, the act of transferring the imperial title from Constantinople to Rome and Aachen, was a revolutionary act because it paved the way for asserting papal jurisdiction over both the emperor's soul and the empire itself, leading by the early thirteenth century to the claim that the imperial office was in the gift of the pope. The notion that two powers, spiritual and secular, ruled mankind remained, but, in papal theory, the pope was clearly the dominant figure. From the papal perspective, if not necessarily from Charlemagne's, the pope could grant and remove the empire and the imperial title when he judged it to be in the best interests of the Church. He did not, for example, ask the pope to provide an imperial coronation for his son, Louis the Pious, but, instead, crowned him himself. As we have already seen, however, some years later Louis did seek papal coronation as well.[13]

Although the imperial coronation of Charlemagne is always seen as one of the most dramatic events in the entire Middle Ages, it is also one of the most perplexing. It is not at all clear what either party understood to be the meaning of the event. Furthermore, it is also not clear that Empress Irene in Constantinople had any idea of its significance either.

From the perspective of Leo III and his contemporaries, the imper-ial coronation appears to have had three functions. In the first place, it was intended to insure the continued Frankish presence in Rome and central Italy in order to protect the papacy from the Lombards and from Leo's Roman enemies, a goal that was achieved. In the second place, by crowning Charlemagne, Leo was reasserting his priestly eminence, his ultimate superiority over the judge who had judged him. Finally, the coronation also restored the right relationship between the two powers, perhaps 'the fulfillment of an Augustinian program of world order, the Christian emperor for the Christian empire, both created to mirror the divine ruler and his universal realm.'[14]

It is easy to say what the empire and the emperor were not. With the possible exception of Rome itself, the imperial name and title were not attached to any specific place. Although Charlemagne's domain was extensive, it did not owe anything except acknowledgement of its size and power to the papacy. One might of course say that he received the imperial title in recognition of his conquest of lesser rulers, that is as a king of kings or as a victorious *imperator*. It would seem, however, that in Pope Leo's mind the title that he conferred upon Charlemagne was not associated with a territory but with an office, a function within the Church. In a curious way, the coronation of Charlemagne can be understood as part of a process that not only expanded Pope Leo's jurisdiction over the secular power, it also reduced the content of the term 'empire' to a functional office within the Church.

The documentary record of the first thousand years of the papal–imperial relationship provided the basis for the eleventh- and twelfth-century canonistic discussion of the nature of the empire. The materials that Gratian employed to create two *distinctiones*, D. 63 and D. 96, provided a history of papal–imperial relations from the Fathers of the Church to Gelasius through the Carolingian era to the Gregorian Reform. It is, of course, a history written to support the reformers' view of the relationship.[15] An analysis of the imperial polemics from the period provides an alternative history of papal–imperial relations, a history espoused by the German kings and their adherents.

Distinctio 63, 'Laymen ought not intervene in any way in [ecclesiastical] elections', contained 36 chapters, many of which dealt specifically with the election of a pope. The elimination of lay participation in ecclesiastical elections was, of course, one of the fundamental goals of the Gregorian reform party. The reformers asserted the right of churchmen to select ecclesiastical officials free from lay interference. At the same time, however, there was a long, documented history of imperial involvement in papal elections, as well as of lay intervention in the selection of priests and bishops, an historical record contained in D. 63. Several of the texts in D. 63 dealt specifically with the role of the emperor in the election of the pope. The problem for the reformers was how to reject this history and thus insulate the Church from lay interference. By denying to the emperor any role in the selection of the pope, the reformers were further reducing the responsibilities and jurisdiction of the emperor, thus contributing to the redefinition of the notion of the *imperium*.

Chapter 22 of D. 63 stated that Pope Hadrian I (772–95) had granted to Charlemagne the right to elect the pope.[16] The following chapter reported that Pope Leo VIII followed Hadrian's example in granting the same privilege to the emperor Otto I in the tenth century.[17] The history of papal–imperial relations in Chapter 63 of the *Decretum* thus included what might be termed the Carolingian view of those relations, a view that made the emperor in some way the superior of the pope even in ecclesiastical matters. While it might be too much to say that this view of papal–imperial relations reduced the pope to the role of imperial chaplain, it does suggest that the emperor played a dominant role in Christian society. The Gelasian balance between ecclesiastical authority and temporal power now seemed weighted in favor of the imperial power.

Other texts in D. 63 and even more in D. 96 demonstrated that the Carolingian image of imperial power contained in D. 63 was in fact erroneous. The theme of D. 96 was that laymen had no right to intervene in ecclesiastical matters. Perhaps the most important text in this *distinctio* was an excerpt from Gelasius's letter concerning the respective roles of the two powers, spiritual and temporal. Gratian provided several ancient texts, starting with a letter from Pope Symmachus (498–514), to prove that laymen, including the emperor, never had any right to intervene in ecclesiastical matters. The second chapter cited emperor Marcian (450–57) who had indicated that his role in the Council of Chalcedon (451) was to support its decisions, not to demonstrate his own power. Several other chapters in this *distinctio* consisted of excerpts from letters of Pope Nicholas I (858–67) that restated the Gelasian balance of power between the pope and the emperor (chs 4–8).[18]

The most assertive chapters in D. 96, however, came from the writings of Pope Gregory VII (1073–85). The overall theme of these chapters (cc.9, 10) was a response to the question: who can deny that 'the priests of Christ as fathers and masters of all mankind can judge kings and princes?' (c.9) The next excerpt, ch. 10, although labeled Gelasius's letter on the two powers, was in fact taken not from that letter but from Gregory VII's recension of it in a letter to Bishop Hermann of Metz. Gregory restated Gelasius's description of the relation of the two powers, stressing that the pope's was the greater responsibility because of his responsibility for the salvation of the emperor as well as for that of all mankind. Gregory added that there were numerous other examples of bishops who judged the actions of emperors: Pope Innocent I (402–17) excommunicated Emperor Arcadius (395–408); Bishop Ambrose of Milan, not even a pope, excommunicated Emperor Theodosius (379–95).[19] Gregory VII not only restored the Gelasian balance in these letters, he tilted it in favor of the Church and the papacy.

Distinctio 96 also contained the text of the Donation of Constantine, one of the most famous and most discussed texts in the history of papal–imperial relations. Briefly put, the Donation alleged that papal jurisdiction over the empire was derived from a grant from Emperor Constantine I (311–37). The origins of the Donation are unclear. It has been dated from as early as the mid-eighth century to as late as the early decades of the ninth.[20] Likewise, its author or authors, are unknown, and the purpose for which it was originally composed is not entirely obvious.

Some scholars have identified the Donation with the efforts of mid-eighth-century popes to obtain the assistance of the Carolingians against their enemies in central Italy, because certain symbolic actions of Charlemagne's father, Pepin, suggest actions that the author of the Donation attributed to Constantine.[21] Our understanding of the Donation and its significance is also complicated by the fact that later generations of medieval lawyers and polemicists employed it for purposes not necessarily envisioned by its authors.[22] What made the Donation important in the history of political thought was its incorporation in the ninth-century legal text known as the Pseudo-Isidore and, subsequently, its inclusion in Gratian's *Decretum*. As Janet Nelson has pointed out, however, the Donation was not employed in the ninth century 'as documentary support for papal imperialism' at this point but for the narrower purpose of serving as 'a proof-text for the inviolability of ecclesiastical property against lay encroachment'.[23]

In the Donation of Constantine, the emperor Constantine, recently converted and baptized, humbly recognizing the superior status of the papacy, declared:

And, to the extent of our earthly imperial power, we decree that his holy Roman church shall be honored with veneration; and that, more than our empire and earthly throne, the most sacred seat of St. Peter shall be gloriously exalted; we giving to it the imperial power, and dignity of glory, and vigour and honour. And we ordain and decree that he shall have the supremacy as well over the four chief seats Antioch, Alexandria, Constantinople and Jerusalem, as also over all the churches of God in the whole world....

...and, through our sacred imperial decrees, we have granted them our gift of land in the east as well as in the west; and even on the northern and southern coast; – namely in Judea, Greece, Asia, Thrace, Africa and Italy and the various islands....[24]

Having made this grant of the West to the pope, Constantine declared:

Wherefore we have perceived it to be fitting that our empire and the power of our kingdom should be transferred and changed to the regions of the east; and that in the province of Byzantium, in a most fitting place, a city should be built in our name; and that our empire should there be established. For, where the supremacy of priests and the head of the Christian religion has been established by a heavenly Ruler, it is not just that there an earthly ruler should have jurisdiction.[25]

Although the Donation was a forgery, it was not a pure invention. The extraordinary claim to imperial jurisdiction that this document contains stems from two undeniable facts: Constantine did grant some properties in the city of Rome to the pope, and he did establish a new capital at Constantinople.[26] Furthermore, Constantine did grant legal recognition to Christianity after the battle at the Milvian Bridge and received baptism at the end of his life.[27]

What is perhaps even more striking in the Donation than the grant of the western lands of the Roman Empire to the pope was the explanation it gave for this grant. The writer [or writers] who produced the Donation did not attribute Constantine's recognition of Christianity to his victory at the Milvian Bridge, the explanation that Constantine's Christian contemporaries provided.[28] Instead, the writer built on a later legend that Constantine accepted Christianity because Pope Sylvester cured him of leprosy. Pagan priests had declared that a cure could only take place if Constantine bathed in the blood 'of innocent infants'. In a dream, however, Saints Peter and Paul appeared to the emperor, telling him that if he went to Pope Sylvester and if he was washed in the saving waters of baptism, he would be cured. Constantine does this, is cured, and in appreciation gives the western lands of the empire to the pope and his successors.[29]

The legendary version of Constantine's 'conversion' placed the responsibility for the conversion not on Christ whose symbol Constantine saw in the sky before his great battle, the meaning of which was explained to him in a dream, but on the pope. The conclusion that the reader should draw from this version of the story is that Christ is approached through the Church whose head, the pope, is the link between man and God. Furthermore, this version of the story emphasized the subordination of the emperor to the pope in place of the direct relationship between Christ and Constantine that the other version of the story implied. The Donation also argued that *de iure*, if not *de facto*, the pope was the legitimate ruler of western Europe and of the other lands specified in the Donation.

Although the precise date of the Donation is unknown, some scholars have argued that it was in circulation by 754 when Pepin met Stephen II at Ponthion, dismounted, prostrated himself before the pope, then rose and led the pope's horse for a short distance, acting as his *strator*.[30] This action appears to have been a carefully staged demonstration of the relationship between the papacy and secular power that employed symbols, Pepin's prostration and then his leading the pope's horse, acts that emulated Constantine's similar act for Pope Sylvester as mentioned in the Donation. In the Donation Constantine reported that he had held 'the bridle of his [Sylvester's] horse, out of reverence for St. Peter ... [performing] ... for him the duty of groom....'[31] This line of argument linked the Donation to the Frankish incursions into Italy at the request of the pope to, as the papacy saw it, restore papal control over the parts of Italy that it had lost to the Lombards. Obviously, the pope wished not only to regain these lands from the Lombards but to bring the secular ruler who acted for the pope in the matter, the King of the Franks, under his control as well. The Donation underscored the subordination of the empire, the greatest symbol of secular power, to the moral authority of the papacy. If the emperor is the groom, the humble helper of the pope, what can a mere king or lesser secular official be in relation to the pope and the Church?

The subsequent history of the Donation suggests that few people took it seriously. As pointed out previously, it survived to be incorporated in the *Decretum* only because it served interests other than papal ones. Two centuries later Emperor Otto III 'was the first to expose the Donation of Constantine before the eyes of Christendom as a forgery....'[32] Otto III claimed that knowledge of the forged nature of the Donation reached the court of his grandfather, Otto I, by way of a cleric who had fled the papal court and revealed the story of the forgery to the emperor. Thus, any papal claims to lands or jurisdiction based on the Donation were invalid. Furthermore, perhaps to under-score the danger of granting lands and power to the bishops of Rome, Otto III pointed to the way in which the popes had wasted the wealth of the city, showing themselves to be poor stewards of the imperial patrimony. Instead of reviving the demonstrably fraudulent Donation of Constantine, out of affection for his old tutor, now Pope Sylvester II (999–1003), Otto III then granted some specific lands to the papacy.[33] In doing this, Otto III was reasserting the superiority of the Roman Emperor over the Roman Pope. Nevertheless, the Donation did not disappear from political debate.

The Donation of Constantine was only one of the elements that contributed to the development of papal and canonistic ideas about the relationship of the papacy to the empire. A second element in the development of the papal claim to oversee the empire was the theory of *translatio imperii*. This theory purported to explain what had occurred between Leo III and Charlemagne at Christmas 800.[34] If the pope was indeed the true ruler of the western half of the Roman Empire, although he did not exercise that power directly, then he had the right to determine who exercised that power in his name. In the eyes of some popes, the coronation of Charlemagne was an assertion of this papal power. The emperor, the papal *strator*, was an official who served the needs of the Church in matters of secular power. It is not at all clear, however, that Charlemagne saw his coronation in the same terms. Charlemagne may have seen the pope as his chaplain.

As we have already seen, the historical roots of the Donation story lay in the fact that Constantine did legalize the Christian Church, although he himself was not baptized until he was on his deathbed, that he did grant some land to the Church, the Lateran area in partic-ular, and that he did build a new capital at Constantinople. Those facts, along with the legend of his baptism by Pope Sylvester, were conflated in the mid-eighth century by an author, or authors, whose apparent goal was to emphasize the pope's power over secular rulers. As Judith Herrin phrased it, the Donation resulted in a theory of Petrine supremacy, in worldly as well as spiritual affairs, that met the pope's needs. It proved that the successors of St. Peter had a historic claim on the loyalty of truly Christian rulers and could be used to put pressure on the Frankish dynasty.[35]

The drawback to the Donation, however, was that it explained papal power in secular affairs in terms of an imperial grant. The Donation could be read as implying the superiority of the secular power over the spiritual authority. It may have been for this reason that Gratian himself did not include it in the *Decretum*. The Donation appears in the *Decretum* because a subsequent editor made some additions known as *palae* to Gratian's text.[36] Furthermore, few canonists appear to have commented on the Donation, suggesting that while the forgery might have been useful in the eighth century, it did not serve the needs of the reforming papacy of the twelfth century.

The decretists, the canonists who commented on, that is, glossed, the *Decretum* dealt with the empire and the emperor not in terms of the Donation but within the larger context of the Gelasian tradition. The major emphasis within the canonistic analysis of secular power was upon the source of the power that secular rulers exercised. The canonists agreed that power, although ultimately originating in God, did not in all cases come directly from Him, so that it was important to determine the channel through which power passed from God to secular rulers. The discussion resolved around two distinct positions, the ecclesiastical tradition, that saw all power within the Christian community as coming from the pope, and a Roman law tradition, which considered the people the immediate source of power by way of the *lex regia*.[37] The position that a canonist took on the immediate source of power was directly related to the position that he took on the problem of the relation of the two powers. Hierocrats, canonists who asserted that the two powers were hierarchically organized with the secular power legally subordinate to the spiritual, argued that the secular ruler's power came from the pope. The opposing school of canonists, the dualists, argued that the two powers were separate and distinct, the spiritual power possessing only a superiority of dignity and that the ruler's power came from the people that he ruled.[38] Finally, in addition to these fundamental positions, there was a third position with regard to the power exercised by kings. Was the power that territorial monarchs possessed derived from the emperor, power from the *lex regia*, that he delegated to them, or was there another source? This last position was intimately linked to the question of the nature of the empire.

The fundamental question was whether secular power was within or outside the Church. The Gelasian tradition implied the powers were functionally distinct, parallel, destined to cooperate, but with the papacy bearing the greater responsibility and so being clearly the superior partner. Within the *Decretum*, however, there was another tradition, one that challenged the conception of the two powers as coordinated equals. The roots of this theme lay in the metaphors of the two keys and the two swords. This metaphor stemmed from the two swords that Christ's apostles possessed and His command to Peter: 'Put thy sword back into its place; all those who take up the sword will perish by the sword.'[39] Medieval thinkers eventually identified the two swords with the two powers, the spiritual and the temporal.[40] This identification, or misidentification, was apparently a later development based upon a misunderstanding of Gratian's use of the phrase. He had used the two-swords metaphor to represent the two forms of coercive jurisdiction that the Church possessed, spiritual, that is excommunication, and physical, that is where the shedding of blood was involved.[41] The actual infliction of physical punishment ordered by the Church was to be performed by a secular official at its command. The *gladius materialis*, the physical aspect of the Church's disciplinary power, was committed to the secular power. Eventually, the canonists confused the secular power's specialized function as the Church's policeman with the Church's superior dignity, leading to the conclusion that the secular power as a whole was identified as a part of the Church's sphere of jurisdiction. Thus, the two swords in the Church's possession came to mean that the Church possessed both spheres of jurisdiction, spiritual and secular.

Once the canonists had placed secular power within the Church, a new question arose. Did the Church possess and exercise secular power or did it delegate the secular power it possessed to secular rulers? Here the metaphor of the keys to the kingdom that Christ had given to Peter came into play.[42] One early canonist, Rufinus, confused the statement about the keys with the following clause in which Christ told Peter that whatever he bound on earth would also be bound in heaven. In this way, the keys became the keys of heaven and earth, or, according to Rufinus, power over clerics and spiritual affairs together with power over laymen and temporal affairs. The pope, Christ's vicar, possessed the two keys but could exercise only the power contained in the spiritual key. The other key, power in temporal matters, he entrusted to the emperors who would then use that power at the direction of the pope. Rufinus did not, however, say that the emperor received his power from the pope, only that he 'confirms' that power which the emperor presumably received from either the people or from the imperial electors.[43]

The generation of canonists that followed Rufinus often referred to the distinction between possessing and exercizing power and in so doing extended its meaning. When, for example, emphasizing the papal origin of the powers that clerics and the emperor possessed, Stephen of Tournai stated that the pope consecrated priests and crowned the emperor.[44]

The next step in the development of the distinction between the two spheres of jurisdiction was to emphasize not Peter's possession of the two swords but Christ's. Some canonists even began to describes Christ as a Priest-King in order to prove that the two powers were united in the same person. With this image of Christ came the indiscriminate use of the symbols of the keys and the swords to represent the two powers. One canonist argued that in His own life on earth Christ had used the two powers. In sacrificing Himself on the cross for the sins of men Christ had acted as Priest. In driving the buyers and sellers from the Temple at Jerusalem, He had acted as King, that is, He exercised secular power.[45] This canonist also argued that Christ was the last person to wield both powers himself because subsequently the spiritual power was granted to the pope while the temporal power was granted to kings. He emphasized that the power of the emperor, and presumably that exercised by other rulers as well, came not from the pope but was derived separately because the two powers are separate.

The most influential commentator on the *Decretum*, Huguccio of Pisa (d. 1210), repeated many of the arguments against the papal origin of secular power found in earlier canonistic writings.[46] In his opinion, the ancient emperors had been both priests and rulers, thus uniting the two powers. Christ, who was both priest and emperor, separated the two offices, granting spiritual power to the pope and temporal to the emperor. Repeating Gelasius, Huguccio noted that man's sinful pride necessitated the separation of the powers. Thus, according to Huguccio, the two powers were separate and distinct so that presumably the imperial or secular power was not derived from the spiritual.[47]

Lest there be any doubts concerning the source of the power exercised by the emperor, Huguccio went to some length to state his position. In the first place, he declared that the two powers were separate, neither being dependent on the other, so that no one could argue for the papal origin of the imperial *gladius*. The pope consecrated the emperor and confirmed the power which he received from the election by the German princes and people, but the only constitutional value of the consecration was that the imperial title could be used by the person elected. The emperor possessed the fullness of his power before the act of papal confirmation.[48] Furthermore, to emphasize the separation of the two jurisdictional spheres, Huguccio added that the pope could not depose the emperor without the consent and the cooperation of the princes who elected him.[49]

The roots of the assertion that the emperor derived his power from the pope can be seen faintly in Rufinus's discussion of the keys that Christ gave to Peter. In describing the distinction between *auctoritas* and *administratio*, Rufinus noted that a bishop appointed a secular administrator, the *yconomus*, to direct the secular functions attached to the episcopal office.[50] This official possessed the *ius administrationis* and functioned under the general direction of the bishop's *ius auctoritatis*. Likewise, after his confirmation and consecration by the pope, the emperor had the *administratio* of the earthly empire while the pope possessed the ultimate *auctoritas*.[51]

Huguccio discussed in much greater detail the relationship between the emperor and the pope, and in so doing gave a more precise formulation to the description of the emperor as in some way an official entrusted with specific secular functions by the pope. He noted that although the statement that the pope possessed the material sword was not true in the broad sense, it was true in one particular case. The pope did possess the *gladius materialis*, the power of temporal coercive jurisdiction, within the city of Rome and its environs.[52] Any ecclesiastic who held a temporal lordship in addition to his ecclesiastical office could be said to possess both swords. But, as Huguccio also emphasized, possession of a material sword by an ecclesiastic did not mean that he possessed it by virtue of Peter's possession of two swords. Such a person possessed the two swords by virtue of exercising two distinct functions, the powers proper to each being derived independently from God, the source of all power. In the case of the pope, the temporal power which he possessed in and around Rome originated with the Donation of Constantine. Although Huguccio did not state explicitly that the Donation was the source of the papal lordship, he did declare that the pope appointed the *patriciatus* or civil governor for the area in and around Rome, a right possibly based on the Donation.[53] In discussing this right of the papacy, however, Huguccio contributed to the later misunderstanding of the traditional interpretation of the papal–imperial relationship. To defend the right of the papacy to grant the coercive power contained in the governorship of Rome, Huguccio observed that the papacy could delegate to another a power which it could not itself exercise. In using this particular terminology, Huguccio was using the same terms as proponents of the papal origin of all secular power employed. What could happen was a failure to realize that Huguccio was considering one special case and analysing it very carefully in order to prevent any confusion. If Huguccio's caution was overlooked, then his position would appear to be that the secular power was derived from the ecclesiastical because the pope possessed the two swords and he delegated the *gladius materialis* to the emperor.

An examination of canonistic glosses from the period 1190–1210 reveals the desire of the canonists to create a synthesis which would present the pope as the source of all earthly power while still respecting the dualistic spirit of the *Decretum*. In order to achieve this, the decretists continued to emphasize the distinction between the possession and the exercise of authority. Various decretists attempted to expand the phrases which suggested that ultimately the secular power was legally subordinate to the spiritual power in order to resolve the question. One canonist discussed the two powers possessed by Christ in terms of possession and exercise, obviously seeking to trace the distinction between *auctoritas* and *administratio* back to the ultimate source of power.[54] Another glossator specifically declared that kings, as well as the emperor, received the exercise of the *gladius materialis* from the pope, thus broadening the scope of papal control over secular power.[55] Yet another canonist dealt directly with the assertion that the powers were separate and distinct. Expanding on Rufinus's distinction between the possession and the exercise of power, this glossator declared that the powers were distinct only at the functional level.[56] To prove the contention that the material sword is in the gift of the pope, the glossator proceeded to argue that the pope may withdraw the sword from any secular ruler who abused his power and then grant the sword to another. Thus, papal possession of the two swords is not simply an abstract principle but a very real fact of political life. Finally, the glossator refuted the objection that the secular ruler's power came directly from God by observing that since the pope can depose secular rulers, he must be able to remove their *potestas gladii* from them and, therefore, he must be the source of the *potestas*.[57]

The increased emphasis on the subordination of the secular to the ecclesiastical power forced the defenders of the dualistic tradition to define with more precision the actual functional relationship between the two powers. Specifically, what relation, if any, existed between the material sword and the spiritual one? No canonist had asserted the existence of an absolute division between the two powers. From Gratian to Huguccio, the need for cooperation between the two powers was constantly voiced. Cooperation was the essential theme of the Gelasian position, a cooperation based on man's twofold destiny, one natural, the other supernatural. In the face of a rising tide of claims for the legal subjection of the secular sphere to the spiritual, there was an ever-increasing need for the defenders of the Gelasian view to make even clearer the difference between cooperation between the two powers and the subordination of one to the other.

The canonist Benencasa d'Arezzo (d. 1206) considered the problem of papal power in terms similar to those employed by Huguccio, but he added some explanatory details involving the relation of the pope to the emperor.[58] Benencasa argued that the pope granted the material sword only to the emperor and to bailiffs within the papal patrimony. Kings received their power not from the pope but from the princes who elected them.[59] Thus, as king of the Germans, the emperor received his power from his election by the electors of the kingdom, but as emperor he received his imperial crown and power from the pope. Furthermore, the linking of the emperor with papal bailiffs suggests that for Benencasa the emperor's role was restricted to the papal lands and only as a papal functionary, further emphasizing the meagerness of the imperial power.

Subsequently, the author of the *Summa Bambergensis* developed the views of Huguccio and Benencasa but with the difference that he demonstrated that Huguccio's concept of the material sword could be reconciled with the view that the pope was the source of all secular power. The author of this *Summa* declared that the pope possessed both swords by virtue of the two swords held by Peter.[60] Furthermore, as if the biblical evidence was not enough, the glossator pointed to the Donation of Constantine as another proof that the pope held both swords. In his opinion, Constantine gave his material sword to the pope in return for being cured of leprosy, thus stating explicitly what Huguccio had implied. Unlike Huguccio, however, this canonist did not define the imperial power in limited terms. Instead of simply referring to power over Rome and its environs, the author of the *Summa Bambergensis* appears to have equated each sword with a universal power, one spiritual, the other temporal. In receiving his sword from the pope, the emperor thus received a papally delegated authority over all secular affairs because the two powers symbolized the two powers necessary for ruling the world.

The various interpretations of the two swords provided a major topic of discussion among late-twelfth- and early-thirteenth-century canonists. Support could be found for the following positions: the pope possessed both swords; the pope possessed only the spiritual sword; the pope possessed the spiritual sword from Christ and the material sword from Constantine. A striking indication of the amount of canonistic interest in the two swords exists in an anonymous gloss that marshalled 14 citations for and against the proposition that the pope possessed both swords. The glossator himself took the position that the pope did indeed possess both swords, although he did not exercise both of them.[61]

About the same time as the canonists began to emphasize Christ's possession of the two powers, the popes began to style themselves vicars of Christ rather than vicars of St Peter as they had done previously. Although this was not an entirely new designation, it became increasingly common after the mid-twelfth century, and the older notion of the Petrine vicariate gradually fell into disuse.[62] Innocent III (1198–1216) completed this trend when he officially adopted the title of Vicar of Christ. This change in title removed a major obstacle in the way of attributing the fullness of both powers to the pope, namely that Peter had never held both powers, so the pope could not either. Although defenders of the claim that the pope did possess both swords attempted to prove that Peter did in fact possess both powers, it was easier to claim to possess both powers directly from Christ because no one would deny that Christ had possessed both powers.[63]

The decretists' discussion of the relationship between the pope and the emperor provided the broad theoretical background to the most complete discussion of papal relationship to the empire, Innocent III's (1198–1216) decretal, *Venerabilem*. Innocent III issued this decretal in an attempt to end the civil war in Germany that had begun at the death of King Henry VI (1190–97). Henry had died unexpectedly young, aged 32, leaving as his presumptive heir the future Frederick II who was not yet 3 years old. The German throne was, however, elective and two adult candidates appeared to contest Frederick's claim to it. The first was his uncle, Philip of Swabia (d. 1208). The other was Otto of Brunswick (d. 1218). In the long run, all three candidates were elected king of Germany. Otto and Philip were each able to win the support of a bloc of the German nobles and to win the votes of some of the seven electors, and each was actually crowned King in separate ceremonies that each candidate claimed was the correct procedure.[64] The claims of Frederick were ignored at this point.

The papacy had a direct interest in the election for several reasons. In the first place, popes had long feared the attempts of the Hohenstaufen kings of Germany to gain effective control of the entire Italian peninsula. Ever since the Ottonians had acquired the Kingdom of Italy in the tenth century, the German monarchs claimed to be the authentic rulers of the peninsula north of the Papal State, the traditional Kingdom of Italy.

In the second place, the marriage (1184) of Henry VI and Constance, the daughter of Roger II (1130–54) and aunt of the last Norman King of Sicily, William II (1166–89), led to Henry VI acquiring that kingdom through the right of his wife after William II died childless in 1189.[65] The Hohenstaufen thus had a legal right to rule virtually all of Italy outside of the Papal State. The papacy found itself in a vise, the jaws of which could squeeze it unmercifully if the handle of the vise was in aggressive hands. The papacy did, however, have a card to play because the Kingdom of Sicily had been a papal fief since 1059 when Robert Guiscard surrendered his kingdom to Pope Nicholas II (1059–61) and received it back as a fief.[66] As the overlord of the kingdom, Innocent III was the guardian of Frederick, the heir to the kingdom. To reinforce that relationship, the young king's mother, Constance, who died toward the end of November 1198, included in her will a clause naming the pope as her son's guardian.[67]

To counter the Hohenstaufen vise that gripped the papal state, the papacy had two legal positions. In the first place, as the Kingdom of Sicily was, in theory at least, a papal fief, the pope could invest anyone whom he wished with that fief after Henry VI's death. In the second place, while the pope had no right to intervene in the election of the German king, he did possess the right to raise the individual whom the electors selected to be king of Germany to imperial rank. As we shall see, on that basis, Innocent III claimed that he possessed the right to determine the fitness of the candidate whom the German electors presented for the imperial office. As this claim did not go unchallenged, Innocent III was forced to defend his position and thereby to define the nature of the empire and the pope's relation to it in *Venerabilem*.

What makes *Venerabilem* even more significant, however, is the fact that there survives in the Vatican Archives a volume containing a file of documents that Innocent III sent and received in the course of the conflict. This file demonstrates how Innocent developed the principles enunciated in *Venerabilem*, providing us with an unusual insight into one pope's process of decision-making.[68]

Innocent III's position on the relation between the two powers in general has been the subject of a great deal of discussion. One line of interpretation sees him as asserting the most extreme papal claims to jurisdiction, claims that would make him in effect the head of a papal world monarchy. On the other hand, there is the argument that although his claims for papal jurisdiction are indeed strong, he did recognize limits on papal power and the existence of an autonomous sphere of secular jurisdiction.[69] In his decision on the imperial crown, Innocent III demonstrated the complexity of his views on the relations between the spiritual and the temporal powers. Innocent himself recognized the importance of *Venerabilem* when he included it in a collection of decretals that he sent to the law school at Bologna.[70]

In the final analysis, Innocent carefully distinguished the imperial office that lay in the gift of the pope from the royal crown of Germany that came from election by the princes of Germany.

> And thus we recognize, as we ought, that the right and power of electing the king [of Germany] who afterwards is to be promoted to the imperial office belongs to the princes.... But the princes ought to recognize that the right and authority of examining the person elected to the kingship and who is to be promoted to the imperial office belongs to us who anoints, consecrates, and crowns him.[71]

This statement was the product of three years of Innocent's involvement in the conflict over the imperial throne between Philip of Swabia and Otto of Brunswick. Each had claimed to be the legitimately elected King of the Germans and therefore entitled to imperial coronation. There were, however, flaws in each election that led to a civil war in Germany as the supporters of the two candidates sought to impose their candidate securely on the German throne. The German civil war itself did not provide a basis for papal intervention. What did necessitate papal involvement was the fact that the king of the Germans was the usual candidate for the imperial throne. Until the Germans settled their conflict and presented a candidate who had the support of all the nobles, the pope was in a legitimate position to intervene in the German situation.

Innocent III developed his theory of a clear-cut division of jurisdiction between the papacy and the empire only gradually. Initially he appears to have been attempting to blur the distinction between the role of the pope and that of the princely electors. For example, in a general letter to the German princes in the summer of 1201, Innocent made only a general allusion to the differences in their roles. After discussing the qualities of the two candidates for the imperial throne, he added that it was not his intention to infringe the 'liberty, dignity, and power' of the princes, but he did not state explicitly what constituted their 'liberty, dignity, and power'. In fact, in the introduction to the letter, the pope seemed to suggest that since the princes had been unable to select a king it was the responsibility of the pope to do it for them.[72]

Innocent never explicitly stated that the pope could select a German king. His arguments always centered on the need of the papacy for its imperial protector. At the same time, he rarely let slip an opportunity to remind the princes that Philip of Swabia and his family were enemies of princely liberties as well as enemies of the papacy. In the same letter to the princes he emphasized that their right to elect the king of the Germans would be impaired by Philip's election because it was Hohenstaufen policy to replace election with hereditary succession.[73] This line of argument suggested that the interests of the princes and of the pope in the election of the king were similar.

In a consistory held at the end of 1200, Innocent discussed the candidacies of Philip and Otto as well as that of Henry VI's young son, the future Frederick II. In evaluating the candidacies of Philip and Frederick, Innocent again blurred the distinction between the imperial and the royal offices, pointing out objections to either man holding these offices. For example, Frederick, being still a child, was clearly unsuitable for any office, much less for the imperial office.[74] Lest his meaning be not completely clear, Innocent added the biblical warning 'Woe to the land whose king is a child.'[75] Turning to the question of Philip's qualifications, Innocent admitted that it would not be proper for him to intervene in a valid election, but the present situation in Germany was clearly not a valid election. He then proceeded to portray Philip as a thoroughly wicked person whom no body of electors would wish to raise to any office. Finally, the pope also again reminded the electors of the threat that Hohenstaufen hereditary succession posed to them.[76]

The confusion of the imperial with the royal office and the denigration of Philip and Frederick were obviously deliberate. With the distinction between the two offices blurred, objections to the candidate for one office were automatically applicable to his candidacy for the other. In arguing that Philip was unsuitable for the royal office, Innocent was applying the arguments he had employed in judging Philip unsuitable for the imperial office. Underlying this confusing – or conflating – of the two offices were 50 years of papal–imperial conflict about the precise relationship between the papacy and the imperial office. Innocent traced the history of the conflict during the twelfth century, even mentioning the letter from Adrian IV (1154–59) to Frederick Barbarossa that had been translated in such a way as to suggest that the empire was a papal fief.[77] While the translation of the term *beneficium* as fief may have been a simple error in translation, it may have been a calculated attempt to test the German response to an extreme definition of the papacy's relation to the empire.[78] The violent reaction of the princes who heard the empire so described had warned Adrian not to push his claims too far.[79] On the other hand, the popes and canonists did not simply define the papal–imperial relationship in terms they thought acceptable to the Germans. For the next 50 years there remained a tension in papal– German relations because the two sides would not or could not agree on a definition of the proper relation that should exist. Innocent III was well aware of this tension.

The conflict between Philip and Otto enabled the pope to benefit from the lack of an agreed-upon definition of the papal–imperial relationship. Otto and his supporters accepted the papal argument that the pope could evaluate the princes' candidate for the imperial office, and that the pope could even reject their candidate if he was unsuitable in papal terms. Philip and his supporters, on the other hand, argued that the pope had no discretion in the matter and he must accept the candidate of the princes. The pope thus had room to manoeuvre between the competing factions, emphasizing or de-emphasizing the papal role in the selection process according to circumstances. Unless the papacy could reach an agreement with the Germans concerning the nature of the papal–imperial relationship in which the papal view of the relationship was fully accepted, the best situation was one in which some flexibility remained.

In *Venerabilem* Innocent did make such a definition, one not completely favorable to the papacy, but necessitated by his failure to win over Philip's supporters. The continued strength of the Swabian's support meant, at best, a stalemate. The papal conception of the emperor as the defender of the Church required an end to the German conflict. Furthermore, Innocent's failure to resolve the problem was a blow to papal prestige. Finally, as Innocent admitted, papal involvement in the electoral process was highly unpopular among the princes in both camps.[80] Philip had drawn upon this antagonism when he attempted to win over Otto's supporters by pointing to the papal legate's role in the election.

The need for a defender of papal interests and the need to placate the princes forced Innocent to demarcate the respective papal and princely roles in the two selection processes. In effect, he rejected any direct papal role in the election of the German king and any direct princely role in the selection of the emperor. The pope's power was clearly the superior one, however, because he could refuse to consecrate the prince's choice if he was unsuitable in the pope's judgement, thus giving the pope veto power over the prince's choice for German king.

In making this choice, Innocent chose between two conflicting streams of canonistic thought about the relation of the pope to the emperor and, by extension, about the relation of the spiritual power to the temporal. On the one hand, he had the arguments of Huguccio who had argued that the two powers were separate and distinct.[81] Regarding the imperial office, Huguccio had gone so far as to say that although the pope consecrates the emperor-elect, the emperor's powers come from his election by the princes and people. In sharp contrast to Huguccio's position, his contemporary, Alanus Anglicus, had viewed Christian society as an organic whole with the pope as its head.[82] In this view, all legitimate secular power, even that of the emperor, came from the pope. Innocent rejected both extremes, absolute separation of the powers or inclusion of all secular jurisdiction within the ecclesiastical.

In the case of the Holy Roman Empire, Innocent reminded the German princes that the empire was in the gift of the pope because its primary function was to defend the papacy from its enemies. The Empire existed to serve the needs of the papacy. It was an office and a function, not a place. At the same time, the autonomy of the German princes in the election of a king was limited by the need of the papacy for a defender.

According to Innocent, the pope had the right to examine the suitability of the candidate for the imperial office because the papacy had long ago 'transferred the Roman Empire from the Greeks to the Germans in the person of the great Charles'. After all, what if the German princes elected as their king, 'a sacrilegious person or an excommunicate, a tyrant, a fool, or a heretic? Ought we to anoint, consecrate, and crown such a man? Of course not.' Furthermore, if the German princes failed to agree on a candidate for the throne, the pope would be within his rights to identify and install on the imperial throne a candidate who would be acceptable. The fact that the princes could not agree among themselves should not prevent the papacy from having the 'advocate and defender' that it needed. Furthermore, history was on the papal side, a pope having chosen between candidates for the imperial crown in an earlier dispute.[83]

In a gloss on *Venerabilem*, the compiler of the *Glossa Ordinaria* to the *Decretales*, Johannes Teutonicus (fl. 1215), expanded on Innocent III's position, spelling out the importance of a papal defender in more detail. He explained that when the Lombards were attacking the papal lands during the eighth century, the pope, Stephen II (752–57) first called upon the emperor at Byzantium.[84] When he failed to come to the pope's aid, Pope Stephen 'transferred the *imperium* to Charles the Great, the son of Pepin' whom Stephen's predecessor Zacharias (741–52) had placed on the Frankish throne when his predecessor had proved incompetent.[85] The glossator was emphasizing the right of the pope to remove an incompetent ruler when their incompetence endangered their own people or the papacy. Here again, the functional nature of government, especially of the imperial government, was being stressed.

The author of the *Glossa Ordinaria* went on to explain that even though the ruler at Constantinople retained the imperial title, he was not a real emperor any more than the king on a chessboard was a real king.[86] The true emperor was the one who did what an emperor should do, in this case defended the papacy, not simply the person who bore the title of emperor. In explaining the transfer of the imperial title from Constantinople to the West, the glossator was echoing the language that had accompanied the deposition of the last Merovingian monarch. According to a chronicler, Pepin had written to Pope Zacharias asking whether the royal crown should be on the head of a powerless monarch. The pope responded 'that it was better for the man who had power to be called king rather than one who remained without royal power....'[87] In effect, according to the author of the *Glossa Ordinaria*, just as one pope had suggested the deposition of the last Merovingian because of his powerlessness, so too another one could remove the imperial title from a Byzantine ruler who failed to perform the functions of a true emperor. That he retained the name of emperor was of no consequence.

In the final analysis, Innocent III's *Venerabilem* provided the fullest development of the papal and canonistic conception of the empire and its place within Christian society. This empire was not a place but an office in the gift of the papacy, and while the elected king of the Germans was the usual candidate for the office, it was open to any Christian. Innocent appears to have had some notion of an orderly Christian world in which the pope and the Christian rulers, headed by the emperor, would direct spiritual and temporal aspects of life in a cooperative manner for the good of all Christians. Innocent's role in the imperial election, in attempting to bring peace between the kings of France and England, and in ending the civil war between John of England and his nobles suggests the role that Innocent III believed the pope should play. It also indicated the place of the empire in his vision of society.

Innocent III's vision of a neatly structured Christian society reached its peak at the Fourth Lateran Council, but it remained a vision and not a reality.[88] Frederick II received the imperial title in 1220 and proceeded on a career that led to almost 30 years of papal–imperial conflict and to his being excommunicated several times. Popes and canon lawyers might see the empire as an office within the Church, a tool to be employed in the service of the spiritual power, but Frederick clearly did not. As it turned out, the papacy was able to destroy the Hohenstaufen attempt to create some kind of imperial power on their own terms. What the popes who defeated the Hohenstaufen could not do was to replace them with more acceptable rulers. The papal crusade against Frederick II's heir Conrad IV (1250–54), the disputed election of 1257 and the Interregnum (1254–73) reflected the inability of the papacy to implement Innocent III's vision.[89] It also demonstrated that the Hohenstaufen attempt to create an empire on their own terms could not succeed either. Popes and emperors thought in grandiose terms that the political scene could not support in practice. Although papal coronation was considered essential to legitimate possession of the imperial crown until the sixteenth century, the papacy had little real impact on the imperial election in the later Middle Ages. Charles V was the last German emperor to receive papal coronation.

4 The Emperor as *Dominus Mundi*

For, if it is agreed that mankind as a whole has a goal (and this we have shown to be so), then it needs one person to govern or rule over it, and the title appropriate to this person is Monarch or Emperor.

Thus it has been demonstrated that a Monarch or Emperor is necessary for the well-being of the world.[1]

Let our first conclusion, then, be: The Emperor is not the lord of the whole earth. This is proved from the fact that dominion must be founded either on natural or divine or human law; but there is no lord of the earth in any of these....[2]

From the perspective of some supporters of papal power, the emperor was an official or a functionary of the papacy, the secular ruler to whom God had entrusted the physical protection of the papacy through the imperial coronation, the *Imperator vicarius papae*. There was another view of the emperor's status, however, that of the Roman legal tradition. With the revival of Roman law in the twelfth century, emperors and their officials came to possess a legal theory that justified imperial power in terms that did not recognize any papal role in the selection of the emperor.[3]

According to the *Digest*, the emperor was 'the Lord of the World'.[4] In the early stages of the re-emergence of Roman law in the twelfth century, however, this concept received little attention. Indeed, Kenneth Pennington has recently argued that 'Modern historians ... have focused on questions of the emperor's and the pope's claims of universality to the exclusion of other issues that had, in fact, more relevance for medieval jurists.'[5] Nevertheless, the theme of the emperor's universal jurisdiction was a important one in subsequent discussions of the concept of empire. In the fourteenth century Dante took the Roman law discussion of the emperor as *dominus mundi*, joined to it a philosophical tradition about the unity of mankind and, in his *Monarchia*, produced a theory of universal imperial rule that would have displaced the papacy as the head of a universal society. Subsequently, in the sixteenth century Charles V seemed on the verge of creating a truly world-wide empire. Writing to Charles V in 1519 Hernan Cortés declared that the lands he was in the process of conquering were so great that 'one might call oneself the emperor of this kingdom with no less glory than of Germany, which, by the Grace of God, your Sacred Majesty already possesses'.[6] Later generations were also impressed with the claims to universal imperial jurisdiction so that, for example, when James Bryce wrote his history of the empire, he stressed the importance of medieval Christian universalism and its links to the theory of imperial universalism.[7] Friedrich Heer's more recent work on the empire, the work of a citizen of the Habsburg heartland, places even more emphasis on the history of imperial universalism, suggesting that the only solution to wars and international conflicts is the establishment of a universal government, a world government in the tradition of the Holy Roman Empire.[8]

The Roman law statement about the emperor as universal lord was, in itself, not enough to make the emperor an equal (or superior) of the pope. The obvious fact was that the empire as it existed in the twelfth and later centuries was not actually universal in scope and a phrase lifted from the ancient law would not change that fact. Nevertheless, the lawyers did debate whether the emperor was *dominus mundi* at least *de iure* if not *de facto*, suggesting that in a rightly ordered world there would be some form of universal jurisdiction.[9]

There is no doubt that Roman lawyers discussed the theory of the emperor as *dominus mundi*. The question remains whether any German ruler who bore the imperial title actually thought of himself as the true *dominus mundi*. The one group of emperors who do seem to have so thought of themselves in those terms were the Hohenstaufen emperors, especially Frederick I (1152–90) Barbarossa and his grandson Frederick II (1212–50). As is well known, Barbarossa encouraged the study of Roman law and, in the view of one scholar, 'sought to apply in practice the universalist conception of the Roman emperorship found in the *Corpus Iuris Civilis*'.[10] Furthermore, with Barbarossa lawyers trained in the Civil Law came to play a larger role in government. Perhaps the most famous illustration of Barbarossa's personal interest in the powers of the emperor was the discussion he was said to have had with several doctors of law regarding the argument that the emperor had the right to dispose of all private property. Frederick obviously preferred the view that the emperor as lord of the world could dispose of all private property.[11] Nevertheless, it is not absolutely clear that as a practical matter Frederick I actually saw himself as the *dominus mundi*.[12]

A more significant application of the theory of the emperor as the *dominus mundi* appeared in Barbarossa's relations with the other kingdoms of Europe. Faced with a double papal election after the death of Adrian IV (1154–59), Frederick Barbarossa asserted his imperial responsibility for calling a council to determine whether Alexander III (whose election was eventually upheld [1159–81]) or Victor IV was the true pope. The language of a letter sent to the German bishops ordering them to attend the council suggested that Frederick saw himself as the lord of all the Christian kings of Europe. He was calling to the council not only the bishops of Germany, his own subjects, but 'those of the other kingdoms as well, France, England, Spain, and Hungary'.[13] Stated this way, Frederick seemed to be asserting that the bishops of these other kingdoms were his subjects as well. On the other hand, in a letter to Henry II of England (1154–89), inviting him to send bishops to the council, Barbarossa did not include the language that implied some kind of imperial jurisdiction over the English clergy.[14] In another situation, however, a chronicler recorded Barbarossa labeling the kings of England and France 'the kings of provinces', suggesting that they were only subordinate rulers who had succeeded to offices equivalent to that of Roman imperial governors, making them subordinate to the emperor.[15]

The career of Barbarossa's grandson, Frederick II, contains some statements that also suggest that he saw himself as the lord over the kings of Europe. In particular, after Pope Innocent IV (1243–54), ordered Frederick II deposed in 1245, Frederick responded with a letter to the kings of Europe rejecting the papal claim to a right to depose rulers. In the letter, Frederick warned the kings of Europe that what the pope had done to him he could do to them. 'You', he wrote, 'and all kings of particular regions have everything to fear' from a pope who claims such powers. Frederick's reference to his fellow monarchs as 'kings of particular regions', however, suggested another threat to their independence because he was echoing his grandfather's description of kings as rulers of provinces.[16] In Frederick II's case, the call for support against the papacy in these terms must be seen primarily as a last-ditch effort to retain his throne in the face of papal opposition and not a thought-out statement of the relation between the emperor and the kings of Europe.

An even more important aspect of the debate about the jurisdiction of the emperor arose not from the legal tradition but from the Christian tradition. The Roman law had attributed the powers of the emperor to the *lex regia*, a law that purported to transfer the power of the Roman people to govern themselves to the emperor.[17] When the Roman lawyers added to this the argument that the power of the people had in turn come from God, it made the emperor equal in some way to the pope. The fourteenth-century Roman lawyer (and canonist) Baldis de Ubaldus (c.1327–1400), representing the 'mainstream juristic interpretation', attributed 'a thoroughly theocratic origin to the power of the emperor, who is God's vicar on earth'.[18]

To the divine origin of the source of the power that the *lex regia* gave to the emperor, the supporters of the empire's universal mission added another support drawn from the Christian tradition. As Baldus pointed out, Christ Himself identified the divine origins of the empire when he spoke of rendering to Caesar that which was his.[19]

Although the Roman lawyers discussed the nature of the empire and produced a theory of empire that enabled them to locate the empire outside the Church, they were not the most imaginative defenders of the empire. It was Dante Alighieri who brought the legal, theological, and philosophical traditions together to create the most powerful defense of the universal empire in his *De Monarchia*. This defense of the empire could compete intellectually with the papal conception of the empire within universal Christian society.

In the *De Monarchia*, Dante presented the issues very directly. In his opinion, the question of the empire can be reduced to three fundamental questions.

> The first is the question whether it is necessary for the well-being of the world. The second is whether it was by right that the Roman people took upon itself the office of the monarch. And thirdly, there is the question whether the Monarch's authority is derived directly from God or from some vicar or minister of God.[20]

Dante's answers to these questions provided the most complete defense and justification for the existence of a universal Christian empire. When later writers discussed the medieval empire, they often did so in the terms that Dante presented. Along with the lawyers Bartolus and Baldus, Dante shaped the views of Mercurino de Gattinara, the advisor who contributed to Charles V's conception of universal empire.[21]

Dante based his argument on the proposition that there is an 'ultimate end of human society as a whole...'.[22] That being the case, there 'can be no substantial objection either from reason or authority' to the statement that 'temporal monarchy is necessary for the well-being of the world'.[23] The leads to the conclusion that the 'title appropriate to this person [who will rule the world] is Monarch, or Emperor'.[24] Lesser political units, kingdoms, in turn 'must be subordinate to one ruler or rule, that is, to the Monarch or to Monarchy'.[25]

In the second section of the *Monarchia*, Dante defended the Roman Empire against the criticism of St Augustine (d. 430) and others. In the *City of God*, Augustine had attacked Rome as having begun in fratricide and then moved on to bloody conquest throughout the known world. Rather than being worthy of admiration, Augustine argued that the Roman Empire was only worthy of condemnation.[26] From Dante's perspective, however, the Romans acquired their empire 'by right, not by usurpation' because the 'Roman people were the noblest' people among mankind.[27]

Furthermore, Dante asserted that 'God did indeed intervene miraculously in the foundation of the Roman Empire', a conclusion he supported with citations from Livy and other pagan writers.[28] Dante then went on to present the history of world empires, a history that began with the ancient Assyrians. In his view, the history of mankind has been the history of a sequence of world empires, one conquering another in a history that climaxed with the victory of the Romans over their enemies, a victory that he termed a triumph 'by divine decree'.[29] For him, the victory of the Romans over their enemies was a kind of trial by combat, a 'duel' that leads to 'the judgment of God' in the conflict between the contending powers.[30]

In addition to being a just empire because it was the product of a duel, the Roman Empire also had the blessing of God upon it. If, Dante argued, 'the Roman Empire was not founded upon right then Christ, by his birth, assented to an injustice'.[31] Throughout His life, Christ obeyed the laws of the Romans, thus demonstrating the righteousness of that empire.

In the final section of the *Monarchia*, Dante turned to the problem of the relationship between the empire and the papacy. Specifically, did the emperor receive his power directly from God or through some intermediary such as the pope? Here he turned to an analysis of the arguments that the popes and the canon lawyers employed to defend the theory of papal superiority over the empire. For example, one of the great clichés of the papal position was that the relationship between the ecclesiastical and the secular powers was similar to that of the relationship between the sun and the moon. Just as the moon gets its light from the sun, so the secular rulers receive their power from the Church. As Dante pointed out, 'it does not follow' because the moon received its light from the sun, 'that the moon is derived from the sun'. That being the case, 'temporal government does not owe its existence to spiritual government, nor its power ... though it certainly receives from the spiritual government the energy to operate more powerfully...'.[32]

In the course of the argument, Dante proceeded to refute the papal claim to superior jurisdiction by rejecting the various biblical proof texts that the popes and the canonists had employed. His argument was that the powers that Christ conferred upon Peter and through Peter to his successors were spiritual in nature and did not authorize the pope 'to bind and loose the decrees of the Empire'.[33] Furthermore, Dante rejected any papal claims to power based on the Donation of Constantine, arguing that 'it did not fall within the power of Constantine to dispose of the Imperial prerogatives, nor within the Church's power to accept them'.[34] The most that Constantine could have done would have been to 'grant the Church guardianship over one part or another of his patrimony' authorizing the pope to act 'not as a proprietor, but as administrator of the fruits for the benefit of the Church and the poor of Christ – as the apostles are known to have done'.[35]

In the final analysis, Dante returned to a modified Gelasian position on the relationship between the two powers. He argued that God designed mankind for a dual end, happiness in this world and in the next. This duality 'explains why two guides have been appointed for man to lead him to his twofold goal: there is the Supreme Pontiff who is to lead mankind to eternal life ... and the Emperor who ... is to lead mankind to temporal happiness'.[36] Each of these figures has a responsibility and power directly from God. The pope's role, however, is a strictly spiritual one while the emperor's is temporal. Neither should intervene in the jurisdiction of the other. The emperor, nevertheless, is 'obliged to observe that reverence towards Peter which a first-born son owes to his father'.[37]

The implications of Dante's conception of the imperial role in the world were grandiose and it is difficult to believe that he actually believed that the world should be directed by the emperor. Although Dante was obviously quite serious about the problem of imperial–papal relations, like the Roman lawyers, there is an element of playfulness in his demonstration of the natural unity of mankind that then requires a single world ruler. Furthermore, Dante's view of human history as a kind of imperial round-robin in the course of which empires defeat one another in a divinely ordained contest contains a rather bleak view of human history.

Dante's conception of empire brought together several strains of medieval thought about empire in a convenient fashion. A. P. d'Entrèves has argued that there was only one original point in the *Monarchia*, the notion of *humana civilitas*, the rest being restatements of traditional positions.[38] Seen in that light, the *Monarchia* might seem of limited interest. Its importance lies, however, not in the originality of the specific points advanced but in the overarching conception of human unity, *humana civilitas*, that it presents, and the logical political consequences that flow from that conception. The *Monarchia* continued to be read by those who found that the constant warfare that afflicted Europe caused not only physical harm but moral and spiritual harm as well.

The Habsburg court in the sixteenth century saw a number of figures interested in Dante's views.[39] Dante was sufficiently important for Hugo Grotius that he went to the trouble of rejecting his views in his *On the Law of War and Peace*. In Grotius's opinion, Dante's conception of a universal empire would never work because it was too large and unwieldy to be effective.[40] Nevertheless, Dante's goal of world peace through a universal government did not die out. Even Grotius and the international law thinkers who succeeded him sought to reduce the severity of wars if not end war entirely just as Dante had. They differed not on the goal but on the means by which such a goal could be achieved. The continuing interest in the *Monarchy* was rooted more in the goal than in the means that Dante supported. James Turner Johnson has suggested that Dante's discussion of world peace was an early stage of a tradition that was to 'be carried on by Renaissance utopianism, the "perpetual peace" movement of the Enlightenment, and the internationalism of the nineteenth and twentieth centuries'.[41]

Grotius's objection to the notion of a universal empire, the impracticality of such a large governmental structure, was related to the actual condition of the Empire in medieval Europe. Even in Dante's own day, the reality of imperial power and of the jurisdiction of the Empire was in almost inverse proportion to his image of it. In practical terms, the most important question concerning the Holy Roman Empire, after the issue of its relation to the papacy, was the relation of the empire to the emerging kingdoms of Europe. If the emperor was 'the true Lord of the World', did that mean that kings were his subordinates? The relations of the Emperor to the emerging kingdoms of

Europe generated some interesting lines of debate, especially among the canon lawyers.

As we have already seen, the papacy saw the empire not as a universal, coordinate power but as an office or function at the disposal of the Church. Nevertheless, the canonistic tradition considered some questions concerning imperial jurisdiction. For example, in the *Decretum* Gratian included a brief excerpt listing the elements of the Roman *ius quiritium*, the law of inheritance, wardship, contract and prescription. The excerpt declared that these particular legal practices were unique and proper to the Romans, suggesting that the use of these practices was a sign of subjection to Rome.[42] Quentin Skinner has attributed the opposition of English lawyers and rulers to the use of Roman Law in England to 'feelings of xenophobia' and a belief that the use of any but the Common Law meant 'foreign interference' in English legal matters.[43] Subsequently, the reception of Roman law into a society raised the issue of whether the use of that law signified subordination of some sort to the Roman emperor.

Only a few of the commentators on the *Decretum*, the decretists, discussed the Empire at any length. One important locus for decretist discussion of the Empire was a letter of St Jerome (c.347–c.420) declaring that every community required a single source of authority. Gratian took an excerpt from this statement to support the contention that there should be but a single bishop within each church, by which he meant each diocese. The reason for this was that the unity signified by a single head was essential for all societies, human and non-human. As in every hive of bees there is a single head (*princeps*), so there should be a single judge within each province and a single emperor within the Empire. In addition to the parallel with the insect world, Jerome pointed out that both biblical and profane history demonstrated that dual leadership could not be sustained. Romulus killed Remus to establish the rule of one man, paving the way for the greatness of Rome, and Esau and Jacob fought while still in their mother's womb. Both cases demonstrated that duality must always give way to unity.[44]

The most important of the decretists, Huguccio, raised several important questions about the Empire, beginning with the status of the emperor at Constantinople. Was he *the* emperor, that is the one true emperor, or a co-emperor with the western holder of the title? Huguccio responded that the ruler at Constantinople employed the imperial title unlawfully, usurping the title that belonged to the Roman emperor, that is the emperor approved by the Romans.

Furthermore, Huguccio added that there was only one emperor and all kings were subject to him. Huguccio did not, however, spell out the precise details of this subjection.[45] Elsewhere Huguccio noted that every province should have its own king and that there should then be a single emperor who would be pre-eminent over all the kings.[46] By using the term 'province' for what were obviously territorial monarchies, Huguccio was suggesting that each of the monarchies was a continuation of an old Roman province and that the kings bore the same relation to the emperor as provincial governors had borne.

Huguccio's position on the relation between the Empire and the emerging kingdoms was not, however, entirely clear.[47] In one place he argued that the Byzantine ruler could not be the true emperor because he did not recognize the papal headship of Christian society, suggesting that imperial jurisdiction was limited to those lands that were subject to the Church of Rome and that the emperor was the senior secular official within that sphere.[48] In another gloss, however, Huguccio recognized that kings were independent of the empire but subject to the pope.[49] This gloss could be reconciled with Huguccio's other statements that stressed the notion of a single universal (or at least Christendom-wide) empire if he meant that those monarchs who did not admit subjection to the empire possessed only a *de facto* independence, not a *de iure* independence.

Another decretist dealt with the status of the Empire in terms similar to those employed by Huguccio, but drew out some of the details that Huguccio had left implicit. This writer argued that Rome was the common *patria* of those who used Roman law, adding that Jews and Latins who used Roman law ought to be subject to the emperor. At the same time, he also admitted that although in his own day many refused to admit this subjection, they did recognize their subjection to the Church and, therefore, to Rome.[50] This argument suggests that in practice the empire was not coterminous with the Church, nor even with those lands using Roman law.

Another decretist rendered the vague discussion of the relation between royal and imperial power in very specific terms. Were the kings of England and France obliged to obey imperial laws? His answer was that they were indeed bound to obey those laws, but that such obedience did not imply subjection to the empire. Those kingdoms that did employ Roman law did so 'not because the emperor issued them but because the Church had confirmed them'.[51] For this decretist, obedience to Roman law was a sign of membership in the Church and not of subjection to the Empire. This argument reduced the Empire to some undefined role within the Church, leaving the universal responsibilities once attached to it assigned to the Church.

The issue of whether the use of Roman law meant subjection to Roman imperial jurisdiction may have played a role in the English rejection of Roman law in the person of the twelfth-century Italian lawyer and teacher, Master Vacarius. He had come to England at the request of Archbishop of Canterbury, Theobald, in whose household he subsequently taught. It is also known that he was forbidden to teach Roman law by order of King Stephen (1135–54) and that although the ban was eventually lifted, Vacarius and the law he taught had little long-term effect in England.[52] In the eighteenth century William Blackstone argued that the ban on the teaching of Roman law in England was the response of a people used to 'a mild and rational system of laws' while only 'the monkish clergy (devoted to the will of a foreign primate) received it with eagerness and zeal'.[53] Further on, Blackstone quoted approvingly an assertion by fourteenth-century nobles 'that the realm of England hath never been unto this hour, neither ... shall it ever be, ruled or governed by the civil law'.[54] At the end of the nineteenth century, another scholar echoed this sentiment, suggesting that, in rejecting Roman and canon law, the English were standing up 'for the law of the Anglo-Normans against the decrees of the Roman popes and emperors'.[55]

Modern scholarship has tended to see the English opposition to canon and civil law in political terms rather than in terms of a conflict between legal systems. 'Vacarius', according to one recent writer, seemed to be 'a formidable opponent and trainer of young men as potential opponents of the crown and dynasty.'[56] Seen in this light, Stephen's ban on the teaching of Roman law becomes a side-effect of the mid-twelfth-century English dynastic crisis and Vacarius a kind of *agent provocateur* whose influence over the coming generation of clerics might prove dangerous to the interests of the monarchs. Nevertheless, there does seem to have been a feeling in England that the laws of the English were, for the English, the equivalent of the Roman laws for the Romans (or for their twelfth-century heirs in Germany).[57]

The *Glossa ordinaria* to the *Decretum* also contained references to the emperor's universal jurisdiction. In commenting on the *ius quiritium*, the glossator stressed the connection between the use of Roman law and recognition of imperial political supremacy. The emperor being the '*princeps totius mundi*', the supreme secular ruler, the kings of the several territorial kingdoms, or provinces (*provinciae*), were only regional governors whom he appointed. Furthermore, this writer stressed that the use of the Roman law of inheritance required recognition of the imperial supremacy.[58] In yet another gloss, the same decretist stated that there were those who believed that the emperor crowned the kings.[59]

Finally, the *Glossa ordinaria* to the *Decretum* repeated the argument that although two rulers claimed the imperial title, there was in fact only one true emperor, the one subject to the Roman Church, because the pope had transferred the seat of empire from east to west.[60] Here again, the true empire was the one whose head recognized the source of his office in the papal *translatio imperii* and accepted the empire's place within Christian society.

For the most part, the commentators on the *Decretales* focused their attention not on the emperor as the source of royal authority but on the exemption of the kingdoms from any imperial jurisdiction. One of the earliest decretalists, Tancred (c.1185–c.1235), did refer to the emperor as 'over all kings ... and all nations are subject to him ... for he is the prince and lord of the world...'. He also argued that the Byzantine emperor was not a true emperor although he was generally termed emperor. His justification for this was the argument that 'outside the Church there is no *imperium*...'.[61] This of course identified the Empire with the Church, placing the true Empire within the Church.

The more important theme within the decretalist tradition, however, asserted that the king within his kingdom possessed the same powers as the Emperor within the empire.[62] The roots of this theory had first appeared in the *Decretum* with Gratian's definition of a *constitutio* as 'an edict or command established or issued by a king or emperor'.[63] Some decretists understood this to refer to the emperor who was King of the Germans until the pope raised him to the imperial office.[64] Other glossators, however, understood this statement to mean that kings could issue laws for their own kingdoms, but that the emperor could issue general laws, binding on all men.[65]

The final stage in the development of a theory to justify the exemption of kings from imperial jurisdiction came in Innocent III's decretal *Per venerabilem*. Innocent issued this decretal in response to a request from Count William of Montpellier to legitimate two of his children. The pope could clearly legitimate illegitimate children in ecclesiastical law, so that, for example they could be ordained priests (canon law forbade the ordination of illegitimate children). On the other hand, it was not clear that the pope could legitimate in secular law outside of the papal state. Making the issue even more complicated was the fact that earlier Innocent III had legitimized two children of the king of France.[66]

In *Per venerabilem* Innocent III rejected Count William's request, pointing out that the French king had requested the pope to legitimize his children because there was no one else the king could ask to do this. The pope pointed out that 'the king [of France] acknowledges no superior in temporal affairs and so, without injuring the right of anyone else, he could submit himself to our jurisdiction and did so'.[67] On the other hand, Count William did have a secular overlord, the king of France, who could grant the request. If the pope was to grant the request, he would be impinging on the jurisdiction of the king. 'It is not', Innocent wrote, 'that we want to prejudice the rights of anyone else or to usurp any power that is not ours...', language that echoes his words to the German princes in *Venerabilem*.[68] In both decretals, however, Innocent's position serves to undercut the independence and jurisdiction of the emperor. In *Venerabilem* the pope made it quite clear that the imperial office was the pope's to award, and he reduced its role to that of an office or function within the Church. In *Per Venerabilem* Innocent further undercut the emperor's jurisdiction by observing that the king of France had 'no superior in temporal affairs', thus rejecting the emperor's claim to universal jurisdiction.

Among contemporary canonists, there were several who echoed Innocent III's rejection of the emperor's claim to jurisdiction over all Christian rulers. Alanus Anglicus (*fl.* 1190–1215), for example, suggested that although there had once been a single emperor and a universal empire, in his own day there were numerous kingdoms that were clearly in fact exempt from imperial jurisdiction. Each ruler of these kingdoms 'possessed the same jurisdiction in his kingdom as the emperor had in the empire'.[69] In Alanus's opinion, the *ius gentium* justified this claim of exemption from imperial jurisdiction and the papacy had approved it. Another English canonist, Ricardus Anglicus, a contemporary of Alanus, made a similar argument about the exemption of kingdoms from imperial jurisdiction. Pointing to the political situation in Europe as it existed in his own day, Ricardus observed, 'it is evident that many kings are not subject to the emperor, for it seems that, just as they were subdued by force, so they can return by force to their proper liberty'. This particular line of argument underscored the notion of empire as the result of conquest but without any suggestion that the history of violence associated with empires was part of some divine plan. Furthermore, Ricardus Anglicus appears to have considered emperors little different from kings. 'And the army elects an emperor, so by the same reason it can elect a king.... Since then both emperor and king are anointed with the same authority, with the same consecration, with the same chrism..., why should there be a difference in their powers?'[70] This in effect flattened the difference between royal and imperial power, suggesting that if the king's power in his kingdom is the same as that of the emperor in the empire, so too, the emperor's power in the empire is the same as that of the king in his kingdom, thus reversing the usual cliché.

While these English canonists discussed the exemption of kingdoms from the empire in general terms, citing no specific examples of such exemption, Spanish canonists provided a concrete case and they did so in terms that have suggested to some scholars that modern nationalism has its roots in these medieval discussions of the relationship of the empire to kingdoms.[71] The Spanish canonists asserted the exemption of the Spanish kingdoms from imperial jurisdiction in response to an assertion found in Johannes Teutonicus's ordinary gloss to the *Decretum*. Johannes Teutonicus explained that although the emperor was the *dominus mundi* and was specifically superior to the kings of Spain and of France, there were those who denied this superiority. He pointed out that the argument for the exemption of the Spanish kingdoms was based on the argument that the Spanish themselves had delivered their lands from the hands of their enemies (obviously the Muslims who had conquered almost all of Spain in the eighth century), and had not relied on imperial assistance.[72]

Johannes Teutonicus seems not to have believed the argument that Spain was exempt from imperial jurisdiction because one Spanish canonist, Vincentius Hispanus (d. 1248) explicitly attacked Johannes's position. According to Vincentius, echoing the argument of Ricardus Anglicus, everyone knew that Charlemagne had been unsuccessful in his attempt to gain control of Spain. Furthermore, 'I, Vincentius, say that the Germans have lost the empire by their folly.... Only the Spaniards have acquired an empire by their valor....'[73] In other words, the Spanish kingdoms freed themselves from Muslim domination by their own actions and so recognized no conqueror or overlord. They were now independent, equal to other independent rulers or even to the Holy Roman Emperor.

The English and Spanish canonists discussed here, as well as lawyers elsewhere, contributed to the process by which the Empire's theoretical pretensions to universal jurisdiction were being reduced to fit the political realities of thirteenth-century Europe.[74] The notion that the king in his kingdom possessed the same powers as the emperor within the empire was a legal doctrine destined to have a long history, as Kenneth Pennington has pointed out. The modern notion of sovereignty, usually associated with Jean Bodin and the development of early modern political thought, was rooted in these medieval discussions of the relationship of the emperor to the kings of Europe. The tension between universal – or at least European-wide – imperial jurisdiction and limited territorial jurisdiction also foreshadowed the early modern conflict between empire and state. In both cases, there was a built-in tension between strong, centralized government over a limited territory with a homogeneous population and government over a large area, the constituent elements of which were not contiguous and the population of which was multi-lingual and multi-cultural and many regions of which had long histories of self-government. The story of the medieval empire might have served as a cautionary tale for the rulers of early modern empires.

5 Empires – Metaphysical and Moral

Westward the course of empire takes its way,
  The four first acts already past;
A fifth shall close the drama with the day –
  Time's noblest offspring is the last.[1]

from the beginning of the newborn world up to this age, as we read, there never was universal peace except when the whole world lifted its eyes to the one Caesar Augustus, as to the celestial kingship.[2]

Thus far, the discussion of the concepts of empire and emperor has dealt with political units and political actors who occupied real political space. The concept of empire involved actual governments and officials or, at the very least, as in papal political theory, individuals who carried out real governmental functions under papal supervision. Empire and emperor could have other meanings, however, meanings that were metaphysical or mystical or moral, not identifying real people and institutions but providing an explanation of God's providential plan for mankind or judging a form of government that morally corrupted those who practiced it.

The first of these uses of the terms empire and emperor had a long history, originating long before the Middle Ages. As the earlier discussion of Dante's *De Monarchia* pointed out, the concept of empire could refer to a divinely ordained sequence of great powers, four world monarchies or empires, engaged in a conflict that would eventually lead to a single great empire.[3] The wars and struggles that characterized the history of the Near East and the Mediterranean world, the known world of the ancient and early medieval eras, could be reduced to a teleological schema that ultimately led to the fullness of God's plan. In other words, the concept of empire could have a metaphysical reality, describing an institution that played a unique role in the providential plan for mankind. In such a perspective, the actual empires were of little significance in themselves, acquiring their importance from their role in the divine plan.

The notion that human history was the story of a continuous series of world monarchies or empires was rooted in the prophetical Book of

101

Daniel. King Nebuchadnezzar had dreamed of 'a statue that was very large and extraordinary in appearance. The sight of it was terrifying. The head ... was of pure gold, its chest and arms were of silver, its belly and hips of bronze, its legs of iron, and its feet partly of iron and partly of terra cotta.' After Nebuchadnezzar's usual sorcerers and other wise men failed to provide an interpretation of the dream, Daniel provided it, saying to the king:

> You, O king – king of kings, to whom the God of heaven has given sovereignty and power, strength and glory, and to whom he has handed over the men, the wild animals, and the birds of the air in the whole inhabited world, making you ruler of them all – you are the head of gold.

His reign would be followed by a series of lesser kingdoms until the day that

> the God of heaven will set up a kingdom that will never be destroyed, nor will this kingdom ever be delivered up to another people. It will crush and put an end to all those other kingdoms, while it itself will stand forever....[4]

This imagery, repeated elsewhere in Daniel, 'suggests a framework of four successive world-kingdoms in this order; the Babylonians, Medes, Persians, and Greeks (or Macedonians)'.[5]

The seventh chapter of Daniel discussed the last of the kingdoms. The Fourth Kingdom, identified as a beast, 'dreadful, terrifying, and exceedingly strong, with great teeth of iron and claws of bronze' will persecute the faithful [7:7] until in turn it is 'slain and its body destroyed, consigned to consuming fire.' [7:11] Then, according to Daniel, there would come someone who would receive

> ... domination – glory and kingship.
>   Every nation, tribe, and tongue must serve him; His dominion is to be everlasting, never passing away; his kingship never to be destroyed. [7:14]

The Jewish apocalyptic tradition subsequently identified the one who was to come as the Messiah.[6] Seen in this light, the theory of the four monarchies becomes part of the millennial and apocalyptic tradition found not only in Judaism but in Christianity as well.[7]

Modern scholarship has demonstrated that the theory of history built around the four world monarchies that the Book of Daniel provided was not unique to the Jewish community (although the apocalyptic aspect of that tradition certainly was unique to Judaism and Christianity). The concept seems to have been known as early as the fourth century BC and seems to have risen in Persia. Thus, 'the Book of Daniel merely reflects the oriental tradition about these empires'.[8]

The theory of the four monarchies/empires subsequently became 'current in Rome at least as early as the first quarter of the second century BC'. For the Romans, the final empire in the sequence, sometimes the fourth, sometimes 'the fifth and more glorious empire' would of course be theirs.[9] Polybius, the Greek hostage who devoted his years of honorable captivity in Rome to a history of the Roman people, alluded to the theory of the cycle of great empires that had ruled the known world. He pointed out to his readers that he would 'compare with the Roman domination the most famous empires of the past, those which have formed the chief theme of historians'. These historical empires were the Persian, the Lacedaemonian, and the Macedonian. The Roman Empire was thus the fourth and last in this cycle. The Roman Empire differed from these earlier empires because 'the Romans have subjected to their rule not portions, but nearly the whole of the world (and possess an empire which is not only immeasurably greater than any which preceded it, but need not fear rivalry in the future).'[10] Polybius went on to explain that the Greeks were not 'well acquainted with the two states which disputed the empire of the world', that is, with Rome and Carthage, so that he was obliged to present their histories to his Greek readers.[11]

For Polybius, the cycle of empires or world monarchies was a consequence of the 'Fortune' that 'has guided almost all the affairs of the world in one direction and has forced them to incline towards one and the same end'.[12] Thus, the Roman domination of the world in his own day was the product of forces similar to those that Daniel saw as the cause of the cycle of empires. The major difference was that Daniel was looking to the Fifth Monarchy as the culmination of the historical process while Polybius saw in the Rome of his day the fourth and final stage in this historical process.

With the development of Christian histories the theory of the cycle of world monarchies took on a new significance. The Christian conception of history, like the Jewish, was linear, showing 'a development with a unique beginning, central event, ultimate goal, told by scripture'.[13] The sequence of empires was teleological because there was to come a fifth and final monarchy. In the first place, this Christian history was found in the Vulgate Bible that offered the story of Daniel and the image of the series of world monarchies. Subsequently, the image appeared in other writings, such as St Augustine's *City of God*. The Bishop of Hippo sought to explain the meaning of human history to his anxious flock, observers of and participants in the collapse of the Roman Empire, the empire sometimes seen as the last in the cycle of great empires. For him, the four kingdoms were the Assyrian, the Persian, the Macedonian, and the Roman. Following Jerome's commentary on the Book of Daniel, Augustine saw this historical cycle in apocalyptic terms, describing the Fourth Kingdom as that of Antichrist. This stage of history would be followed by a spiritual kingdom, not a temporal one, that would be the end of the historical cycle.[14]

Augustine's contemporary Orosius, author of a universal chronicle, also repeated the theme of the four world monarchies, having apparently learned of it by way of a now-lost Roman historian, Pompeius Trogus (third century AD), whose writings had been later summarized by a writer identified as Justin (third century).[15] In his version of the historical cycle, 'Babylon, a city of the Assyrians' was the first empire while 'Rome, which today equally dominates the world', is 'the last empire'.[16]

The image of the four monarchies continued to surface occasionally in various later chronicles as the writers sought to place their own eras within a larger framework of meaning. Notker the Stammerer (c.840–912), for example, began his biography of Charlemagne with a reference to the 'all-powerful Disposer of events, [who] having destroyed one extraordinary image, that of the Romans, which had, it was true, feet of iron, or even feet of clay, then raised up, among the Franks, the golden head of a second image, equally remarkable, in the person of the illustrious Charlemagne'.[17] Clearly, for Notker, the Frankish monarchy, the possessor of the *imperium* granted by Leo III, was the Fifth Monarchy of Daniel's prophecy. In the next century, Liutprand of Cremona identified the Ottonians as the leaders of the Fifth Monarchy because of their role in stopping the advance of the Muslims.[18]

Thus, by the beginning of the high Middle Ages, there were available to Christian thinkers several variations on the theme of universal empire that linked World Monarchy or World Empire with the divine plan for mankind. Furthermore, as Notker and Liutprand made clear, the empire that Leo III had transferred from Byzantium and granted to the Franks could be identified with the Fifth Monarchy that was the climax of the divine plan.

The high point of this line of historical development came in the twelfth century when a German bishop related to the Hohenstaufen family, an uncle of Frederick Barbarossa, Otto of Freising (d. 1158), produced the most important work of world history from a Christian perspective since Augustine and Orosius. His *The Two Cities* was a history of the world from its beginning to his own day, shaped by the historical outlook of Augustine, as the title makes clear, and of Orosius.

For Otto, the traditional cycle of empires fitted within Augustine's theory of two cities, the two fundamental communities that comprised all mankind. For him, the most important of these empires were the first, the Babylonian, and the last, the Roman, identified with gold and with iron.[19] When writing *The Two Cities* Otto concluded that 'we who live in the closing days of that kingdom are experiencing that which was foretold concerning it, and expect that what we have yet to fear will soon take place'.[20] That is, for Otto his own age was the final phase of the Roman Empire, the iron age of the cycle of empires. This empire was to be the last in the cycle of empires so that he was compelled to place within that empire all human history from the rise of the Roman Empire to his own day and beyond. For example, Otto saw Constantine as initiating the *translatio imperii* when he moved the imperial capital from Rome to Constantinople so that 'the sovereignty of the Romans [was] transferred to the Greeks'.[21] Subsequently, when Leo III crowned Charlemagne, the empire was returned to the West.[22] Thus, the *translatio imperii* became a part of the cycle of empires that carried out God's plan for mankind.[23] Furthermore, according to Janet Nelson, 'Otto's Augustinianism could be espoused by the *politiques* of Barbarossa's court; it supported claims to superiority over all the *regna* of Christendom…'.[24]

In the Eighth and final book of *The Two Cities*, Otto of Freising then explained the events that would mark the end of the Roman Empire and thus the end of the world as men know it. The Antichrist will appear and the members of the Church, the City of God in Otto's view, will be tested. The faithful members of the Church will attain 'the highest blessedness' while the members of the other 'will fail and descend to the utmost misery'.[25]

For Bishop Otto,

the empire of the Romans, which in Daniel is compared to iron on account of its sole lordship – monarchy the Greeks call it – over the whole world, a world subdued by war, has in consequence of so many fluctuations and changes, particularly in our own day, become, instead of the noblest and the foremost, almost the last.

Otto then saw the subsequent course of imperial history as one of decline and decay. The empire having been

> transferred from the City [i.e. Rome] to the Greeks, from the Greeks to the Franks, from the Franks to the Lombards, from the Lombards again to the German Franks, that empire not only became decrepit and senile through lapse of time, but also, like a once smooth pebble that has been rolled this way and that by the waters, contracted many a stain and developed many a defect. The world's misery is exhibited, therefore, even in the case of the chief power in the world, and Rome's fall foreshadows the dissolution of the whole structure.[26]

In the final book of *The Two Cities*, Otto of Freising discussed the end of the Roman Empire and the appearance of the 'Antichrist, and the resurrection of the dead and the end of the Two Cities'.[27] As he pointed out, these images linked

> the Apocalypse of John ... to the visions of prophets of old, particularly Daniel and Ezekiel, and that the earlier prophecies were necessarily explained by it. In the final vision he describes – the vision of the temple and of Jerusalem – he is like Ezekiel; in that of the last judgment and of the kingdom of Christ he is like Daniel. ... and that Daniel prophesied not, as the Jews believe, concerning a judgment of the Gentiles and an earthly kingdom of the Messiah, but of the true heavenly and eternal judgment and kingdom of Christ.[28]

By making this argument, Otto linked the Book of Daniel's vision of a cycle of empires with the apocalyptic and millenarian tradition identified with the writings, authentic and otherwise, of Joachim of Fiore (1145–1202) as well as with Augustine's conception of history as the struggle of the two cities.[29] The Calabrian abbot employed a different historical schema than did Otto of Freising (or anyone else), one that saw the history of the world as a tripartite process, the successive ages of God the Father, God the Son, and God the Holy Spirit. The age of the Spirit, the final stage of human development, would be 'preceded by a period of incubation' during which 'Antichrist would have his reign'. The Antichrist 'would be a secular king who would chastise the corrupt and worldly Church until in its present form it was utterly destroyed. After the overthrow of this Antichrist the Age of the Spirit would come in its fulness.'[30]

In Joachim's writings, the Antichrist was unnamed, but among those who took up his ideas and developed them, there emerged a body of pseudo-Joachite prophecies that identified the Antichrist who would reform the Church before the end as the Emperor Frederick II. Those who developed the pseudo-Joachite literature perceived Frederick in more than one way. For the German Joachites, Frederick II was their saviour, a positive image, while to Italian Joachites, he was the Antichrist, a clearly negative image. Frederick's unexpected death in 1250 'was a catastrophic blow' to both of these groups.[31]

The solution to this blow, at least for the German Joachites, was to deny that Frederick II had died. Instead, as Peter Munz has pointed out, Germans linked Frederick II to tales of a good emperor who would bring on a new golden age. Frederick slept within a mountain, perhaps Mount Etna, perhaps Kyffaüser, until the time was ripe to commence the new golden age.[32] Periodically during the fourteenth and fifteenth centuries peasant rebellions and millenarian fantasists proclaimed the re-emergence of the sleeping emperor and the beginning of the end of the world as it had existed. The once and future emperor was the avenging force who would reform both the spiritual and temporal orders, paving the way for Christ's kingdom on earth.

In contrast to those who saw the empire in apocalyptic terms in the later Middle Ages and the Renaissance, there were others, especially among the conciliarists and the humanists, who saw the meaning of empire in positive moral terms. The humanists, for example, debated the best form of government not in terms of power and conquest, the usual explanation for empire, but in terms of moral worth. What form of government was best designed to nurture the qualities of the good citizen, the republic or the empire?[33] As a result, the humanists were less interested in the effectiveness or efficiency of governmental forms than in the moral consequences of those structures.

Although there were numerous discussions of the significance of the empire in the writings of fourteenth- and fifteenth-century scholars, both humanists and non-humanists, these later discussions of empire have been seen as only restating traditional positions and consequently have received little scholarly attention.[34] Recently, however, some scholars have begun to find significance in discussions of empire in the writings of those associated with the conciliar movement and in the writings of Renaissance humanists. For a conciliarist such as Nicholas of Cusa (1401–64), the emperor shared with the pope responsibility for the right order of Christian society. Although in recent years the humanists have generally been identified with republican government, it was possible for a humanist such as Aeneas Sylvius (1405–64), Pope Pius II (1458–64), to provide a defence of the moral role of the empire in Christian society without denying the value of republics.

Let us first consider the concept of empire in connection with the conciliar movement. It should not come as a surprise that conciliar thinkers considered the nature and function of the empire. They were after all seeking to create a new ecclesiastical structure, one that would resolve, among other issues, the relationship between the Church and secular society.[35] While much of this literature has something of an antiquarian air about it, repeating older ideas and language somewhat mechanically, not all of it has this flavor.

For Nicholas of Cusa, a leading conciliarist whose *Catholic Concordance* provided a powerful discussion of the right order of Christian society (and which has recently appeared in an English translation), the relationship between the pope and the emperor, their 'concordance', was the key to an orderly Christian world. Cusa, for example, rejected the Donation of Constantine and the theory of the *translatio imperii*.[36] Instead of a papally dominated Christian society with the emperor as chief papal agent, Nicholas of Cusa envisioned a Christian world order headed by pope and emperor jointly. As the pope is the head of the ecclesiastical hierarchy, so the emperor is, or ought to be, head of the temporal hierarchy with kings and lesser officials subject to his oversight.[37] Cusa's conception of a 'concordance' of powers, spiritual and temporal, provided a more balanced relationship between the two powers than previous ones.

Nicholas of Cusa's re-ordering of the relationship between papal and imperial powers was only one way in which fourteenth- and fifteenth-century thinkers reconsidered the concept of empire. At least one significant Renaissance humanist saw the concept of *imperium* in moral terms, though not in the same terms as did the spiritually minded thinkers. For many, though certainly not all, humanists, the Roman Empire, and thus the imperial form of government in general, was a corruption of a better form of government, the Roman Republic. The intellectual debate could even be reduced to the way in which humanists responded to one situation. Did one side with Julius Caesar who established the empire, or with Cicero who supported the

Republic? Seen in graphic terms, did one agree with Dante who placed Brutus and Cassius, along with Judas, in Lucifer's mouth at the very heart of the Inferno, or did one condemn Dante for his support of the empire?[38] Were the defenders of the Republic seeking to restore a dying way of life or were they attempting to block God's providential plan for mankind? As Hans Baron concluded: 'Dante appeared to be wrong in his appraisal of Caesar and his enemies; the view of the ancient and medieval Empire enshrined in the *Divina Commedia* became alien to Florentine readers.'[39]

The major focus of scholarship has been the development of republican thought and its implications for modern political development. Republics were associated with virtue while empires were associated with moral corruption. One result of this outlook was the humanists' interest in the Roman Republic and the causes of its degeneration into the empire.[40] As John Pocock has pointed out, some humanists re-evaluated Julius Caesar and his assassin Brutus, rescuing 'Brutus from the depths of infamy into which Dante had cast him'.[41] In the final analysis the argument was not about the most effective form of government but about which form of government would be most congruent with the development of man as a fully developed moral actor.

The debate about the degree to which Renaissance humanists supported republicanism and rejected empire has played a significant role in scholarly debate since the publication of Hans Baron's work on Italian civic humanism. Baron sought to identify Renaissance humanism with republican government and as the enemy of tyranny and imperialism. As he phrased the situation, the fourteenth century saw 'the emerging alternative between the building of one absolute, empire-like monarchy on the one hand, and regional independence with the preservation of civic liberty on the other...'.[42] Specifically, Baron saw in Florentine opposition to the expansionist policies of the despotic Visconti of Milan a tyrannical spirit than was countered by the republican spirit of the Florentines that foreshadowed the opposition of the democracies to the Nazism in the twentieth century.

For Hans Baron, the Florentines, the epitome of the Renaissance humanistic spirit, produced 'a Humanism which refused to follow the medieval precedent of looking upon the Rome of the emperors as the divinely guided preparation for a Christian "Holy Empire" and the center of all interest in the ancient world...'.[43] In taking this position, Baron stood in sharp opposition to Jacob Burckhardt, whose *Civilization of the Renaissance in Italy* had dominated the study of the Renaissance since its first appeared in 1860. For Burckhardt, the central figures of the Renaissance were the forceful, ruthless men who seized power and asserted their dominance over other men, his true individuals. Despotism ... fostered in the highest degree the individuality not only of the tyrant or Condottiere himself, but also of the men he protected or used as his tools...'.[44] For Burckhardt, men like Caesar were characteristic of the Renaissance and the glories associated with that age were the product of such men and their striving.[45] These men were the moral opposite of the citizen of the humanist city-state. The heroes of Burckhardt's Renaissance were the villains of Baron's.

Baron's work has generated a good deal of controversy and also a good deal of work on the concept of civic humanism and its role in the shaping of early modern political thought. The work of Quentin Skinner and J.G.A. Pocock, to cite the most influential scholars in this area, has both criticized and developed Baron's work.[46] What it has also done has been to suggest that the civic humanists were part of a mainstream of political thought that rejected any notion of empire because of its association with tyranny.

Recently, however, a younger student of political thought, Cary Nederman, has begun to re-examine the Renaissance humanist attitude toward the concept of empire. He contends that at least some humanists saw a positive value in the Empire, thus rejecting Baron's equating of humanism and republicanism.[47] From this perspective, fourteenth- and fifteenth-century thought on the issue of the empire is potentially more interesting than previously believed.

The focus of the recent interest in the positive view of the empire in the ranks of the humanists is Aeneas Sylvius Piccolomini, better known as Pope Pius II (1458–64). Before becoming pope, Aeneas was a well-known humanist who had followed a familiar career-pattern for humanists, that of secretary for a secular ruler, in his case for the Emperor Frederick III (1440–93).[48] Some scholars have found Aeneas Sylvius's defense of the empire as of little significance because in their view he was an opportunist who simply articulated views that supported his employer's interests.[49] More recently, however, Nederman has pointed out that Aeneas Sylvius's 'political thought is treated (at least implicitly) as an anachronistic reversion to the mental constructs and categories of the Latin middle ages rather than as the reflection of an authentically renaissance perspective on politics'. Even those scholars who rejected Baron's equating of humanism with republicanism have not considered Aeneas Silvius's work on the empire as an example of humanist support of an imperial vision.[50] This suggests that even without Baron's argument, scholars had already written off any defense of empire as little more than an antiquarian exercise.[51]

While in the service of Emperor Frederick III, Aeneas Silvius wrote the *De ortu et auctoritate imperii Romani*, a defense of the universal jurisdiction of the emperor. Instead of seeing the empire as a vast war-machine designed to crush republican city-states, Aeneas Sylvius stressed that the right order of the world demanded that 'all people and powers are by right under the Roman emperor in temporals and seculars as under the Pontifex Maximus in spirituals'.[52] In making this argument, the future pope was not simply asserting imperial power but rather he was restating the Gelasian view of the world, i.e. that the world was directed by two powers working jointly to achieve the ultimate good of all men. He also argued that those who argued that their kingdoms were no longer subject to imperial jurisdiction because of their own actions, clearly a reference to Spanish canonistic tradition, which had made this argument, were in error.

> But some say that by their own virtues they have earned that privilege, even without the intervening authority of the emperor. For they say that they had conquered, by their own arms and by their own blood, the provinces which were occupied by barbarians or by enemies of the Christian name and which did not recognize the Roman empire.[53]

Like Dante, Aeneas Sylvius saw in the empire the guardian of world peace and order, although he placed more stress on the papal role in world order than did the future pope.

According to Nederman, the imperial perspective of Aeneas Sylvius even reflected a tension in the writings of Cicero himself, the exemplar of humanist republicanism. In his view,

> Aeneas recognizes that Cicero's own work embraced an unresolved tension between what might be termed 'nationalism' (or more properly, if less elegantly, 'civism') and a 'supernationalism' or 'transnationalism' which might be used as the foundation for a theory of universal empire.[54]

In Nederman's view, this tension arose in Cicero's writings because of the Stoic influence on his outlook. In the Stoic view 'Reason itself is the bearer of the communal bond' that causes men to 'congregate because reason reveals to them the advantages that stem from co-operation'. On the other hand, 'Cicero also recognizes that rational self-interest is insufficient as the basis for a stable and harmonious society.' One consequence of this is 'the appointment of governors and the formulation of laws whose purpose is to maintain social order by imposing justice on the community'.[55] The result was the creation of numerous political units, each with its own laws and customs, within which men sought to live virtuously and in accordance with justice.

The creation of numerous political units as a result of the natural desire of men to live peacefully with one another meant wars and conflict as local rulers, even with the best of intentions on both sides, seek the interests of their own societies. Since 'the very purpose for which civil justice was instituted', that is, 'the maintenance of harmonious relations among human beings,' is frustrated by such conflicts, some means to mediate disputes among political units must exist.[56] It is the emperor who sits at the apex of human power who will serve this function because in the 'empire alone does political power finally attain a form consistent with the universalistic tendencies of sociability implicit within human nature'.[57]

The conception of empire that Nederman finds in Aeneas Sylvius' writings suggests that the concept of empire was still evolving and had applications for even the world of republican city-states. This conception of empire has roots in medieval thought about the nature of human society, but it also reflects a harsh political reality – the emerging kingdoms of Europe are constantly at war with one another, as were the Italian city-states. As the experience of the Florentines with the Visconti of Milan made clear, in order to maintain the city-state, the ideal form of human society, it might be necessary to have some overriding authority that could protect the virtuous from the less-virtuous.

Furthermore, as any humanist must have realized, even the Greek city-states had been unable to cooperate peacefully in the work of creating a truly just society. Thucydides, after all, made that point quite clear.[58] The Roman Empire, however, the age of mankind apparently most favored by God (or why would Christ have been born under its banner?) provided both world order and room for men to develop just local and regional societies. This empire was neither an all-powerful conqueror nor simply a stage in the providential plan for mankind, it was a natural and rational institution that would guarantee the fullest flowering of human sociability. Thus, instead of being a symbol of corruption and tyranny, the murderer of the republic and republicanism, so to speak, for Aeneas Sylvius the empire was the guardian and guarantor of republicanism.

In many ways, the metaphysical and the moral concepts of empire were destined to have a major impact on the way in which later generations understood empires and emperors. The Protestant Reformation let loose a wide variety of religious ideas, including the notion of the Fifth Monarchy, the final world empire that would appear near the end of time.[59] In the seventeenth and eighteenth centuries, even as the Holy Roman Empire of the German Nation was declining into political irrelevance and becoming transformed into the Austrian Empire, the concept of empire continued to attract the interest of politically involved individuals who feared the moral implications of imperial government and preferred republican government instead.[60] Above all, empires were by definition expansionist, a fact that inevitably led to the moral corruption of their citizens.

6 The Golden Age of Empire

... for I wished Your Highness to know all the things of this land, which ... are so many and of such a kind that one might call oneself the emperor of this kingdom with no less glory than of Germany, which ... Your Sacred Majesty already possesses.[1]

If the colonies are not subject to the authority of parliament, Great Britain and the colonies must be distinct states, as completely so, as England and Scotland were before the union, or as Great Britain and Hanover are now.... Let us suppose ... allegiance due from the colonies in the person of the king of Great Britain. He then appears in a new capacity, of king of America, or rather in several new capacities, of king of Massachusetts, king of Rhode Island, king of Connecticut, etc. etc.[2]

Although historians of political thought have generally identified the Middle Ages as the age of empire and the modern world as the age of the state, in fact, the most extensive period of imperial development was from the sixteenth to the nineteenth centuries.[3] No medieval monarch ruled a domain as extensive as that of the Holy Roman Emperor Charles V, or that of the Spanish monarch Philip II (1556–98) who ruled more than twenty kingdoms, or even that of George III of England (1760–1820). What is of special interest here is that with the exception of Charles V, and then only in part of his domains, these rulers were not labelled emperors. What John Adams said of the British Empire, that there was no such institution in either the law or the constitution, was also true of the Habsburg family possessions outside the boundaries of the Holy Roman Empire. There was no Spanish Empire any more than there was a British Empire. What existed were several medieval personal monarchies, dynastic agglomerations of territories that had little in common except that they shared the same ruler.

In spite of the fact that the terms empire and emperor were not employed in the legal and constitutional sense that John Adams noted, nevertheless these terms were employed in discussions of governance from the sixteenth to the eighteenth centuries. We will consider here some of the ways in which these terms were employed, the relationship of those usages to medieval usage, and the significance of those usages for the history of political and legal thought.

The career of Charles V provides a striking illustration of the difficulties that the use of the terms empire and emperor created. In his capacity as Holy Roman Emperor, he was the heir of Charlemagne, of the Ottonians, and of the Hohenstaufen, the *dominus mundi* of the Roman Law, and the agent of the papacy. In practice he was the ruler of a collection of German principalities over which he had little control outside of his own dynastic territories. Guided by Archbishop Berthold of Henneberg (d. 1504), his grandfather, Maximilian I (1493–1519), had proposed unsuccessfully to create institutions that would provide a common imperial superstructure in matters of defense and justice.[4] While these reforms would not have transformed the Holy Roman Empire from a loose confederation into a modern state, they might have prepared the way for such a transformation.

Charles V was also the last emperor to receive the imperial crown from the hands of the pope and was thus emperor in the papal understanding of the term, that is the Church's protector and agent.[5] Subsequent emperors rejected any papal role in their office and any imperial role as an agent or official of the papacy. The Peace of Westphalia (1648) that ended the religious wars in Germany completed the process whereby the Germans severed the Holy Roman Empire from the papacy. The pope played no role in the peace negotiations, and the subsequent papal condemnation of the terms of the peace reflected the anger that the papacy felt at that action.[6] From the papal perspective, Westphalia undid the knot that had joined the empire to the papacy since the coronation of Charlemagne eight centuries earlier. In place of pope and emperor resolving disputes among the kingdoms of Europe along religously based lines, by the mid-seventeenth century there emerged the modern 'secular system of international relations' associated with the name of Hugo Grotius (1583–1645).[7]

In Spain, as Charles I of Castile, Charles I of Aragon, etc., Charles was also the heir of the legal tradition that stressed the independence of the Spanish monarchs from *the dominus mundi*. In Castile, for example, he was sovereign, a *rex in regno suo*, a king who possessed the powers of an emperor within the boundaries of his own kingdom because the emperors had not protected the people of Spain from their enemies.

Finally, Charles was an emperor in the sense that Hernan Cortés used the term – he was at the head of a vast territory brought under his control by force of arms. In Cortés's opinion, the size and scope of his conquests in Mexico 'are so many and of such a kind that one might call oneself the emperor of this kingdom with no less glory than of Germany'.[8] This was an empire in the ancient Roman sense, the product of armed conquest. Charles was in fact occasionally identified as the Emperor of the Americas.[9]

As Frances Yates has demonstrated, the reign of Charles V seemed to many contemporaries, especially writers and scholars, as the revival of the medieval conception of universal empire. She pointed out in *Astraea*, her discussion of the imperial image in the sixteenth century, that the imperial themes found in the work of writers and painters 'raised again the phantom of empire which had haunted the Middle Ages, but in a modernized form'. The voyages of Columbus and his successors were at the same time revealing to European eyes previously unknown lands, suggesting to some 'that these discoveries were themselves a portent of a new world monarchy'.[10] Indeed, there were some contemporaries such as the historian Johann Sleidan (1506–56) who saw Charles V as the last in the prophet Daniel's list of emperors.

> The prophet has foretold that the Roman Empire should be the last, and the most powerful.... Yet after all, God has at last given us the most potent emperor that has reigned in many ages. For in the person of this prince are united the succession of many rich and powerful kingdoms and inheritances, which by reason of their situations have afforded him the opportunity of performing great things, by sea and land.

In Sleiden's opinion, Charles was the last in a line of 'illustrious and great princes' whom God appointed 'when the ecclesiastical or civil state were to be changed'. These included 'Cyrus, and Alexander the Macedonian, C. Julius Caesar, Constantine, Charles the Great, and the Ottos of Saxony...'.[11]

The sixteenth-century revival of Daniel's imperial imagery and its appropriation by the supporters of the house of Habsburg led to a critique of the concept. Jean Bodin devoted an entire chapter of his *Method for the Easy Comprehension of History* to the 'Refutation of Those Who Postulate Four Monarchies and the Golden Age'. He specifically rejected Sleiden's work among others, pointing out that if any ruler deserved to be identified as the fourth world monarch, it was 'the sultan of the Turks', who ruled a far larger area and was far more powerful' than any other ruler, presumably including Charles V.[12]

In effect, the career of Charles of Habsburg in the first half of the sixteenth century involved several of the meanings medieval thinkers and writers had attributed to *imperium* and *imperator*. Scholars have debated for decades how Charles and those around him understood his imperial role. To what, if any, extent, did they see his role as that of a universal ruler or, at the very least, as a ruler whose domains were coterminous with Christendom? In recent years, a great deal of scholarly attention has been paid to Charles V's chancellor, Mercurino de Gattinara (1465–1530) as the inspirer of grandiose imperial claims for Charles V.[13] The work of John Headley has been especially important in this regard, using as he did an extensive array of archival materials, including those found in the long-closed Gattinara family archive.[14] Headley has pointed to the role of late medieval imperial thinkers, especially Dante and the lawyers Bartolus and Baldus, in shaping Gattinara's outlook.[15] Gattinara even sought the publication of a new edition of Dante's De *Monarchia*, 'the classic text for imperial claims', although this project came to naught.[16]

In many ways, however, the imperial vision attached to the reign of Charles V remained a literary and artistic movement, not a real empire in the sense of a coherent governmental structure. Charles's empire consisted of the dynastic lands and claims of the Habsburg family. What was lacking were the basic components of a governmental infrastructure that cut across the boundaries of the various kingdoms and units that formed this inheritance. The question is, as Headley has pointed out, 'whether there ever was an imperial chancellery under Gattinara that attempted to function not simply for the Holy Roman Empire but for the entire Habsburg *monarchia*'.[17] There is some evidence that Gattinara wished to undergird the empire of literary and religious theory with imperial institutions, but this effort never achieved the full articulation of an imperial government. Charles V remained in fact truly emperor only in the Holy Roman Empire.

When Charles V resigned his various crowns and offices over a period of several months in 1555 and 1556, the dynastic union that had joined the Habsburg possession was broken permanently, although that was not Charles's original intention.[18] The imperial title remained with the Austrian branch of the family and for all practical purposes it became the hereditary possession of that family although the imperial electoral college remained in existence. Under the leadership of the Austrian Habsburgs, the Holy Roman Empire eventually declined into political irrelevance until Napoleon officially ended its existence in 1806.

The real power of the Habsburgs lay with the Spanish branch of the family, beginning with Philip II who ruled an even larger domain than had his father. In addition to the Spanish kingdoms and numerous principalities in Europe and the Spanish overseas possessions that he inherited from Charles V, in 1580 Philip II obtained the Portuguese throne as well. As king of Portugal as well as king of Castile, Philip, in theory at least, had claims to exclusive rule over all of the newly discovered lands covered by Alexander VI's bull *Inter caetera*, making him ruler of virtually the entire world. He bore numerous titles, including a score of royal titles, among which were King 'of the Islands of the Indies, East and West, and the mainland of the Ocean-Sea' and 'lord in Africa and Asia'.[19] What Philip II was not, at least not in law, was an emperor.

Spanish lawyers and bureaucrats wrestled with the problem of defining the nature of Philip's possessions. At the beginning of his reign, the fundamental problem was that Philip and his ministers 'had no ... plan or programme, certainly not during the first 25 years of the reign'. In fact, the dilemma was especially great because an earlier attempt at a program had ended when 'Charles's and Gattinara's universalist plans had clearly failed in the middle of the sixteenth century.'[20]

Philip II's problem was more complex than his father's. Although Charles had reigned over numerous lands, his major focus was the Holy Roman Empire, where he faced the Protestant Reformation internally and the Muslim threat externally. Furthermore, his interests were not administrative and bureaucratic. Like his medieval predecessors, Charles V had seen himself as a warrior king. Philip II, on the other hand, was the first modern, desk-bound ruler, famous for the long hours he spent at his desk writing state documents and annotating memoranda from officials throughout his dominions.[21] Although Philip II may not have had a formal, written program of government, several themes did characterize his reign. Within Europe he was anxious to rationalize and modernize the government of his scattered possessions. In this sense, he was anxious to create a state out of the collection of dynastic lands that he had inherited. Outside Europe he had to wrestle with the governance of a wide variety of foreign possessions that posed particular problems. How were these possessions, especially the vast lands of the Americas, to be included within his realm? Finally, transcending these two structural problems, was Philip's desire to be the sword and shield of the faith, a role traditionally associated with the emperor. Was it possible to achieve all of these goals? The eventual outcome indicated that it was not possible.

The bedrock problem that Philip faced was that the scores of European kingdoms and other principalities that he ruled had created their own legal and constitutional systems over a period of several centuries and were quite unwilling to surrender them. His war in the Netherlands, for example, simplistically seen as an attempt to impose Spanish Catholic absolutism on the liberty-loving Protestant Dutch, was in reality an attempt to rationalize and modernize an outdated ecclesiastical system that best served the interests of an entrenched aristocracy.[22] The result would have been to increase Philip's control of the Netherlands. Located at some distance from the heartland of his territories, occupied by a wealthy and energetic population that had connections with other Protestant powers, possessing a long history of local rule, the Netherlands could not easily be transformed into a subordinate unit of a Spanish-Habsburg state governed from Madrid. As John Elliott phrased it: 'the problem of the Netherlands was ultimately the problem of the Spanish Monarchy as a whole – of its future direction and constitutional structure'.[23]

The problems that Philip II faced in the Netherlands were representative of all attempts at state-formation in the sixteenth and seventeenth centuries. Even at home, within Spain itself, Philip's power was limited by local traditions and institutions. He was, after all, king in both Castile and Aragon, and his powers were different in each kingdom. Each was in fact a small empire in at least two senses of the term, the products of previous consolidation that had brought, for example, the crowns of León and Granada under the Castilian crown and those of Valencia and Majorca under the Aragonese crown. Furthermore, as the Castilian crown possessed an empire in the Atlantic, the Aragonese had one in the Mediterranean.[24] In a sense, Philip was the emperor of two empires within Spain itself. The problems that he faced with the Aragonese were not very different from those that he faced with the Dutch.

As for Philip's overseas possessions, the fundamental issue was how to prevent the colonists from creating institutions that would make them as hard to control as the Dutch and the Aragonese. What the government at Madrid feared was the creation of a series of feudal societies ruled by a hereditary aristocracy of the kind that the rulers of Castile had tamed in the fifteenth century. A key element in retaining control was restricting major offices in the Americas, secular and ecclesiastical, to natives of Spain, indeed, originally to Castilians, and requiring officials to return to Spain after the end of their term of service. This meant that the descendants of the original conquerors who chose to make their homes in the Americas and who intermarried, thus retaining their Spanish purity of blood – the *criollos* – were excluded from holding major offices, a source of continuing resentment.[25]

The obvious difficulty with the governance of Philip II's possessions was their vast scope and the size of the civil administration and military and naval forces necessary to make his government effective. Philip governed as if Mexico and Peru were little further distant than Catalonia or the Netherlands. In practice, the state model of government that Philip followed required contiguous territories through which royal messengers and officials could travel rapidly to enforce the ruler's commands. The unwillingness or the inability of Spanish officials overseas to obey their monarch's order was legendary.[26]

Although it is conventional to describe Philip II as the first modern monarch, it is not entirely accurate. Like that of his medieval predecessors, his was a personal rule to a great extent. That is, although there existed extensive governmental structures in this various possessions, Philip saw himself as ruling these territories directly. His unwillingness to trust his officials, like their unwillingness to obey him, was legendary. Furthermore, Philip's conception of himself as the defender of Christendom was medieval in origin. In a sense, Philip and those around him seem to have believed that there had been a kind of *translatio imperii ad Hispanos*, a sense that with the collapse of Charles V's imperial vision, the Castilian monarch was now the heir to the role of Charlemagne.[27]

One proposed solution to the problem of identifying Philip II's lands was to refer to them as forming a '*monarquia del mundo*', a world monarchy, a phrase that had some currency in the sixteenth century.[28] The notion of world monarchy also possessed some overtones of the monarchies that Daniel had foretold. Tomasso Campanella (1568–1639), for example, suggested that the world monarchy that had begun in the ancient Near East was reaching its final incarnation in the Spanish monarchy.[29]

One of the most important contributors to the debate about the nature of the Spanish ruler's domain and powers was Juan de Solórzano Pereira, whose *De Indiarum Jure* was perhaps the longest and most complex defense of the Spanish conquest of the New World ever produced.[30] Solórzano's career placed him in a unique position to observe the nature of the Spanish domain. He spent almost 20 years as a member of the *Audiencia* in Peru and, after returning to Spain, he served on the Council of Castile and that of the Indies. In addition, he laid the foundation for the great collection of laws dealing with the Americas, the *Recopilación de leyes de las Indias*. His *De Indiarum Jure* synthesized more than a century of Spanish debate about the conquest and possession of the Americas.[31]

In discussing the Spanish world Solórzano did not employ the terms *imperium* and *imperator* in his treatment of his monarch, Philip IV (1621–65). Philip was not, in Solórzano's opinion, the emperor of Spain or of anywhere else. He did recognize, however, that some writers referred to the lands of the Spanish monarchs as an empire. After all, various biblical, classical and contemporary authors had employed the term imperial to describe vast assemblages of territory that had been formed in their own days. As Solórzano pointed out, if such 'hyperbolic' language, clearly literary in nature, not legal or constitutional, could be used to describe the vast territories ruled by the Romans or the Chinese, why could it not be employed to describe the domains of the Spanish?[32] In the case of the Spanish monarchs, however, as Solórzano pointed out, using the language of empire would not be rhetorical exaggeration, only the truth.[33]

At the same time, the association of the imperial title with ancient Rome posed a serious problem for Solórzano and his contemporaries. It was all well and good that literary figures in their enthusiasm compared the Spanish monarch's possessions with the Roman Empire, but lawyers and governmental officials had to restrain that sort of hyperbole. There was the awkward issue of the Holy Roman Empire, *the empire* of the Civil Law. The problem of the nature of the Empire was not simply a matter of antiquarian interest for Solórzano and the other Spanish lawyers who dealt with this issue with regard to the New World.

Because the King of Aragon and the King of Castile was also the King of Germany and the Holy Roman Emperor during the greatest period of Spanish expansion in the New World, the period that saw the conquest of the Aztecs and the Incas, it was possible to see the conquest in terms of an imperial claim to universal jurisdiction. The argument could be made that the conquest of the New World took place under imperial auspices. When Charles V divided the Habsburg possessions at the end of his life, however, he clearly severed the empire from the Spanish monarchy.[34]

Solórzano then went on to consider the argument that from the beginning of imperial power, the rulers of the Roman people took the position that they possessed imperial jurisdiction over the entire world.[35] The Roman law used the phrase *dominus mundi*, Lord of the World, to describe the emperor.[36]

It was not only the pagan Romans who identified Roman imperial rule with universal jurisdiction, however, according to Solórzano. The canon law also contained a number of statements supporting the opinion that the empire possessed universal jurisdiction. For example, the *Decretum* contained a statement from St Jerome that pointed out that as there 'is one head among the bees', there is also but 'one emperor [and] one judge in a province'. Solórzano then noted that the glossators added that in consequence of there being but a single ruler of the world, 'all kings ought to be crowned by the emperor' as a sign of their subordination to him.[37] In reality, of course, this was not the case. Nevertheless, according to this interpretation of the principle that the emperor was the *dominus mundi*, there would be an orderly world if all rulers subordinated themselves to imperial oversight. Even the New Testament supported the universal claims of the Roman Empire, according to the proponents of this opinion. When, for example, Christ pointed out that there were things that belonged to Caesar and things that belonged to God, He was in effect upholding the Roman claim to universal jurisdiction.[38]

On the other hand, as Solórzano pointed out in the next stage of this argument, while under Augustus and the other pagan emperors, Rome did possess universal jurisdiction, subsequent events led to the shrinking of such a claim. For example, the emperor Constantine (312–37) gave the city of Rome to the Church and removed the seat of the Empire to Constantinople. Thus the Donation of Constantine gave the western regions of the Roman Empire to the papacy and the Church, reducing the territory subject to the Roman Emperor and effectively eliminating the basis for any claim to universal jurisdiction by the emperors. Furthermore, in either 800 or 801, the pope crowned Charlemagne, King of the Franks, as emperor, thus transferring the seat of the empire from Constantinople back to the West (*a Graecis ad Gallos Transierit*). Subsequently, in the tenth century, after the extinction of the Carolingian family, the papacy again transferred the empire, this time from the Franks to the Germans in the person of Conrad, King of the Germans.[39] Nevertheless, even though the Roman Empire has become only a vestige of its former self, the image of a world subject to Roman domination remained in the political and legal vocabularies.[40]

Solórzano ended this stage of the discussion by pointing out that 'almost all the peoples who obey Holy Mother, the Church of Rome, are also members of the Roman people or empire. Thus, if any deny that the emperor is the Lord of the World', they reject the very words of the Gospel. At the same time, citing contemporary opinion, Solórzano added that 'if the emperor is not the Lord of the World, at least he should be recognized as the overseer [*moderator*] of the whole world....' In other words, even if the emperor no longer possessed coercive juris-diction over the world, he should be recognized as the ruler to whom all conflicts between lesser rulers should be presented for resolution. In the next stage of the discussion, Solórzano considered one of the most important consequences of the claim that the emperor was, in theory at least, Lord of the World. If the emperor did possess such power, then defenders of the conquest of the New World could argue that he pos-sessed the power to deprive the infidels of their lands and jurisdiction.[41] He cited a number of canon lawyers in defense of this position, includ-ing Hostiensis who had commented that 'the emperor was lord of every-thing, everywhere...'.[42] Further along in the same discussion, Solórzano cited commentators on the Roman law who argued that the emperor possessed universal jurisdiction and he was 'the natural lord of the entire world' with the power 'to divide up and to unite lands and those things which pertain to them...'.[43]

Having presented arguments about universal imperial jurisdiction that he admitted were well developed and defended, Solórzano then went on to present the other side of the question. The 'more true and safer opinion is that of those who deny that the Roman Emperor can have any right [*jus*] in the lands and provinces of the infidels, and especially [in the lands] of those barbarians discovered by the Spanish...'. The reason for this is that the 'Roman Caesars did not possess [those regions], indeed, they did not even know of their exist-ence...'.[44] In effect, the jurisdiction of the Roman Empire was limited, not universal, and so the emperor could not possibly have given the New World to Christian rulers, as some had alleged.

After presenting the arguments in support of the Emperor's claim to universal jurisdiction, Solórzano then went on to deal with what he termed 'the more true and more general' opinions about the extent of imperial jurisdiction. According to the authors of these opinions, 'neither when Rome flourished long ago nor afterwards, when the Roman Empire was transferred to the Greeks, the French and the Germans' did the emperors have jurisdiction over any peoples other than those directly subject to them.[45] Imperial jurisdiction was thus limited to the defined borders of the Empire, that is, to the territory and the people over which the Emperor clearly exercised governing power. The history of the Roman Empire itself at the time of its greatest extent demonstrated that there were nations that Rome had never controlled. Some lawyers argued that the Persian empire and other peoples may have possessed 'exemption from the Roman Empire on a *de facto* basis but not *de jure*...', an argument that Solórzano found unacceptable, even 'silly and shallow'. Furthermore, not only were such arguments baseless with regard to the jurisdiction of the ancient Roman Empire, they were also irrelevant to the status of the Empire in the contemporary era. In fact, the freedom of the ancient Persians and the seventeenth-century Indians from imperial jurisdiction was not *de facto* but *de jure*. Indeed, 'it was not just nor was it appropriate or was it even possible for the whole of mankind to dwell under a single ruler and overseer...'.[46]

The final step in this stage of the argument about the extent of imperial jurisdiction was to refute the argument of St Jerome about the need for a single world ruler along the lines of the single head of a beehive. Solórzano argued that Jerome only meant that within any beehive there is a single leader whom the others follow. Thus, 'in any well-established republic, kingdom or province a specific emperor, king or rector exists' to render justice to all who are subject to him.[47] It does not follow logically, at least on the analogy of the beehive, that all mankind formed a single entity requiring a single head.

Having proved that the imperial claim to universal jurisdiction was, at best, a rhetorical statement, Solórzano then proceeded to demonstrate that the Emperor could not award the New World to the kings of Spain or to anyone else. The Emperor's jurisdiction extended only to his subjects. He has no right 'to take from them [the inhabitants of the New World] their *dominium* of goods and lands'.[48]

Finally, Solórzano described the Spanish monarchs as possessing in their own kingdoms the power that the emperor possessed in his empire, in other words, these rulers were the emperor's equals, not his subordinates.[49] In such circumstances the Emperor could not legitimate any action of the Spanish rulers because he possessed no basis for exercising jurisdiction over them. Furthermore, lest anyone think that Charles V's possession of the imperial throne along with the Spanish thrones meant that the empire had regained some kind of jurisdiction over Spain, Solórzano pointed out that Charles V had publicly promised to recognize the independence of Spain from the

Empire's jurisdiction.[50] In support of this, Solórzano added that Charles V also promised that any titles of nobility and other privileges that he granted to his Spanish subjects in his capacity as Emperor would be valid only in the Empire and not in Spain.[51] In fact, the Spanish were so sensitive to potential imperial infringements of their sovereignty that one legal writer even asserted the existence of a law in Spain making it a capital offense to attempt to use imperial laws in the Spanish courts.[52] Thus, to term the Spanish territories an empire would be to expose the Spanish to the possibility of endless legal wrangling about the nature of imperial power, a fruitless activity.

Solórzano did, however, employ the terms *imperium* and *imperator*, but in reference to the Aztecs and the Incas, not the Spanish. Among the justifications advanced for the legitimacy of the conquest of the New World was the argument that the peoples of the Americas did not live at a civilized level of existence. If this was the case, then the Spanish, according to some writers, could lawfully conquer these people in order to raise them to a civilized level of existence, that is, until they learned to live 'in a political fashion'.[53] It is in this context that Solórzano employed a number of terms from the traditional European political vocabulary. In order to be considered as living at a civilized level of existence, the inhabitants of the New World would have to demonstrate that they possessed *regna*, *imperia*, or *respublicae*, that is, the kinds of political units that European political thinkers deemed indicative of civilized living.

For Solórzano, living in a political fashion meant to live in a society with fixed rules and defined rulers. In making this judgement, he was drawing on Joseph Acosta's (c.1539–1600) threefold classification of non-European, non-Christian societies. These categories reflected standards of behavior, activity, institutional and cultural development, not the moral or intellectual capacity of the people involved, and provided a scale for determining the place of any society along a spectrum of social and political evolution.[54]

The crucial standard for judging the place of any society within Acosta's categories of development was thus the level of organization that a society had attained. Societies that were orderly and disciplined, where there was what Solórzano defined as a *respublica*, that is a recognizable form of orderly government, were the equivalent of European kingdoms. In effect, societies everywhere were being judged according to an Aristotelian standard of social order. Furthermore, Europeans presumably could deal with such societies through their rulers and other officials just as they dealt with one another in Europe. Diplomatic relations, as it were, could exist with such societies.

Solórzano used the terms empire and kingdom as synonyms for living in an orderly fashion as well. Thus, the Mexicans, the Peruvians and the Chileans had 'empires, republics, laws and institutions', the existence of which made them part of the second class of societies. As a result, he could refer to Montezuma, the ruler of the Aztecs, as an emperor and to the ruler of the Incas as a king. The Aztecs and Incas possessed empires or kingdoms, that is recognizable political and governmental units.[55] Furthermore, this classification of the Incas and Aztecs also meant that the Spanish could not legitimately conquer them on the grounds that they were too barbarous, primitive, or undeveloped to govern themselves. Obviously these people did govern themselves in such a way as to satisfy Aristotle's and Acosta's definition of the level of political life required of a *respublica*.

Solórzano also used the term *imperium* in another way. In addition to meaning a form of government, it could simply mean power or jurisdiction, what it had originally meant to the Romans. As a consequence, Solórzano could refer to the Indians as 'living peacefully under the *imperium*' of their kings.[56] Here again, the point was that the Aztec, Inca and other Indian rulers who fitted Acosta's second category exercised the same kind of power as their European counterparts.[57] In addition to this morally neutral use of the term *imperium*, there was also the connotation of ruling over other peoples by force, a usage that also applied to the Aztecs and Incas who had conquered their neighbors.[58] Seen in the latter light, the Aztecs or Incas could be seen as peoples who expanded their domain, their *imperium*, in illegitimate ways, thus justifying the Spanish conquest of the Americas as a means of protecting the subject peoples of these empires from their evil masters.[59]

For Solórzano the Spanish monarchs had a world mission that came from God. The lands that these monarchs had acquired in the New World they had acquired under the terms of Alexander VI's *Inter caetera*, a fact that would suggest that the pope, not Charles V or Philip II or any of their successors, was the true *dominus mundi*. Solórzano was able to avoid that conclusion by arguing that the papal role in the conquest of the Americas and the work of converting them to Christianity ended with the issuance of Alexander VI's bull.[60] He suggested that the Spanish role in the Americas was implicitly derived from God's will, so that the Spanish monarch was the true *dominus mundi* of the Roman law even though he was not officially called by that title.

Solórzano's discussion of the nature of the Spanish governmental structure reflected the complex burden attached to the terms *imperium* and *imperator*. His career as an official of the *Audiencia* in Lima and subsequently as a members of the Councils of Castile and of the Indies made him quite aware of the practical problems of administering his master's vast possessions. One of these was the status of the descendants of the original conquerors and of the original inhabitants. On the one hand, Solórzano 'sought to present the Indies as fully formed kingdoms, similar in status to their European counterparts'. That being the case, the descendants of the original conquerors and the Indians ought to lead the government of the Indies just as the local nobility in each of the monarchy's constituent kingdoms dominated the local administration. Yet this did not come to pass, because of what D.A. Brading has termed 'the morass of native debility' and the fear within the royal court that 'creole nobles, jurists and churchmen', the very classes that dominated the European kingdoms of the monarchy, would not in the long run remain loyal to the monarchy.[61] The centralizing monarchs of Spain were not about to create a nobility in the Americas that would act in defense of local interests in the same way as the nobles of Castile or of the Netherlands or of Naples had opposed the extension of royal power. In other words, try as he, and others, might, Solórzano could not construct a model of an empire that would allow for strong central authority and strong local leadership at the same time. The creoles would remain blocked from the higher offices of Church and State because these were restricted to *peninsulares*, Spaniards, like Solórzano himself, who returned to Spain after their tour of duty.[62] This policy created a colonial class that was increasingly wealthy and identified with the Americas yet unable to exercise the level of political power its members believed was their due. It was this class that led the revolutions of the nineteenth century that created the modern independent nations of Spanish America.

The problems that the Spanish monarchs faced in dealing with their extensive possessions within and beyond Europe and the tension between domestic centralization and imperial governance were not unique to them. The English kings faced similar problems in their domains as they wrestled with the problems associated with the governance of Scotland, Ireland and the American colonies. There is no evidence that John Adams knew of Solórzano, although some of his contemporaries certainly did, but if he had read Solórzano's work, he would have understood the problems that the Spanish lawyer and bureaucrat examined.[63]

As mentioned earlier, John Adams denied the existence of an English or British empire. Nevertheless England was in fact an empire, at least Henry VIII (1509–47) had termed it such in various documents involving England's relation to the papacy and also in relation to conquered territories such as Wales and Ireland. In the Act of Supremacy (1534), for example, he asserted that the King of England was not subject to the pope, because

> by divers sundry old authentic histories and chronicles it is manifestly declared and expressed that this realm of England is an empire, and so hath been accepted in the world, governed by one supreme head and king having the dignity and royal estate of the imperial crown of the same, unto whom a body politic, compact of sorts and degrees of people divided in terms and by names of spirituality and temporality, be bounden and owe to bear next to God a natural and humble obedience....[64]

Henry VIII not only asserted the imperial nature of the English crown, he also emphasized the antiquity of that imperial crown and, presumably, the fact that the imperial stature of the English crown was well-known.

In other acts that created the Church of England, Henry VIII restated the imperial nature of the English crown. For example, a parliamentary act aimed at ending ecclesiastical payments to Rome referred to such payments as being 'in great derogation of your imperial crown and royal authority'. Subsequently, another act established the king as 'the only supreme head in earth of the Church of England called *Anglicana Ecclesia*, and shall have and enjoy annexed and united to the *imperial crown of this realm* [my emphasis] as well the title and style thereof, as all honours, dignities ... to the said dignity of supreme head of the same Church belonging and appertaining'.[65]

In employing the term imperial in these contexts, Henry VIII and his advisors were using the term imperial in its medieval sense of sovereignty, the notion that the king within his kingdom was as the emperor within his empire.[66] Henry VIII and his advisors simply took the traditional arguments about limitations of imperial jurisdiction in temporal matters and employed them against the papacy, asserting the sovereign status of the English crown in ecclesiastical matters as well as in temporal.

Henry VIII also employed the term 'imperial crown of this realm' in several statutes that affected his standing in temporal matters as, for example, in an act of 1536 aimed at reasserting royal control over 'Liberties and Franchises'.[67] This was part of a policy of reasserting the monarch's power against nobles who had acquired various rights and privileges from Henry's predecessors to the detriment of the king's power. In a sense, this was a stage in the formation of the English state, that is, in the centralization of governmental power.

Like his contemporaries on the continent, Henry VIII wished to strengthen the monarchy at the expense of the nobles and, like them, he defined sovereignty not only in terms of exemption from imperial and papal jurisdiction but also in terms of royal control within England as well.[68]

Imperial language also appeared in statutes dealing with Wales and Ireland, at first glance a more obvious use of such language. For example, the Act for the Government of Wales (1536) began:

> An act for laws and justice to be ministered in Wales in like form as it is in this realm. Albeit the dominion, principality, and country of Wales justly and righteously is and ever hath been subject to and under the imperial crown of this realm as a very member and joint of the same....[69]

A few years later, in 1541, Henry VIII employed similar language in the act that changed his title in Ireland from Lord of Ireland to King of Ireland. Under the terms of the new title, as king of Ireland he would possess with all the 'honours, pre-eminences, prerogatives ... and other things whatsoever they be, to the estate and majesty of a king imperial appertaining or belonging' and the kingdom of Ireland is 'united and knit to the imperial crown of the realm of England'.[70]

In both of these cases, Henry VIII was asserting the English crown's sovereignty, that is its unopposed domination, 'a commitment to effective and total rule' in Wales and Ireland.[71] The Irish situation posed a particular problem for the theorists of Tudor rule because, according to English officials there, '"the Irish have a foolish opinion that the Bishop of Rome is King of Ireland".'[72] This, of course, reflected the fact that English rule in Ireland began with Pope Adrian IV's (1154–59) bull *Laudabiliter* (1155) authorizing Henry VIII to go there in order to reform the Irish Church.[73] Henry VIII's use of the title King of Ireland was designed to underscore the theory that he was supreme in Ireland and that he did not owe his title to anyone outside Ireland nor was he subject to any supervisory authority in his governance there. Henry VIII's imperial crown thus represented his unchallenged position as supreme head of both Church and State within all of his domains, subject neither to the pope nor to the Holy Roman Emperor.[74]

The imperial language that Henry VIII employed was rarely used by his heirs, at least not officially. Apparently neither Edward VI (1547–53) nor Mary I (1553–58) used it at all. During the reign of Elizabeth I (1558–1603) the phrase 'this realm and the imperial crown thereof' did appear in a few documents. Her very first statute, the Act of Supremacy of 1559 (I Eliz. I, c.1), designed to restore 'to the Crown the ancient jurisdiction over the state ecclesiastical and spiritual and abolishing all foreign power repugnant to the same', rejected any papal jurisdiction. According to the statute, Queen Mary had brought her subjects 'under an usurped foreign power and authority', an action that was detrimental 'to the imperial crown of this ... realm'.[75] Furthermore, the oath that the act required of all lay and ecclesiastical officials obliged them to defend 'all jurisdictions, preeminences, privileges and authorities ... united or annexed to the imperial crown of this realm'.[76] Subsequently, in a response to Pope Pius V's (1566–72) bull ordering her deposition on the grounds of heresy and related crimes, Elizabeth retorted that the pope was attempting 'to bring this realm and the imperial crown thereof ... into the thralldom and subjection of that foreign, usurped, and unlawful jurisdiction, preeminence and authority claimed by the said see of Rome ...'.[77] This suggests that for the later Tudors, the conception of empire remained identified with exemption from papal or any other kind of external jurisdiction. In other words, for Elizabeth, like her father, *imperium* was the equivalent of sovereignty.

Although official documents of the later Tudors made little use of imperial language, Frances Yates has shown how literary figures often used imperial language to describe Elizabeth, drawing upon the entire arsenal of imperial terminology to describe her.[78] Here again, the emphasis was upon the religious role of the ruler and served to justify not only English exemption from papal jurisdiction but also the English monarch's role as Supreme Head (or in Elizabeth's case, Supreme Governor) of the church as well. In Yates's view, England under Elizabeth saw a shift in the theory of empire from 'universal medieval aspirations' to 'a nationalist direction, towards a golden age for England'.[79] Thus it became possible to attribute to Elizabeth qualities and responsibilities that humanists attributed to ancient Roman emperors. For example, the first edition of John Foxe's massive history of the English Church contained a dedication to Elizabeth, comparing her to the Emperor Constantine who had ended the persecution of Christians and brought it peace.[80] The union of temporal and spiritual powers that the Tudors claimed was, according to Foxe, a return to the early Christian world, a world that existed until the wicked, self-aggrandizing bishops of Rome corrupted the Church and took advantage of the generosity of secular rulers who had endowed it with great wealth.

Yates suggested that the imperial symbolism in Elizabeth's reign was 'influenced in many ways by imitation, conscious or unconscious, of the dazzling figure of Charles V, in whom the imperial theme, in all its aspects had shone forth with renewed splendour'.[81] While there is no doubt much truth in this observation, it should also be noted that the imperial theme in England partook of another tradition as well, one that Yates did not discuss, the prophet Daniel's vision of the Four World Monarchies or Empires. For Yates, the theme is Elizabeth as 'the Virgin Astraea, or Justice', an image from Virgil's Fourth Eclogue that prophesied 'that the golden age was about to return, and with it the reign of the Virgin Astraea, or Justice, and that a child would be born destined to rule a reconciled world'.[82] This echoes the theme of the Fifth Monarchy that came to play a role in the roiling world of religious ideas that marked seventeenth-century England. The vision of the Fifth Monarchy 'made a considerable impact on some of the higher-ranking officers" of the parliamentary army at the beginning of the English Civil war.[83] This would have made England, not some universal empire, but the final stage of the historical process that Daniel had outlined. The conception of Elizabeth as Astraea and the biblically based theories of the Fifth Monarchy Men shared a vision of England as the climax of a process leading to some kind of imperial golden age, though not necessarily a universal one.

The use of imperial language continued to appear occasionally in official documents of the seventeenth and eighteenth centuries, often in connection with control of territories outside England. Charles I (1625–49), for example, referred to Virginia, the Somers Islands, and New England as 'part of his royal empire', a phrase that might seem redundant except for the fact that it meant that the King of England was as sovereign in these regions as within England itself.[84]

The Act of Union (1707) that joined the kingdoms of England and Scotland might have provided an opportunity to discuss the concept of empire, but no such discussion emerged. The Act of Union with Scotland abolished the Parliament of Scotland and provided instead

seats in both Lords and Commons for the Scots.[85] With one exception, the Act avoided the use of imperial language, usually referring to
the union as the 'Monarchy of the United Kingdom of Great Britain
and of the Dominions' and to the 'Parliament of Great Britain'.[86] The
only point at which imperial language appears in the Act was in connection with succession to the throne. In language recalling Henry
VIII's assertion of England's imperial status *vis-à-vis* the papacy, the
Act declared 'that all Papists and persons marrying Papists, shall be
excluded from and for ever incapable to inherit possess or enjoy the
Imperial crown of Great Britain...'.[87] In this sense, the United
Kingdom was imperial because it not only rejected the papacy but any
person who accepted its jurisdiction as well. At the same time, the new
structure was not a British or an English Empire. The term United
Kingdom underscored the equality of the two partners in the arrangement. Scotland was not a conquered kingdom now brought under
English control but a full partner. To have used the term empire
would have blocked the union.

The two Declaratory Acts of the eighteenth century in which the
English Parliament asserted its jurisdiction over Ireland (1719) and
then over British North America (1766) emphasized the unique, non-
imperial, nature of the United Kingdom created in 1707.[88] Each of
these acts was a response to an assertion of independence from
Parliament's jurisdiction.

In the Irish case, the Irish Parliament, following a longstanding line
of argument, claimed that the English House of Lords had no right to
overturn decisions of the Irish Parliament. Although the English
Parliament had long claimed jurisdiction over Ireland, there had
always been some question about the validity of that assertion. By the
terms of Poynings' Law (1495), the Irish Parliament could meet only
with royal permission and only after the matters to be treated in the
Parliament had received royal approval.[89]

In the seventeenth century, the Protestant leadership in Ireland,
restive under English control of the politics and the economy of
Ireland, asserted the status of Ireland as a kingdom, answerable only
to the King of Ireland, that is to the King of England in his role as
King of Ireland. If, however, the people of Ireland were to be subject
to laws passed in the English Parliament then the Irish, that is, the
Protestant landowning class, should elect members to sit there. There
is an element of 'no legislation without representation' here, foreshad-
owing the famous American revolutionary slogan about taxation. The
most famous statement of this position was William Molyneaux's

(1656–98) *The Case of Ireland ... Stated*. Molyneaux provided a history of the English in Ireland designed to demonstrate that

> it is manifest that there were no Laws Imposed on the People of *Ireland*, by any Authority of the Parliament of *England*; nor any Laws introduced into that Kingdom by *Henry* the Second, but by the *Consent* and *Allowance* of the People of *Ireland*: For both the Civil and the Ecclesiastical State were settled ther ... solely by the Kings Authority, *and their own good Wills*....[90]

Furthermore, Molyneaux made the striking argument that only 'a meer handful of the Antient *Irish*' remained in Ireland, the present population of Ireland being almost entirely descended from 'the *English* and the *Britains*, that came over and Conquered with' Henry II and these people 'retain'd all the Freedoms and Immunities of *Free-born* Subjects ... [and neither] they nor their descendants could in reason lose these'.[91] That being the case, those inhabitants of Ireland who derived their origins from the Norman and English invaders were being unlawfully deprived of their right to elect members of Parliament or to be governed by an Irish Parliament that answered to the King of Ireland. This also meant that the English did not have to concern themselves with the rights or the legal status of indigenous peoples, but only with the status of Englishmen abroad. At the same time it underscored the fears of the English settlers in Ireland that they were being treated as subject people, not as the possessors of the legal rights of Englishmen, an argument that was to reappear in eighteenth-century America.

The position that Molyneaux articulated underlay the case that produced the Declaratory Act. In response to the claim that the English Parliament could not overrule actions of the Irish Parliament, the act 'declared ... that the said kingdom of Ireland hath been, is and of right ought to be, subordinate unto and dependent upon the imperial crown of Great Britain, as being inseparably united and annexed thereunto' and so 'the king's majesty, by and with the advice and consent of the lords spiritual and temporal, and commons of Great Britain in parliament assembled' possessed the right 'to make laws and statutes ... to bind the kingdom and the people of Ireland'.[92]

In 1766, the English Parliament issued another Declaratory Act, this time asserting the Parliament's right to legislate for the British North American colonies. The language of the Declaratory Act for the American colonies was virtually identical with that of the Irish act.

In the American case, 'the said colonies and plantations in *America* have been, are, and of right ought to be, subordinate unto and dependent upon the imperial crown and parliament of *Great Britain*; and that the King's majesty, by and with the advice and consent of the lords spiritual and temporal, and commons of *Great Britain* ... [has] full power and authority to make laws and statutes ... to bind the colonies and peoples of *America*, subjects of the crown of *Great Britain*, in all cases whatsoever'.[93]

The two declaratory acts had both traditional and novel elements and marked a new stage in the development of the concept of empire. In spite of the fact that both dealt with overseas possessions, they concerned sovereignty, not empire in the sense of conquered possessions. Furthermore, they were concerned with claims that English subjects living abroad had raised, not with the interests of conquered peoples. What was new about the claims made in these acts was the fact that they concerned parliamentary sovereignty, a claim made most assertively in the American act where the colonies were defined as 'dependent upon the imperial crown and parliament of *Great Britain*'.[94] It would appear that this parliamentary claim was limited to those territories directly dependent upon the monarch in his capacity as king of the United Kingdom. Both Ireland and the American colonies were described as 'subordinate' and 'dependent' upon the crown of the United Kingdom. The Parliament of England was asserting the claim that its jurisdiction was coterminous with that of the king and crown of the United Kingdom and the territories directly dependent upon them. It did not, however, extend to all of the territories that the monarch of the United Kingdom ruled in his other capacities, such as Elector of Hanover.[95]

A second issue that the Declaratory Acts confronted was the question of who constituted the imperial people. Both the ruling Protestants in Ireland and the English inhabitants of North America claimed that moving from England did not abrogate their rights as Englishmen. Neither William Molyneaux nor John Adams argued that the indigenous people of the lands they occupied possessed the rights of Englishmen; only those of English descent did so. The Irish and the Indians were clearly subjugated populations (if indeed, as Molyneaux said of the native Irish, they existed at all), the proper objects of imperial control. The Irish Protestants and the American colonists, however, did not see themselves as conquered peoples but, if anything, the conquerors. They were then only demanding the rights of Englishmen, rights that included either a parliament of their own or seats in the Parliament at London. In a sense they were asking that the relation of their land to the English Parliament, the Parliament of Great Britain, be like that of either Wales or Scotland. When Henry VIII's government fully incorporated what had been the Dominion of Wales into England, Wales was assigned seats in the Commons.

The writings of Molyneaux and Adams suggest they believed that the concept of government that the English were employing was incomplete in that it did not deal adequately with the problem of Englishmen overseas. They were suggesting that either full incorporation into England, as Wales was incorporated, or a union of equals, the solution for Scotland, should be employed for Ireland and for North America. What these writers and those who believed as they did overlooked were the differences in the situations. In the first place, Wales and Scotland were contiguous with England, making their status more important than that of lands beyond the sea. In the second place, although Ireland was labelled a kingdom, it was not so in the sense that Scotland was, that is, possessing its own monarchy, laws, institutions of government, etc. Its status as a kingdom was nominal, not real. It was more like Wales than Scotland. As for the American colonies, the North American settlements did not form a single unit, although by the mid-eighteenth century some steps were being taking to provide some form of union for these colonies. As John Adams pointed out, the King of England was King of Massachusetts, etc., not King of North America.

The problem that the English faced regarding the nature and structure of their monarch's multiple possessions was, in comparison with the problems facing the Habsburgs on the continent, relatively simple. It was not until 1763, when the English ousted the French from North America and from India, that the English government had to focus a great deal of attention on the governance of far-flung territories, in other words to confront the problem of imperial government in the modern sense.[96]

One of the best examples of this debate appeared in two series of polemical essays published in Boston newspapers between December 1774 and April 1775. The first series, the Massachusettensis Letters, consisted of 17 essays defending the English Parliament's right to tax the American colonies, that began to appear at the end of 1774. At the outset, Massachusettensis, in reality a Boston lawyer named Daniel Leonard, summed up his basic argument thus:

However closely we may hug ourselves in the opinion, that the parliament has not right to tax or legislate for us, the people of

England hold the contrary opinion as firmly. They tell us we are a part of the British empire; that every state, from the nature of government, must have a supreme, uncontrolable power, co-extensive with the empire itself; and that this power is vested in parliament.[97]

In the fifth of these essays, Leonard developed his argument about the jurisdiction of the English Parliament over the North American colonies:

If the colonies are not subject to the authority of parliament, Great Britain and the colonies must be distinct states, as completely so, as England and Scotland were before the union, or as Great Britain and Hanover are now. *The colonies in that case will owe no allegiance to the imperial crown* [my emphasis], and perhaps not to the person of the king. .... Let us wave this difficulty, and suppose allegiance due from the colonies in the person of the king of Great Britain. He then appears in a new capacity, of king of America, or rather in several new capacities, of king of Massachusetts, king of Rhode Island, king of Connecticut, etc. etc.[98]

For Daniel Leonard, the notion that George III's titles might include the title of King of Massachusetts was the *reductio ad absurdum* that demonstrated the existence of a British Empire and the universal jurisdiction of the English Parliament within that empire.

After the first six of the pieces by Massachusettensis had appeared, a new series of essays appeared to refute the arguments that Leonard had made. These essays, the Novanglus essays, were the work of John Adams, a friend of Leonard's and a fellow Boston lawyer, as well as future President of the United States. In the third of his essays, Adams rejected one of Massachusettensis' fundamental concepts, the notion that a British Empire actually existed. He argued that

the terms 'British Empire' are not the language of the common law, but the language of newspapers and political pamphlets; ... the dominions of the king of Great Britain have no power coextensive with them. I would ask, by what law the parliament has authority over America?[99]

In subsequent essays, Adams sketched the constitutional history of what popular writers, and Massachusettensis, called the British Empire. He outlined the manner in which the kings of England had acquired and governed Ireland, Wales, the Channel Islands, various parts of France, and other territories during the Middle Ages. The central issue, as Adams saw matters, was that these territories, as well as the palatinates of Durham and Chester within England, claimed exemption from the jurisdiction of the English Parliament although they were obviously the possessions of the King of England.

Adams derived his argument about the exemption of the American colonies from the jurisdiction of Parliament from the argument about the relationship between Ireland and the English Parliament that defenders of the autonomy of the Irish Parliament had made during the last half of the seventeenth century. Employing a line of argument that had much in common with Molyneux's *The Case of Ireland*, Adams asserted that a situation similar to that of Ireland's relation to the English Parliament existed in the colonies in the New World. The settlers of the American colonies had made agreements with the king of England, not with the Parliament, and thus the Parliament had no right to insert itself between the king and the colonists. The result of this argument was that the King of Great Britain was not only also King of Ireland, and King of France, he was also 'King of Massachusetts, King of Rhode Island, King of Connecticut, etc.'[100] There was no British Empire, only a collection of separate and distinct political units of various sizes and shapes, joined vertically, so to speak, to the individual who happened to bear the title of King of Great Britain, but not joined in any other way. Using Adams's legal approach to the situation, one might even be inclined to say that there was no British Empire because there was no British emperor. To identify George III as the King of Massachusetts was, in Adam's opinion, not a *reductio ad absurdum*, simply a statement of legal fact.

John Adams was not only making a debater's point when he denied the existence of a British Empire. His point had real meaning in the contemporary political context. Put in anachronistic terms, Adams's denial of the existence of a British Empire stemmed from the absence of the term empire in the community of discourse that united the common lawyers and made them an intellectual community. The common law knew nothing of a British Empire and so, regardless of the realities of the political and constitutional situation, in legal terms there was none. The significance of Adams's point about the lack of an imperial constitutional structure must have been clear not only to his immediate audience in Boston but to any British official who thought about the issue. The Act of Union with Scotland in 1707 had already made clear, and the Act of Union with Ireland in 1800 was to

Empire and Order

re-emphasize and the Durham Report of 1839 was to emphasize yet again, that the existing structure, or lack thereof, within what was loosely called the British Empire needed to be redressed. Above all, the relationship between the English Parliament and the governments of the various territories that the king of England ruled required rationalizing. For practical purposes, the King of England ruled an Empire so it was necessary to provide a theoretical basis upon which to construct an imperial constitution. The British Empire was, so to speak, an empire in search of a theory to justify it and a constitutional structure to incarnate it.[101]

Conclusion: Empire and State

Empire is one of the most evocative words in the political vocabulary, suggesting as it does a wide range of political situations. In a general sense, it suggests some great territorial expanse, inhabited by a wide variety of peoples. More specifically, to the Greeks, empire meant the vast reaches of the Persian Empire. To later generations of Europeans, empire could mean Roman rule over the known world, a vision of Roman legionnaires marching across the Mediterranean littoral, bringing all they encountered under imperial domination. To the biblically inclined, empire recalled the series of great powers that marked the stages of God's plan for mankind.

These visions of empire also had moral connotations as well. Herodotus contrasted the Persian emperors ruling 'nameless millions who bowed the knee to a tyrannical master', with the free, self-governing, and, above all, victorious, citizens of Athens.[1] Roman critics of the Empire compared it unfavorably to the republican era and argued that the Republic fostered moral virtue, while the Empire only fostered moral decay. Renaissance humanists often followed Tacitus and other critics of imperial Rome, arguing that the Empire meant the end of Roman civic virtue. Leonardo Bruni asserted that Florentine love of liberty was rooted in their hatred of those who destroyed 'the liberty, honor, and dignity of the Roman people'.[2] In turn, eighteenth-century Americans, shaped by the humanist educational program, often saw themselves as Roman Republicans with England playing the part of Julius Caesar whose imperial grasp destroyed the Republic.[3]

Even in the twentieth century, empire continues to have a pejorative meaning for many people. When President Reagan identified the USSR as the 'evil empire', at least some of his listeners must have thought that he was being redundant because empires are always intrinsically evil.[4] The audience that the President was addressing had no doubt of the evil nature of the imperial USSR.

Empire can also have a positive meaning, when, for example, medieval writers identified the Roman Empire as an aspect of God's plan for humanity, under whose *imperium* Christ was born, or when Christian emperors such as Charlemagne came to the aid of

139

beleaguered popes. Even in the Renaissance, those who proposed to identify virtue with republics faced opposition from those who saw in a universal empire the basis for a Christian world order.

In the history of the United States, empire has been an ambivalent term. On the one hand, the revolutionary generation rebelled against the growing imperial claims of the British government. On the other, J.G.A. Pocock has pointed out 'the paradox that the new republic, born of the revolt against empire, had a commitment to empire – and to empire of settlement – built into its structure in a way that the parent system never had'. The expansion of the United States across North America in the nineteenth century was by almost any standard imperial expansion, but expansion with a difference because, in Jefferson's terms, it would create an 'empire of liberty'.[5]

Following the logic of this positive view of empire, late nineteenth-century American publicists saw the acquisition of oceanic possessions in the aftermath of the Spanish-American War not as the creation of an empire in the negative sense but as the beginning of the democratization and modernization in lands that had remained backward too long. Rudyard Kipling's 'White Man's Burden' was a call to humanitarian imperial responsibility as the United States began to rule the newly acquired territories in the Caribbean and the Pacific, an echo of the role that the Romans played according to Virgil.

In the 1950s, a popular American historian, Bernard de Voto, was able to title a laudatory history of the United States from the period of discovery to the early nineteenth century as *The Course of Empire*.[6] DeVoto was echoing Bishop Berkeley's famous lines, 'Westward the course of empire takes its way…', lines that in turn echoed the image of the biblical providential Five World Empires as well as the medieval *translatio imperii*. In this view, the United States becomes the final stage of the providential plan, the final empire in the sequence of divinely ordained empires. Recently, without using imperial language, Francis Fukuyama constructed a similar vision of history, arguing that 'liberal democracy may constitute the "end point of mankind's ideological evolution" and the "final form of human government," and as such constituted the "end of history"'.[7] Fukuyama based his conception on Hegel's view of history, a theory of historical development rooted in Christian conceptions of providential order. In this sense, Fukuyama's end of history is the age of the Fifth World Monarchy or World Empire. Writing about the current American role in international affairs in the *Wall Street Journal*, Irving Kristol observed that 'an American imperium – a more subtle term than empire – has come (and is coming) into existence.' In his opinion, no European country can any longer chart its own path in foreign affairs, dependent as they are on the United States in military and political matters. These countries 'are dependent nations, though they have a very large measure of local autonomy. The term "imperium" describes this mixture of dependency and autonomy.'[8] Kristol's use of the term "imperium" would sound familiar to some of the peoples whom the Romans had brought under their jurisdiction. Even some of the proponents of the Holy Roman Empire's universal role might identify their empire with Kristol's 'imperium'.

All of these uses of the terms empire, emperor, and related words have roots in the ancient and medieval use of these terms. It is a mistake to believe that there was only one medieval notion of empire, the universal Christian empire. It has also a mistake to assume a fundamental opposition between empire and state, identifying empire with medieval universalism and the state with modernity. To make this error is to overlook the roots of the idea of state sovereignty in the application of the concept of imperial jurisdiction to kings, the theory that the king in his kingdom possessed the powers of the emperor within the empire. It also overlooks the obvious fact that the great age of imperial development was not in the Middle Ages but in the modern world.

The most dramatic image of empire in medieval thought was, of course, the conception of the universal Christian empire, and it has been this usage that has received the most attention. In the early Middle Ages, however, the meaning most widely employed was rule over other rulers and other peoples, a meaning that could include universal empire within it. While this use of the term emperor obviously possessed a territorial significance, when an Anglo-Saxon chronicler referred to powerful Anglo-Saxon rulers as emperors or when a king of León identified himself as an emperor, what they meant was that these rulers had conquered equally powerful kings and thus were now kings of kings, the wearers of more than one crown, so to speak.[9] Even the German ruler's use of the imperial title had links to the emperors as kings of kings because he was king of Italy and of Arles or Burgundy as well as king of Germany. The term clearly meant rule over a wide expanse of territory, a wide variety of peoples, and, above all, rule over other monarchs.

Although a medieval ruler might not employ imperial language, he could be labeled an emperor in the sense that he ruled over a variety of territories that he and his family acquired over time. As twentieth-century historians have noted, the Angevins clearly ruled over a diverse set of lands and peoples that for all practical purposes formed an empire in the sense that their Anglo-Saxon predecessors had possessed empires. They even claimed rule over the Kingdom of Scotland. In fact, all the major medieval kingdoms, consisting as they did of a conglomeration of dynastic lands, were empires whether or not anyone chose to employ the term. When Joseph Strayer termed the Kingdom of France a mosaic state he was defining it as an empire in the loose sense.[10] The fact that the French monarchs did not choose to label their possessions as such for reasons best known to themselves does not mean that they did not rule an empire, only that they did not find the term useful.[11]

By the end of the twelfth century, the term empire was becoming generally restricted to the Holy Roman Empire, *the Empire* of Roman law and of medieval political thought. Even when restricted to the Holy Roman Empire, however, the term empire had more than one meaning. From the papal perspective, the empire was an office within the Church, the secular arm that enforced papal decrees when necessary. Basing its position on the *translatio imperii*, the papacy argued that possession of the imperial title could only be based on papal grant and that the papacy could transfer the imperial office and title from an incompetent ruler to a more effective one as its – and the Church's – needs dictated. When Innocent III issued the decretal *Venerabilem*, he resolved, at least as far as the papacy was concerned, the definition of the empire and its relation to the papacy.

As the German monarchs grew stronger in the twelfth and thirteenth centuries and once they had come to employ the Roman law tradition to defend their possession of the imperial title, the papal conception of the empire faced a serious intellectual and political challenge. It became possible to defend the existence of the empire as a political institution that did not obtain its legitimacy from the papacy. Even the German monarchs' decline in real power after the death of Frederick II did not end the assertions of the autonomy of the empire's power. When Emperor Charles IV (1347–78) issued the Golden Bull in 1356, he was asserting the independence of the empire from papal oversight, although he did not reject papal consecration of the emperor elect.[12] The relationship between the empire and the Church was not so much severed as attenuated. The pope must crown the emperor but had no subsequent power over him any more than the archbishop of Canterbury had power over the king of England after he crowned him. The emperors continued to see their role in religious terms, not purely secular ones, but they carried out their religious responsibilities answerable to God but not to the pope. At the same time, the defenders of German possession of the imperial title also encouraged a narrowing of the territorial scope of the empire. It became the Holy Roman Empire of the German Nation, something much less than the universal imperial authority that some earlier lawyers had identified.

The political realities of the later Middle Ages also contributed to a decline in imperial power and to a narrowing of the concept. When a Spanish canonist denied that the Holy Roman Emperor possessed any jurisdiction over the Spanish kingdoms that had freed themselves from the Muslim yoke, he was speaking for the lawyers and rulers of all the other European kingdoms that had emerged out of the ruins of the Roman Empire. The collapse of that empire and the failure of its rulers to provide the most basic function of government, protection from attack, meant that the empire had lost the basis of its legitimacy. Any claim to universal jurisdiction based on law or history or tradition was absurd. What mattered was effective governance.

In a sense, the emerging kingdoms of Europe had performed their own *translatio imperii*, claiming for themselves the kind of *imperium* within their own borders that the German emperors claimed within the borders of the empire. When Innocent III asserted that a king within his kingdom possessed the powers of the emperor within the empire, he was providing a legal statement of the situation that actually existed in thirteenth-century Europe. In fact, regardless of what Roman law or the commentators said, the emperor's power was restricted to those territories that he actually ruled in his capacity as King of the Germans and associated peoples.

The theoretical conception of the empire as possessing universal jurisdiction, the emperor as *dominus mundi*, did not, however, die in the later Middle Ages. Dante in particular developed a theory of universal Christian empire that, if implemented, would have brought the entire Christian world into a coherent governmental structure headed by the Christian emperor who, rather than the pope, would act as God's agent in the direction of the world. In effect, Dante reversed the papal conception of the imperial role, placing the pope and the Church under the empire's protection. Other writers, facing the wars and conflicts within later medieval Europe, continued to find the idea of a universal authority capable of imposing order on Europe attractive. To a greater extent than is often appreciated, the early modern search for a world legal order, a search associated with Hugo Grotius and the international law theorists who followed him, was an attempt to replace the medieval notion of a papal–imperial order of the world with a secular one.

By the end of the fifteenth century, the Europe of nation states was beginning to emerge. Even before the Reformation the papal claim to universal jurisdiction over the Christian kingdoms of Europe was increasingly ignored, and the weakness of the Empire made any claims to universal jurisdiction on its part ludicrous. The various medieval kingdoms were now participating in a process that would transform them from loose confederations of dynastic possessions into modern states. In the course of that process some dynastic possessions would be lost, as the Spanish monarchs lost the Netherlands. In other cases, monarchs had to develop new modes of territorial incorporation, as the English did with the Act of Union with Scotland in 1707. In fact, however, these European kingdoms were not yet states in the twentieth-century use of the term. Furthermore, they were not nations, that is, they did not consist of a single linguistic and cultural group. They continued to include a variety of linguistic groups and cultural traditions, regional differences that were to be markedly reduced by the policies of nation-building rulers in the nineteenth and the twentieth centuries. Furthermore, the monarchs continued to possess several titles, not a single one, reflecting the fact that the politically and culturally homogeneous state was still in the future.

Under these circumstances, it is not easy to accept the argument that the medieval notion of universal empire necessarily gave way to the notion of the nation-state, a narrowly conceived political structure that dealt realistically with the problem of political order in Europe. The transition from empire to state was a lengthy process. Furthermore, when we consider the fact that at the same time as the state was beginning to emerge within Europe, European rulers were also becoming the masters of various overseas territories, we can see that the concept of empire, in one or another of its meanings, was taking on new life as European rulers, officials, and theoreticians sought to fit these new lands within the existing political order. In the sixteenth century, as European monarchs were beginning the process of transforming their dynastic possessions into states, they were acquiring overseas territories that they treated as if they were dynastic possessions, in effect recreating in these new possessions something like the medieval dynastic monarchies that they were trying to transform into states domestically. The history of the Spanish and the English monarchs in the early modern era demonstrates the dilemma of state–empire formation, consolidation at home and expanding territories abroad. Could a European state find a way to dominate an overseas empire?

In recent years, historians have begun to develop some new terms to identify the political forms that emerged in early modern Europe. James B. Collins has suggested that, in the seventeenth century, France was a 'polyglot empire', a term that could apply equally well to Spain, the Holy Roman Empire, or even England.[13] H.G. Koenigsberger has suggested that these sixteenth-century collections of dynastic territories might be termed 'composite monarchies', a term that reflects the existence of several language groups, cultures, legal systems, political structures and economies joined in some way under a single ruler. When considered from the perspective of the mid-twentieth century, composite monarchies (or polyglot empires), as Sir John Elliott has pointed out, seemed to be 'an unsatisfactory prelude to the construction of a more effective and permanent form of political association', that is, the nation-state. At the end of the twentieth century, however, the composite model that sought to recognize the existence of diversity within the political structure has taken on a positive aspect because it was an attempt 'to reconcile ... the competing aspirations towards unity and diversity that have remained a constant of European history'.[14]

The central issue with regard to overseas possessions in the early modern world was how they were to be incorporated within the structure of governance. The situation was complicated by the existence of European colonists in the newly acquired lands who claimed the same political status as they would have possessed in Europe had they remained there. The situation would have been easier if the European conquerors had been able to take over existing governmental units and govern through them as medieval conquerors often had done, in other words to extend the composite model to the newly acquired lands overseas.

In English and in Spanish America, however, the situation was complicated by the presence of colonists who claimed the rights of their countrymen at home. The *criollos* of the Spanish Americas and their counterparts in British North America posed an uncommon but not unique problem in the history of empires, the settlers who saw themselves not as the conquered or colonized but as conquerors and colonizers. The English settlers in Ireland had posed a similar problem for the medieval English government.[15]

The writings of John Adams presented the problem of overseas empire from the perspective of the Englishman abroad. When he argued that the King of England was also the King of Massachusetts or King of Virginia he was arguing for the existence of a medieval dynastic empire composed of a variety of territorial units, each a principality in its own right, that had affiliated with the English monarchs. In making this argument, Adams was not asserting that the indigenous population of British North America had entered into a relation with the English kings, only the English-born population. He was asserting the right of Englishmen abroad to retain the rights and legal status that they would have possessed had they remained in England. The Indians of Massachusetts were viewed either as a conquered people, the legitimate subjects of imperial rule, or, as Molyneaux had said of the Irish, no longer present and therefore of no concern.

What Adams did not know, or did not admit to knowing, or as a lawyer refused to admit, was that England was in fact an empire in a sense other than he was employing the term. Furthermore, as David Armitage has recently pointed out, by 'the second quarter of the eighteenth century, the anglophone inhabitants of the Atlantic world began for the first time to describe their community as collectively and structurally an empire'.[16] Adams of course had carefully restricted his rejection of the concept of a British Empire to the legal tradition, reflecting some caution among lawyers about employing the imperial title because of the legal implications it contained. Henry VIII had termed it such in the Act of Supremacy (1534) when he asserted that the king of England was not subject to the jurisdiction of the pope and pointed to the 'imperial crown of this realm'. In doing so, he and his advisors were using the term imperial in its medieval sense of sovereignty, the notion that the king within his kingdom is as the emperor within his empire, just as Solórzano and other Spanish writers had done.[17] That is, just as the emperor was not answerable to any temporal authority, so, by the thirteenth century, canon lawyers were arguing that various kings of the new European kingdoms were exempt from the jurisdiction of the Holy Roman Emperor whose lawyers occasionally cited the Roman law cliché about the emperor as the *dominus mundi*. The canon-law tradition was developing in such a way as to reduce the territorial extent of the imperial sway, denying the claim to universal imperial jurisdiction contained in the Roman law.[18] Henry VIII simply took the traditional arguments about limitations of imperial jurisdiction and employed them against the papacy, asserting the sovereign status of the English crown in matters ecclesiastical as well as temporal.

Henry VIII's use of imperial language to explain his break with the pope helps us understand why, although to us there was a clear need to provide a formal definition of the form of government that was emerging in sixteenth-century Spain and eighteenth-century England, rulers did not simply adopt the title emperor and label their possessions as an empire and have done with it. In the early modern world, the term *imperium* did not have the limited range of meanings that we routinely attribute to it.

This brief history of the term *imperium* suggests why Philip II or George III did not describe himself as an emperor and why John Adams was literally correct in denying the existence of a British Empire. The terms emperor and empire possessed very definite meanings in the legal and the cultural traditions that extended across the Middle Ages into the early modern world. The result was that these words bore a heavy burden of meaning that worked against their use in the early modern world. To those in the tradition of civic humanism, the terms empire and emperor reflected the decline from republican virtue that the civic humanists sought to restore. To the lawyers who made up a large part of the bureaucracy that administered Spain, for example, the empire meant a weak office within the Church and the possibility of confusing Castile, Aragon and the other possessions of the Spanish monarchs with the Holy Roman Empire. The English Common Law, never having received Roman law and having rejected canon law in the Reformation, had no place for the concept of *imperium* other than as a synonym for sovereignty. For these reasons alone, the medieval baggage attached to the term *imperium* meant that the term would not be employed in official discourse.

If the term empire was not to be used to describe the new constitutional structure, what was to be used? The work of Skinner and Pocock, focused as it is on the coming of the modern state and on the development of republican thought, suggests that the issue of defining the nature of these large-scale governments was in fact a non-issue. There is a hint of the Whig interpretation of history in this. After all, so the argument seems to go, republicanism won out in the eighteenth century and the Spanish and the English empires, such as they were in the eighteenth century, lost, so why bother trying to understand their intellectual substructure? The failure to develop a theory of government that would include all of the territories that a Philip II or a George III ruled was a real issue to men such as Solórzano and Adams and their contemporaries. The series of rebellions and revolts that characterize the political history of Spain and Great Britain from the sixteenth to the nineteenth centuries suggest that some sort of constitutional theory and structure was essential if the vast territories that these monarchs ruled were to cohere.

To some extent, the new United States created a federal structure that might have suggested how empires might be constructed. The federal solution was not, however, a popular one outside the new country. John Adams wrote his three-volume *Constitutions of Government of the United States of America* (1786–87) to defend the existence of thirteen states that comprised the new country. The *philosophe*, economist, and French royal official Anne Robert Jacques Turgot (1727–81) had written a widely publicized letter criticizing the failure of the Americans to create a centralized governmental system.

> In the general union of the states with one another, I do not see a coalition, a melting of all the parts together, so as to make the body one and homogeneous. It is only an aggregate of parts, always too separate, and which have a continual tendency to divide themselves, from the diversity of their laws, their manners, their opinions.... It is only a copy of the republic of Holland....[19]

Turgot's complaint was that the Americans, like the Dutch, were refusing to accept modern, centralized government, preferring in effect a medieval, decentralized constitutional structure.

What is striking in these legal discussions of the nature of existing governments is the way in which medieval experience, language and ideas continued to shape political and constitutional debate. In the case of the term empire, the various medieval usages of this term shaped the development of the early modern analysis of large political units. These units remained what they would have been in the Middle Ages, personal monarchies, numerous individual political units, joined only at the top by the fact of sharing the same ruler. Part of the reason for the failure to transform them into unitary states of an imperial sort was that to do so would require a new, more sophisticated political language that was not yet available. Furthermore, any such political and constitutional language would have to be acceptable to the inhabitants of the European territories of such empires as well as to the indigenous peoples of the newly acquired lands overseas. The one existing language that was available, the language of the *imperium*, could not be used. Only with the *philosophes* did there develop a language that would articulate the realities of modern large-scale states. In this sense, John Adams and his contemporaries were as much the defenders of traditional legal rights as any medieval estate or region.

The American Revolution may even have been the last medieval political conflict.

The problems created by what we may loosely call empires were part of the process by which modern constitutionalism developed. Out of the crisis that George III faced came two new political traditions. On the one hand, with the Durham Report of 1839 the English government finally began to deal with the constitutional complexities of the territories under English rule. In addition, it is not exactly a coincidence that the great experiment in republican government beginning in the late eighteenth century took place in a group of former colonies that began a revolution by seeking to clarify their legal and constitutional relationship to their mother country.

One final note about empire is in order. It is striking that it was only in the nineteenth century that the word empire came into official use in western Europe outside the Holy Roman Empire. Only at this point had the term lost its unacceptable medieval meanings. Not only did it lose its links to the Church and its identification with moral decay; the connotation of empire as conquest became acceptable. The first such use of the title, Napoleon's adoption of it in 1804, marked another *translatio imperii*, one that Napoleon's subsequent abolition of the Holy Roman Empire of the German Nation confirmed in 1806. The last Holy Roman Emperor, Francis II, had begun styling himself Francis I of Austria in 1804, keeping the imperial title but giving it a new meaning. In 1852, Napoleon III revived the imperial title in France and in 1871, the Prussian king became the first emperor of the new German (or Prussian) empire. All of these uses of the term empire emphasize military conquest. Napoleon's image was one of world conqueror; Austria, the Ostmark, was to have its *imperium* over the Slavs of the east; the new German empire was the product of a series of Prussian conquests. Empire as understood in these countries had much in common with what the Romans saw as empire, the conquest of lesser peoples.

Even in the nineteenth century, the use of the term empire did, however, retain some negative implications that made its use in western European political discourse unacceptable. Disraeli and Queen Victoria seem to have understood these residual connotations when Victoria was created Empress of India, not of Great Britain. Empress was a suitable title for the ruler of a conquered people but not for the ruler of Englishmen.[20]

Notes

PREFACE

1. 'Depend on it, Sir, when a man knows he is to be hanged in a fortnight, it concentrates his mind wonderfully.' *Familiar Quotations*, ed. John Bartlett, 15th edn (Boston: Little, Brown, 1980), 355, col. 2.
2. For a forceful statement of the consequences of overestimating the importance of Aquinas in political thought and underestimating the full range of medieval thought on politics, including the role of the lawyers, see Brian Tierney, 'Hierarchy, Consent, and the "Western Tradition"', *Political Theory* 15 (1987): 646–52.
3. Alexis de Tocqueville, *Democracy in America*, ed. J.P. Mayer, trans. George Lawrence (Garden City, NY, 1969), p. 264.
4. Manlio Bellomo, *The Common Legal Past of Europe 1000–1800*, trans. Lydia G. Cochrane (Washington, DC, 1995).

INTRODUCTION

1. Thomas Noble, *The Republic of St. Peter* (Philadelphia, 1984), p. 291.
2. Quentin Skinner, *The Foundations of Modern Political Thought*, vol. 2, *The Age of Reformation* (1978), pp. 349.
3. Ibid., 1: x.
4. A reader for use in western civilization courses reflected the view that medieval political life was anarchical when a selection of medieval documents and twentieth-century historians' opinions about early medieval government was headed 'Feudalism – Cause or Cure of Anarchy' in *Great Issues in Western Civilization*, ed. Brian Tierney, Donald Kagan, and L. Pearce Williams, 3rd edn (New York, 1976), p. 280. Recently some medievalists have been reconsidering the entire concept of feudalism: see Susan Reynolds, *Fiefs and Vassals: the Medieval Evidence Reconsidered* (Oxford, 1994).
5. On the concept of Christendom, see Denys Hay, *Europe: the Emergence of an Idea* (Edinburgh, 1957; reprint edn New York, 1966), pp. 16–36; Robert Bartlett, *The Making of Europe* (Princeton, 1993), pp. 5–23; Alberto Melloni, *Innocenzo IV: la concezione e l'esperienza della cristianità come regimen unius personae* (Genoa, 1990), esp. pp. 4–7.
6. George H. Sabine, *A History of Political Theory*, 3rd edn (New York, 1961), pp. 260–1.
7. Ibid., pp. ix–x.
8. J.W. Allen, *A History of Political Thought in the Sixteenth Century*, rev. edn (London, 1957; reprint, 1960), p. xiv.

9. Quentin Skinner, *Machiavelli* (New York, 1981); Jean Bodin, *The Six Books of a Commonweal*, trans. Richard Knolles, ed. Kenneth D. McRae (Cambridge, MA, 1962); Sabine, p. 351.
10. Sabine, p. 344.
11. Some scholars have argued that Bodin's claims to originality are overstated: see Pennington, *The Prince and the Law* (Berkeley, 1993), pp. 276–78.
12. William Robertson, *History of the Reign of Charles the Fifth*, 2 vols. (London, 1878), 1: 80–1. The two meanings of 'state' in this extract suggest the multiple meanings attached to this term in the eighteenth century.
13. Ibid., 2: 486.
14. Ibid.
15. Tierney, 'Hierarchy, Consent, and the "Western Tradition"', *Political Theory* 15 (1987): 646–52 at 647.
16. A.P. d'Entrèves, *Dante as a Political Thinker* (Oxford, 1952), p. 26.
17. For other late medieval thinkers who dealt with the issue of universal Christian society, see Michael J. Wilks, *The Problem of Sovereignty in the Later Middle Ages* (Cambridge, 1963), esp. pp. 15–64.
18. Anthony Pagden, *Lords of All the World: Ideologies of Empire in Spain, Britain and France c. 1500–c. 1800* (New Haven, 1995). Pagden has written several important works on imperial concepts, especially Spanish, increasingly stressing the importance of taking a comparative approach: see also his *The Fall of Natural Man: the American Indian and the Origins of Comparative Ethnology*, 2nd edn (Cambridge, 1986); *Spanish Imperialism and the Political Imagination* (New Haven, 1990); *European Encounters with the New World* (New Haven, 1993).
19. This work has been reviewed, not entirely sympathetically, in Cary Nederman, 'The Politics of Mind and Word, Image, and Text: Retrieval and Renewal in Medieval Political Theory', *Political Theory* 25 (1997): 716–32.
20. The best introduction to the study of medieval canon law is James A. Brundage, *Medieval Canon Law* (London, 1995). The bibliographical essay, pp. 231–42, provides a fine guide to the literature in the field.
21. Gaines Post, *Studies in Medieval Legal Thought* (Princeton, 1964), p. 10; see also Joseph R. Strayer, *On the Medieval Origins of the Modern State* (Princeton, 1970); H. Mitteis, *The State in the High Middle Ages*, trans. H.F. Orton (Amsterdam, 1975). Skinner has acknowledged this work and began his survey of modern political thought in the thirteenth century: *Foundations*, 1: ix.
22. Machiavelli's *Prince*, for example, has been placed in the tradition of the medieval 'Mirror of the Prince' literature: see A. Gilbert, *Machiavelli's "Prince" and its Forerunners* (Durham, NC, 1938). The literature on Machiavelli is vast. A useful introduction is Quentin Skinner, *Machiavelli* (Oxford, 1981): see also Nicolai Rubinstein, 'Italian Political Thought', *The Cambridge History of Political Thought 1450–1700*, ed. J.H. Burns and Mark Goldie (Cambridge, 1991) pp. 30–65 at pp. 41–58; J.H. Hexter, 'Il Principe and lo stato', in his

The Vision of Politics on the Eve of the Reformation: More, Machiavelli and Seyssel (London, 1973), pp. 150–78; Maurizio Viroli, *From Politics to Reason of State* (Cambridge, 1992), esp. pp. 126–77. On Bodin, see Pennington, *The Prince and the Law*, p. 283; and see Julian H. Franklin, 'Sovereignty and the Mixed Constitution: Bodin and His Critics', Burns and Goldie, pp. 298–328.

23. John Neville Figgis, *Political Thought from Gerson to Grotius 1414–1625*, 2nd edn (Cambridge, 1916; reprint New York, 1960), p. 26.

24. Gaines Post, *Studies in Medieval Legal Thought* (Princeton, 1964); Joseph R. Strayer, *On the Origins of the Modern State* (Princeton, 1970); Brian Tierney, *Religion, Law, and the Growth of Constitutional Thought, 1150–1650* (Cambridge, 1982). Most recently, Pennington, *The Prince and the Law*.

25. For Machiavelli's role in the development of the concept of the state, see J.H. Hexter, '*Il Principe* and *lo stato*', *Studies in the Renaissance* 4 (1957): 113–38.

26. On the medieval meanings of *status*, see Post, *Studies*, pp. 241–414.

27. An interesting example of this is the continuing debate about the layout of computer keyboards: see Paul A. David, 'Clio and the Economics of QWERTY,' *The American Economic Review* 75 (1985): 332–37; and Donald A. Norman, *The Psychology of Everyday Things* (New York, 1988), pp. 145–50.

28. One scholar who has asserted the unity of medieval and early modern political thought is Viroli, *From Politics to Reason of State*, pp. 1–2: see also Hagen Schulze, *States, Nations and Nationality: from the Middle Ages to the Present*, trans. William E. Yuill (Cambridge MA, 1996).

29. Allen, p. xiv.

30. H.G. Koenigsberger, *Politicians and Virtuosi: Essays in Early Modern History* (Rio Grande, Ohio, 1986), p. 12.

31. Thomas Hobbes, *Leviathan* (Oxford, 1957), p. 82.

32. Robertson, *Charles V*, 1: 86.

33. Concerning proposals for perpetual peace in Europe, see James Turner Johnson, *The Quest for Peace* (Princeton, 1987). Specialists in the history of international law generally see this law as beginning with Hugo Grotius's *De Iure Belli ac Pacis* in 1625: see, for example, Michael Akehurst, *A Modern Introduction to International law*, 5th edn (London, 1984), pp. 12–16. For a different perspective, one reflecting the role of medieval canon lawyers in the development of international law, a role that Grotius understood, see James Muldoon, 'The Contribution of the Medieval Canon Lawyers to the Formation of International Law', *Traditio* 28 (1972), 483–97.

34. Carl L. Becker made a similar argument about eighteenth-century French thinkers: see his *The Heavenly City of the Eighteenth-Century Philosophers* (New Haven, 1932).

35. The creoles in Spanish America 'were haunted ... by a sense that they had lost their birthright', the right to govern the Americas: see D.A. Brading, *The First America: the Spanish Monarchy, Creole Patriots, and the Liberal State 1492–1867* (Cambridge, 1991), p. 3.

36. Richard Kroebner, *Empire* (Cambridge, 1961); Anthony Pagden, *Lords of All the World: Ideologies of Empire in Spain, Britain and France c. 1500–c. 1800* (New Haven, 1995).

37. Some writers used the term 'World Monarchy', for example: see Bohdan Chudoba, *Spain and the Empire* (Chicago, 1952), p. 190; Pagden, *Lords of All the World*, pp. 42, 43.

38. John Adams and Jonathan Sewall, *Novanglus and Massachusettensis* (Boston, 1819; reprint edn, New York: 1968), p. 143. Daniel Leonard was not identified as the author of the anonymously published Massachusettensis letters until the 1820s. Adams believed for a long time that Jonathan Sewall was the author.

39. Ibid., p. 171.

40. On the use of the terms British and English with regard to the terms empire and state, see John Robertson, 'Union, State and Empire', *An Imperial State at War: Britain from 1689 to 1815*, ed. Lawrence Stone (London, 1994), pp. 224–57 at pp. 224–9.

41. John Adams, *Life and Works*, ed. Charles Francis Adams, 10 vols (Boston, 1850–6), 4: 37.

42. Ibid., 4: 114–15.

43. Adams was not quite correct in identifying George III as the King of Great Britain. He ruled the United Kingdom of Great Britain: see 'The Treaty of Union of the Two Kingdoms of Scotland and England', in *The Treaty of Union of Scotland and England, 1707*, ed. George S. Pryde (London, 1950; reprint edn, Westport, CT, 1979), p. 83.

44. 'After 1707 Britain meant north and south Britain, that is, Scotland and England and Wales.' John Brewer, 'The Eighteenth-Century British State: Contexts and Issues', in *An Imperial State at War: Britain from 1689 to 1815*, ed. Lawrence Stone (London, 1994), pp. 52–71 at p. 66. The precise nature of the union was a matter of much debate. The Scots favored some kind of federal union while the English favored incorporation of Scotland and England into 'a common, indivisible sovereignty for the two countries'. Robertson, 'Union, State and Empire', pp. 242–3.

45. Massachusettensis, p. 171.

46. Adams, *Works*, 4: 38.

47. Act of Appeals (1533: 24 Henry VIII, c. 12), *The Tudor Constitution*, 2nd edn, ed. G.R. Elton (Cambridge, 1982), pp. 353–8 at p. 353; also, the Act for exoneration of exactions paid to the see of Rome (1534: 25 Henry VIII, c. 21), ibid., pp. 360–4, passim.

48. *Tudor Constitution*, p. 428.

49. Act of Settlement, 1701, *English Historical Documents 1660–1714*, ed. Andrew Browning, *English Historical Documents*, vol. 8 (New York, 1953), pp. 129–34 at p. 132.

50. Ibid., 8: 134.

51. George I considered separating the two offices but was dissuaded from doing so: see Ragnhild Hatton, *George I, Elector and King* (Cambridge MA, 1978), pp. 157–8.

52. William MacDonald, *Charters and Other Documents Illustrative of American History 1606–1775* (New York, 1899), 317; Curtis, Edmund

and R.B. McDowell, *Irish Historical Documents 1172–1922* (London: Methuen, 1943; reprint edn New York, 1968), p. 186.

53. John Robertson, 'Union, State and Empire: the Britain of 1707 in its European Setting', *An Imperial State*, pp. 224–57.

54. The debate about the status of Ireland and its Parliament is echoed in the American debate about the relationship of the American colonies to England. For example, John Adams's position on the relationship of the North American colonies with England bears a striking resemblance to William Molyneaux's *The Case of Ireland Stated* (Dublin, 1698: reprint edn Dublin, 1977).

55. William the Conqueror (1066–87) had created the great palatinates, Lancaster, Chester and Durham. These existed outside 'the sphere of the Common Law courts', although by the eighteenth century only Durham had retained its autonomous status: David L. Keir, *The Constitutional History of Modern Britain since 1485*, 8th edn (Princeton, 1966), pp. 31–2. The basic book on Durham is G.T. Lapsley, *The County Palatine of Durham* (Cambridge MA, 1924). It is worth noting that the Charter of Maryland (1632) had given Lord Baltimore the same 'ample rights, jurisdictions, privileges ... as any bishop of Durham, within the bishopric or country palatine of Durham. ...', *English Historical Documents: American Colonial Documents to 1776*, ed. Merrill Jensen, *English Historical Documents*, vol. 9 (New York, 1955), pp. 84–93 at p. 86.

56. One can see the problem when one examines the attempts of the Spanish monarchs to impose tight control over their possessions in the Americas to avoid the divisions found in their European possessions.

57. Hugo Grotius's first publication, *Mare Liberum* in 1608, dealt with the question of access to ports in the Indian Ocean: see Richard Tuck, 'Grotius and Selden', *The Cambridge History of Political Thought, 1450–1700*, ed. J.H. Burns and Mark Goldie (Cambridge, 1991), pp. 499–529 at p. 504.

58. John A.F. Thomson, *Popes and Princes, 1417–1517* (London, 1980), p. 38.

59. Janet Nelson, 'Kingdom and Empire', *The Cambridge History of Medieval Political Thought c. 350–c. 1450*, ed. J.H. Burns (Cambridge, 1988), pp. 211–51 at p. 230.

60. On the influence of the humanists, see Anthony Grafton, 'Humanism and Political Theory', Burns and Goldie, pp. 9–29; and Nicolai Rubinstein, 'Italian Political Thought, 1450–1530', ibid., pp. 30–65.

61. Concerning the various meanings of 'state', see Viroli, *From Politics to Reason of State*, pp. 128–32, 284–5.

62. 'In the Middle Ages, Europeans recognized no significant difference between themselves and the ancients.' John Howland Rowe, 'The Renaissance Foundations of Anthropology', *American Anthropologist* 65 (1965): 1–20 at 8.

63. Ibid., 10.

64. Richard Koebner, *Empire* (Cambridge, 1966), p. 4. This is the fundamental book on the overall history of the concept of empire and *imperium* in English. Most recently, Anthony Pagden has developed the

study of empire from a comparative perspective in his *Lords of All the World*. In addition, see: 'Imperialismus', in *Geschichtliche Grundbegriffe*, ed. Otto Brunner, Werner Conze, Reinhart Koselleck, 6 vols. (Stuttgart, 1972–1990), 3: 171–88.

65. Koebner, p. 6.
66. J.S. Richardson, *'Imperium Romanum*: Empire and the Language of Power', *Journal of Roman Studies* 81 (1991): 1–9 at 1.
67. Andrew Lintott, 'What was the "Imperium Romanum"?', *Greece & Rome* 28 (1981), 53–67 at 53: see also his *Imperium Romanum: Politics and Administration* (London, 1993).
68. Koebner, p. 5.
69. Lintott, 53.
70. A.N. Sherwin-White, *The Roman Citizenship*, 2nd edn (Oxford, 1973), pp. 258–9.
71. Virgil, *The Aeneid*, trans. Rolfe Humphries (New York: Scribner's Sons, 1951), p. 173.
72. See below, pp. 109 ff., for a discussion of the way in which Renaissance humanists understood empire and imperialism.
73. James Muldoon, *The Americas in the Spanish World Order* (Philadelphia, 1994), pp. 47, 172.

1 FROM THE CAROLINGIAN EMPIRE TO THE HOLY ROMAN EMPIRE OF THE GERMAN NATION

1. Einhard and Notker the Stammerer, *Two Lives of Charlemagne*, trans. Lewis Thorpe (Harmondsworth, 1969), p. 81.
2. James Bryce, *The Holy Roman Empire*, rev. edn (New York, 1886), p. 48.
3. The crown he surrendered had not been that of Charlemagne but 'was probably made for the coronation of Otto the Great in 962'. Heer, p. 22. After surveying the various arguments about the provenance of this crown, and discussing the other possibilities, Peter Lasko concluded: 'It therefore still remains the best hypothesis that it was made in Italy for the imperial coronation of Otto I in Rome.' Peter Lasko, *Ars Sacra 800–1200*, 2nd edn (New Haven, 1994), p. 82. For the material remains of Charlemagne's age, see Donald Bullough, *The Age of Charlemagne* (New York, 1966).
4. Eventually the imperial regalia came to rest in the Hofburg in the Habsburg capital, Vienna: see Friedrich Heer, *The Holy Roman Empire*, trans. Janet Sondheimer (New York, 1968), p. 283.
5. Robert Folz, *L'Idée d'Empire en occident du Ve au XIVe Siècle* (Paris 1953), p. 31.
6. Noble, *The Republic of St. Peter*, p. 291.
7. Einhard, *Two Lives*, p. 81. *The Coronation of Charlemagne*, pp. 2–3, contains the relevant excerpts from the contemporary sources.
8. Einhard, *Two Lives*, p. 81; see also the version of the story that the monk Notker told in ibid., pp. 122–4.

9.   Einhard, *Two Lives*, p. 55. On the significance of the events surrounding the ousting of the last of the Merovingians and the beginning of the Carolingian dynasty, see Janet Nelson, 'Kingship and Empire', *The Cambridge History of Political Thought, 350–c. 1450*, ed. J.H. Burns (Cambridge, 1991), pp. 211–51 at 213–16. Noble, *The Republic*, p. 257, refers to the papal–Frankish relationship as 'the Franco–papal alliance'.

10.   Noble, *The Republic*, pp. 65–94.

11.   Notker, *Two Lives*, p. 122. This was an error. Michael I only became emperor in 811. One East Roman chronicler wrote that 'In this year in the month of December, Charles, the king of the Franks, was crowned by Pope Leo.' Theophanes, *Chronicle*, in Easton and Wieruszowski, p. 128.

12.   Notker, *Two Lives*, p. 123.

13.   'The Frankish Royal Annals', Easton and Wieruszowski, p. 127.

14.   There is an extensive literature on the events of 800. Two old but still useful introductions to the literature concerning the coronation are Folz, pp. 240–41, and *The Coronation of Charlemagne: What did it Signify?*, ed. Richard E. Sullivan, Problems in European Civilization (Boston, 1959). For further bibliographical information, see Edward James, *The Origins of France: from Clovis to the Capetians, 500–1000* (London, 1982), pp. 213, 223; Noble, *The Republic of St. Peter*, pp. 291–9.

15.   Procopius, *The Secret History*, trans. and ed., G.A. Williamson (London, 1966; reprint edn 1981), p. 192; Walter Ullmann, *The Growth of Papal Government in the Middle Ages*, 2nd edn (London, 1962), p. 144.

16.   In the twelfth century, the Roman senate 'undoubtedly saw in its claim to crown the Roman emperor a *renovatio* of pre-Carolingian constitutional practice'. Robert L. Benson 'Political *Renovatio*: Two Models from Roman Antiquity', *Renaissance and Renewal in the Twelfth Century*, ed. Robert L. Benson and Giles Constable (Cambridge MA, 1982), pp. 339–86 at p. 347.

17.   Procopius, *Secret History*, p. 192.

18.   Ullmann, *Growth*, pp. 55–6.

19.   It is worth noting that in a meeting between Louis the Pious and Pope Stephen IV (816–17) at Paderborn, 'Louis dismounted from his horse and prostrated himself three times before the pope.' Ullmann, *Growth*, p. 144.

20.   Einhard, *Two Lives*, p. 67; Charles R. Bowlus, *Franks, Moravians, and Magyars: the Struggle for the Middle Danube, 788–907* (Philadelphia, 1995), pp. 55–6. For a survey of the full extent of Charlemagne's conquests, see Julia M.H. Smith, '*Fines Imperii*: the Marches', *The New Cambridge Medieval History, vol. II c. 700–c. 900*, ed. Rosamund McKitterick (Cambridge, 1995), pp. 169–89.

21.   Noble, *The Republic*, p. 145.

22.   On the East Romans in Italy, see Noble, *The Republic*, pp. 15–60.

23.   Einhard, *Two Lives*, pp. 55–6.

24.   Edward M. Peters, *The Shadow King: Rex Inutilis in Medieval Law and Literature, 751–1327* (New Haven, 1970), pp. 48–54. For a general reconsideration of the Merovingian era, see Patrick J. Geary, *Before*

France and Germany: the Creation and Transformation of the Merovingian World (New York, 1988) esp. pp. 180–1, 226–31. It might be worth noting that Geary refers to the Merovingian lands as 'the Frankish empire' (p. 157), a reference to the fact that in the Merovingian world there were several, usually three, kingdoms at any one time. As Geary phrased it: 'Although there might be a number of Frankish kings and sub-kingdoms, the Frankish kingdoms ruled by Clovis's sons continued to be conceived of as a unity: there was only one *regnum Francorum*' (p. 117). Seen in this light, the Merovingian lands approximate one of the definitions of empire, a form of governance in which there were several kingdoms subordinate to a superior ruler, a king of kings. In this case, there was an empire, a collection of kingdoms, but not an emperor, because no ruler was clearly superior to the others and, of course, the arrangement was not the result of conquest. Nevertheless, Geary's use of the term suggests yet another way in which it can be employed.

25. On Charlemagne's building program, see McKitterick, pp. 9–11; P. Riché, *Daily Life in the World of Charlemagne*, trans. J.A. McNamara (Philadelphia, 1978), pp. 41–7, 153–8; Friedrich Heer, *Charlemagne and his World* (New York, 1975), pp. 201–19. On the building program as a *translatio*, see Heer, p. 16.
26. Einhard, *Two Lives*, pp. 77–8.
27. Noble, *The Republic*, p. 296.
28. 'Karolus serenissimus augustus, a deo coronatus magnus pacificus imperator, Romanum gobernans imperium, qui et per misericordiam Dei rex Francorum atque Langobardorum ...'. This language is found, for example, in the document outlining the division of Charlemagne's lands among his sons in 806: *Monumenta Germaniae Historica, Capitularia Regum Francorum*, vol. 1, ed. A. Boretius (Hanover: Hahn 1883; reprinted, 1980), pp. 126–30 at p. 126. See Noble, *The Republic*, pp. 296–7 for the use of this language.
29. Noble, *The Republic*, p. 296.
30. Folz, p. 35. It should be noted here that such a vision of empire was Christian but not clerical or papal.
31. *Two Lives*, Einhard, p. 81; Notker, p. 124.
32. For the papal conception of the empire, see Chapter 3.
33. *MGH, Capitularia Regum Francorum*, vol. 1, p. 127. At another point, the capitulary refers to 'these three kingdoms' (*haec tria regna*), ibid., p. 128.
34. Noble has suggested a reason why Charlemagne did not identify an heir to the imperial title at this point: 'It cannot be without meaning that Charlemagne did not bequeath his imperial title until after the Byzantine emperor had recognized its legitimacy.' Noble, *The Republic*, p. 297.
35. This also may reflect the Roman concept of empire as containing 'many dependent *regna*': Nelson, 'Kingship and Empire', p. 230.
36. Reuter, *Germany*, p. 45; see also Nelson, 'Kingship and Empire', p. 224.
37. Reuter, *Germany*, p. 46.
38. *Two Lives*, p. 83.

39. Janet Nelson suggests that the events of 806 reflect the new role of the Franks 'as an imperial people and of Francia as the seat of empire.' Nelson, 'Kingship and Empire', p. 232.

40. *MGH, Capitularia Regnum Francorum*, vol. 1, p. 129.

41. Walter Ullmann, *Growth of Papal Government*, pp. 143–8. Ullmann argued that the recrowning was 'due to the initiative of the pope himself' (p. 143). More recently, Janet Nelson has argued that Louis 'organised his own recoronation ... as emperor', 'The Frankish Kingdoms', pp. 814–98: 'The West', *New Cambridge Medieval History* 1: 110–41 at p. 111.

42. Noble, *The Republic*, p. 302. The pope was probably seeking to use the Frankish monarch to assist him in asserting control of lands in the Exarchate, a role similar to that played by Pepin and Charlemagne: see T.S. Brown, 'Louis the Pious and the Papacy: a Ravenna Perspective', in *Charlemagne's Heir: New Perspectives on the Reign of Louis the Pious (814–840)* (Oxford, 1990), pp. 297–307 at p. 303. This volume, among the most recent in a series of scholarly works on the successors of Charlemagne, contains articles by a number of scholars and has extensive bibliographical notes. Other recent works include: Rosamund McKitterick, *The Frankish Kingdom under the Carolingians* (London, 1983) and Janet L. Nelson, *Charles the Bald* (London, 1992).

43. Noble, *The Republic*, p. 302.

44. On Louis's family problems, see Nelson, *Charles the Bald*, pp. 75–104; for a contemporary view, see *Son of Charlemagne: a Contemporary Life of Louis the Pious*, trans. Allen Cabaniss (Syracuse, 1961), pp. 90–117.

45. There is a convenient translation of this document in Henderson, *Select Historical Documents*, pp. 201–6.

46. The most recent brief survey of these events and their implications is Janet Nelson, 'The Frankish Kingdoms', pp. 110–20.

47. Ibid., p. 117.

48. The text of the capitulary on the *missi* is in Henderson, pp. 189–201.

49. Liutpold Wallach, *Alcuin and Charlemagne: Studies in Carolingian History and Literature* (Ithaca, 1959), 20–2. These lines from Virgil's *Aeneid*, VI: 851–3, reappear in connection with early modern empires. For their appearance in Spanish imperial thought, see James Muldoon, *The Americas in the Spanish World Order* (Philadelphia, 1994), pp. 47–8. For an echo of them in English thought, see James Muldoon, 'The Indian as Irishman', *Essex Institute Historical Collections* 111(1975): pp. 267–89 at pp. 276–7. For their use in the twelfth century, see Friedrich Lotter, 'The Crusading Idea and the Conquest of the Region East of the Elbe', *Medieval Frontier Societies*, ed. Robert Bartlett and Angus MacKay (Oxford, 1989; reprint edn 1992), pp. 267–306 at p. 287.

50. Werner Ohnsorge, 'The Coronation and Byzantium' [an excerpt from his *Das Zweikaiserproblem*], in *The Coronation of Charlemagne: What Did It Signify?*, ed. Richard E. Sullivan, Problems in European Civilization (Boston, 1959), pp. 80–91 at p. 81.

51. See Nelson, 'The Frankish Kingdoms', pp. 119–27. There is a convenient translation of the relevant texts in *Documents of German History*, ed. Louis L. Snyder (New Brunswick, 1958), pp. 27–30.

52. McKitterick, *The Frankish Kingdom*, p. 173.
53. Ibid., p. 305, has argued that the weakness of these later Carolingians has been exaggerated; see also Reuter, *Germany*, pp. 126–37, who points out that the later Carolingians were more successful soldiers than is often realized.
54. McKitterick, pp. 179–81.
55. Or, as Geoffrey Barraclough phrased it: 'The significance of the empire and the imperial title changed from generation to generation and from emperor to emperor, reflecting the varying characters of the different rulers and the different *Zeitgeist* of succeeding ages.' *The Origins of Modern Germany*, 2nd edn (Oxford, 1947), p. 56.
56. Otto of Freising, *The Two Cities: a Chronicle of Universal History to the Year 1146 A.D.*, Records of Civilization, trans. C.C. Mierow (New York, 1928), pp. 358–9.
57. Ibid., p. 377.
58. On the German monarchy in this period, see Barraclough, *Origins*, pp. 18–30; Reuter, pp. 126–47. James Bryce pointed out that Italian writers did not identify Conrad I and Henry I as emperors because they never received the imperial crown from the pope: Bryce, *Holy Roman Empire*, p. 191.
59. Widukind described Henry I as '*imperator multorum populorum*': Folz, p. 60. Barraclough, p. 68, points out that Otto I's rule over three kingdoms meant that in effect he rules an *imperium*. See Chapter 2 for this use of the imperial title in other kingdoms.
60. Widukind, *Rerum Gestarum Saxonicarum*, III, 49, ed. G. Waitz and K.A. Kehr, 5th edn rev. Paul Hirsch and H.-E. Lohman, *Scriptores Rerum Germanicarum in Usum Scholarum ex Mon. Germ. Hist. separatim editi* (Hannover, 1935), p. 128. The discussion of the battle of Lechfeld is translated in *The Eagle, the Crescent, and the Cross: Sources of Medieval History*, vol. I, c. 250–c. 1000 (New York, 1967), pp. 228–30; see also Karl Leyser, *Communications and Power in Medieval Europe: the Carolingian and Ottonian Centuries*, ed. Timothy Reuter (London, 1994), p. 146; Reuter, *Germany*, p. 142.
61. Heer, 39.
62. See below, Chapter 2.
63. Karl Leyser, 'Theophanu divina gratia imperatrix augusta: Western and Eastern Emperorship in the Later Tenth Century', in *The Empress Theophano: Byzantium and the West at the Turn of the First Millennium*, ed. Adelbert Davids (Cambridge, 1995), pp. 1–27 at pp. 6–7.
64. K.J. Leyser, *Rule and Conflict in an Early Medieval Society: Ottonian Saxony* (Bloomington, 1979), pp. 19–20.
65. Heer, p. 19.
66. Charles V, in 1530, was the last emperor crowned by a pope, although the ceremony took place in Bologna not Rome.
67. By the terms of both the papal bull *Venerabilem* (1202) and the *Golden Bull* (1356), the German electors elected a king of the Germans who then also bore the title King of the Romans until he received imperial consecration at the hands of the pope.
68. Barraclough, *Origins*, p. 54.

69. Ibid., pp. 65–71.
70. The archdiocese of Magdeberg was established ten days after Otto I's imperial coronation, suggesting a link between the Empire and German eastward expansion: see Leyser, *Carolingian and Ottonian*, pp. 148, 154; Reuter, *Germany*, pp. 162–6.
71. The most extensive discussion of the marriage and its implications is Davids, *The Empress Theophano*. The precise place of Theophano in the imperial family has been disputed. She appears to have been a niece of the usurper John Tzimiskes (969–76), but she has been identified as a daughter of the emperor Romanus II (959–63); see Leyser, *Carolingian and Ottonian*, p. 156 and note 68.
72. Heer, p. 46.
73. Ibid., p. 44; see also Reuter, pp. 280–2.
74. Leyser, *Carolingian and Ottonian*, pp. 149–50.
75. Heer, p. 39.
76. 'Neither Otto I nor any of his successors during the following century entertained ambitions of dominating the western world.' Barraclough, *Origins*, p. 68.
77. This is an enormously complex and extensively studied issue: for a introduction to the issues and an extensive bibliography, see Uta-Renate Blumenthal, *The Investiture Controversy: Church and Monarchy from the Ninth to the Twelfth Century* (Philadelphia, 1988).
78. Brian Tierney, *The Crisis of Church and State 1050–1300* (Englewood Cliffs, NJ, 1964), pp. 59–60. The statement that only deviation from the Faith would justify the removal of an emperor parallels the later statement that the only basis for removing a pope was deviation from the faith. *Decretum*, Dist. 40 c.6; translated in Tierney, *Crisis*, p. 124.
79. For an extensive discussion of what was involved, see Karl Morrison, 'Canossa: a Revision', *Traditio* 18 (1962): 121–48.
80. In 1184, having captured Rome and installed an anti-pope, Clement III (1084–1100), Henry IV received imperial coronation: Fuhrmann, *Germany*, p. 68. Until this point, Henry's letters identified him as 'Henry, King by the grace of God' or, on rare occasions, 'Henry, by the grace of God King of the Romans'. After his coronation at the hands of Clement III, he was identified as 'King Henry, by the grace of God Emperor of the Romans and Augustus'; 'Henry, by the grace of God Emperor Augustus of the Romans' or 'Henry, by the grace of God Emperor Augustus'; or 'Henry, the Emperor': see *Imperial Lives and Letters of the Eleventh Century*, trans. Theodor E. Mommsen and Karl F. Morrison, ed. Robert L. Benson (New York, 1962), pp. 138, 141, 165, 180.
81. Fuhrmann, *Germany*, p. 152.
82. Ibid., p. 156.
83. Ibid., p. 131.
84. Heer, p. 81.
85. Otto of Freising, *The Deeds of Frederick Barbarossa*, trans. C.C. Mierow (New York, 1953), pp. 181–3; Tierney, *Crisis*, pp. 105–6 at p. 105.
86. Otto of Freising, 199–200; Tierney, *Crisis*, 109. On the double meaning of the term *beneficium* at this time, see Susan Reynolds, *Fiefs and Vassals: the Medieval Evidence Reinterpreted* (Oxford, 1994), pp. 443–4.

87. Otto of Freising, pp. 183–4; Tierney, *Crisis*, pp. 106–7 at p. 106.
88. Otto of Freising, pp. 184–6; Tierney, *Crisis*, pp. 107–8.
89. Otto of Freising, p. 193; Tierney, *Crisis*, p. 108.
90. For a brief introduction to the revival of Roman law in the twelfth century, see Stephan Kuttner, 'The Revival of Jurisprudence', in *Renaissance and Renewal in the Twelfth Century*, ed. Robert L. Benson and Giles Constable (Cambridge MA, 1982), pp. 299–323; for the relation between the revival of Roman law and the creation of canon law, see also Brundage, *Medieval Canon Law*, pp. 44–61.
91. Robert L. Benson, 'Political *renovatio*: Two Models from Antiquity', *Renaissance and Renewal*, pp. 339–86 at p. 346.
92. Otto of Freising, 146–8; Tierney, *Crisis*, 103–4.
93. Benson, 'Political *renovatio*', p. 356. The text is in Tierney, *Crisis*, pp. 102–3 at p. 103.
94. Benson, 'Political *renovatio*', p. 363.
95. Ibid., pp. 365, 367.
96. Ibid., p. 375.
97. Ibid., p. 376.
98. Fuhrmann, *Germany*, pp. 180–6.
99. Ibid., p. 184. As we shall see, the papacy employed a similar tactic in seeking to extend its jurisdiction, even acquiring England as a fief from John in 1214.
100. Ibid., p. 186.
101. Barraclough, p. 284.
102. Frederick II's life has spawned an enormous literature which is surveyed most recently in David Abulafia, *Frederick II: a Medieval Emperor* (London: Allen Lane, 1988): reprint edn Oxford: Oxford University Press, 1992), pp. 440–57.
103. Benson, 'Political *renovatio*', p. 363.
104. Concerning the relationship of Byzantium to Christendom, see Denys Hay, *Europe: the Emergence of an Idea* (Edinburgh, 1957; reprint edn New York: Harper & Row, 1966), pp. 51–2, 84.
105. One marriage, that between the Byzantine imperial family and the Romanovs, did have some long-term significance because it gave rise to the theory of Moscow as the Third Rome, see Dimitri Obolensky, *The Byzantine Commonwealth* (New York, 1971), pp. 363–7.
106. Benson, 'Political *renovatio*', p. 378.

2   OTHER MEDIEVAL EMPIRES

1. *Glossa ordinaria ad Decretales ad* 1.6.34.
2. John Gillingham, *The Angevin Empire* (New York, 1984), p. 2.
3. Sullivan, *Coronation of Charlemagne*, pp. 2–3; Einhard, p. 81. For the Byzantine reaction, see W. Ohnsorge, *Das Zweikaiserproblem im früheren Mittelalter* (Hildesheim, 1947); G. Ostrogorsky, *History of the Byzantine State*, rev. edn (New Brunswick, 1969), pp. 185–6.

4. The Byzantine government did know about the increasing reliance that the papacy was placing on the Carolingians to assist in its retention of its lands in Italy: see Noble, *Republic*, pp. 71–98.

5. *Annales Laureshamenses*, trans. in Sullivan, *Coronation*, p. 2.

6. Joseph Vogt, *The Decline of Rome*, trans. Janet Sondheimer (New York, 1969), pp. 179–83, 224; Walter Goffart, *Barbarians and Romans* (Princeton, 1980), p. 36.

7. Folz, p. 31. There is also an English translation: *The Concept of Empire in Western Europe from the Fifth to the Fourteenth Century*, trans. Sheila Ann Ogilve (n.p., 1969).

8. Folz, pp. 31–2; Heer, p. 13. Ostrogorsky, *History of the Byzantine State*, p. 186.

9. As we have seen, a marriage between a member of the western imperial family and a member of the eastern family remained a part of Ottonian and Hohenstaufen policy.

10. Folz, p. 34.

11. Ibid., p. 33.

12. A learned advisor might even have pointed out to his Byzantine imperial master that Charlemagne's description of his role and title had some echoes of the role played by barbarian *magister militum* in the fourth and fifth centuries.

13. The text of the letter is in *Monumenta Germaniae Historica, Epistolae Karolini Aevi*, ed. P. Kehr (Berlin, 1928), 7:386–94. There are extracts from the letter in Folz, p. 197–8. As to the debate about the authenticity of this letter, see R. W. Carlyle and A. J. Carlyle, *A History of Medieval Political History in the West*, 6 vols (Edinburgh and London, 1903–36), I:284.

14. *MGH, Ep. Kar.,* 7:388.

15. Rather like the Carolingians, who received a kind of legitimation of their seizure of the throne from the papacy, 'Basil I could only have been expected to seek in the repertory of imperial ideology demonstrative evidence for the aptness of his rule.' Michael McCormick, *Eternal Victory: Triumphal Rulership in Late Antiquity, Byzantium, and the Early Medieval West* (Cambridge, 1986), p. 152.

16. For Louis the Pious, see Folz, p. 197, note 7; for Charlemagne, see Ostrogorsky, pp. 198–9.

17. *MGH, Ep. Kar.,* p. 389; Folz, p. 197.

18. *MGH, Ep. Kar.,* p. 389; Folz, pp. 197–8.

19. Steven Fanning, 'Imperial Diplomacy between Francia and Byzantium: the Letter of Louis II to Basil I in 871', *Cithera* 34(1994): pp. 3–17.

20. *MGH, Ep. Kar.,* p. 390; Folz, p. 198.

21. Ostrogorsky, p. 198, note 2.

22. Folz, p. 198; *MGH Ep. Kar.,* p. 386.

23. Fanning, 'Imperial Diplomacy', p. 10, suggests that the letter to Basil is better understood 'as a diplomatic document' than as a statement of 'imperial theory'.

24. See below, Chapter 3, for a fuller discussion of the theory of the *translatio imperii*.

25. On Liutprand, see Karl Leyser, 'Ends and Means in Liudprand of Cremona', *Communications and Power*, pp. 125–42.

26. Liutprand of Cremona, 'Report of His Mission to Constantinople', *Select Historical Documents of the Middle Ages*, trans. and ed., Ernest F. Henderson (London, 1925), pp. 441–77 at p. 450: see also Jon N. Sutherland, 'The Mission to Constantinople in 968 and Liudprand of Cremona', *Traditio* 31(1975): 55–81.
27. Henderson, p. 467.
28 Ibid., p. 467; Leyser, *Carolingian and Ottonian Centuries*, p. 136.
29. The Macedonian line of Byzantine emperors (867–1050) led one of the most successful periods in Byzantine history: see Ostrogorsky, pp. 210–315.
30. Dimitri Obolensky, *The Byzantine Commonwealth: Eastern Europe, 500–1453* (New York: Praeger, 1971), p. 108. In 913, the East Roman government authorized the coronation of the ruler of the Bulgarians as Emperor of Bulgaria (*basileus Boulgarius*) by the patriarch of Constantinople, ibid.
31. Donald M. Nicol, 'The Byzantine View of Western Europe', *Greek, Roman and Byzantine Studies* 8(1967): pp. 315–39 at pp. 317–18; reprinted in Donald M. Nicol, *Byzantium: Its Ecclesiastical History and Relations with the Western World* (London: Variorum, 1972).
32. Ostrogorsky, p. 199.
33. Anna Comnena, *The Alexiad*, trans. Elizabeth A.S. Dawes (London, 1928; reprint ed New York, 1967), p. 2.
34. Ibid., p. 35.
35. Ibid., p. 34.
36. Anna Comnena's reference to the Council of Chalcedon (451) concerns a decree of that council that equated ecclesiastical and civil administrative status so that the civil and the ecclesiastical heads of a city would be of the same status. The Byzantines argued that as Byzantium was now the head of the imperial administrative structure instead of Rome, the bishop of Constantinople should now be recognized as the head of the Church in place of the bishop of Rome, whose city had been reduced in status: see Ullmann, *Growth*, p. 77.
37. Hubert Jedin, *Ecumenical Councils of the Catholic Church*, trans. Ernest Graf (New York, 1960), p. 38. For the text, see Bettenson, pp. 116–17.
38. Post, p. 487.
39. Noble, *Republic*, p. 331.
40. Wilhelm Levison, *England and the Continent in the Eighth Century* (Oxford: Clarendon Press, 1946), pp. 121–22.
41. Bede, Book 2, ch.5.
42. F.M. Stenton, *Anglo-Saxon England*, 3rd edn (Oxford, 1971), p. 34; Levison, p. 123.
43. Bede, *Opera Historica*, 2 vols, ed. C. Plummer (Oxford, 1896; reprint edn, 1 vol., 1946), 1:45, 46, 89; 2:43, 86.
44. Levison, p. 123.
45. Ibid.
46. Ibid., pp. 124–5. Recently, Steven Fanning has argued that Bede used *imperium* only to mean 'a wide rule, authority of many nations, peoples, or kingdom' and that the 'entire concept ought to be abandoned'.

Steven Fanning, 'Bede, Imperium, and the Bretwaldas', *Speculum* 66(1991): 1–26 at pp. 25–6.
47. Levison, p. 125.
48. Ibid.
49. Alfred P. Smyth, *King Alfred the Great* (Oxford, 1995), p. 480.
50. Stenton, *Anglo-Saxon England*, p. 336.
51. Ibid., p. 340.
52. H.R. Loyn, *Anglo-Saxon England and the Norman Conquest* (London, 1962), p. 265; see also Leyser, *Carolingian and Ottonian*, p. 76.
53. 'Anglorum basileos et curagulus Bryttannie', Leyser, *Carolingian and Ottonian*, p. 82.
54. Folz, pp. 52–3.
55. Stenton, p. 348.
56. Folz, pp. 52–3.
57. Herrin, *Formation of Christendom*, p. 232.
58. Joseph F. O'Callaghan, *A History of Medieval Spain* (Ithaca, 1975; reprint 1983), p. 121: see also Folz, pp. 64–9, 207–8.
59. O'Callaghan, p. 202.
60. Ibid., pp. 202–4.
61. Ibid. On the papal policy of creating a feudal relationship with the kings of Europe, see Jane Sayers, *Innocent III: Leader of Europe* (London, 1994), pp. 82–7; and A. Luchaire, *Innocent III*, 6 vols (Paris: Hachette, 1904–8), vol. 5, *Les royautés vassales du Saint-Siège*.
62. O'Callaghan, p. 215.
63. Ibid., pp. 25–6.
64. Ibid., p 362. It is worth noting that at the same time as the Aragonese ruler was rejecting any potential Castilian claims to imperial jurisdiction over Aragon he was laying the foundations for a kind of empire of his own. 'Whether one cares to call it an empire or not, the loose dynastic agglomeration that constituted the Arago-Catalan world of the thirteenth and fourteenth centuries was meant to function cohesively as a kind of fraternal alliance ...'. Felipe Fernàndez-Armesto, *Before Columbus* (Philadelphia, 1987), p. 41.
65. Gaines Post, *Studies in Medieval Legal Thought: Public Law and the State, 1100–1322* (Princeton, 1964), pp. 488–91. Post first discussed Vincentius in '"Blessed Lady Spain" – Vincentius Hispanus and Spanish National Imperialism in the Thirteenth Century', *Speculum* 29(1954): 198–209. It is worth noting that, even in the sixteenth century, when the 'Hispanic empire of León was no more, scarcely even a memory' (O'Callaghan, p. 675), the acquisition of the Holy Roman imperial title by Charles I of Castile and of Aragon, making him Emperor Charles V of the Holy Roman Empire, posed problems for the Spanish. Charles publicly recognized the independence of the Spanish kingdoms from imperial jurisdiction: see Muldoon, *The Americas*, p. 153.
66. O'Callaghan, pp. 232–3.
67. Frank Barlow, *William Rufus* (Berkeley, 1983), p. 4.
68. Frederick W. Maitland, *Roman Canon Law in the Church of England* (London, 1899), p. 100.

69. The medieval notion of the people (*gens*) or the nation (*natio*) reflected 'linguistic and cultural groups, not ... breeding stocks'. Robert Bartlett, *The Making of Europe* (Princeton, 1993), p. 197.
70. John le Patourel, 'The Plantagenet Dominions', *History* 50 (1965): 289–308 at pp. 307–8. Reprinted with the same pagination in his *Feudal Empires Norman and Plantagenet* (London, 1984), VIII. It might be pointed out here that the existence of the nation, the foundation of the modern nation-state, is often taken for granted. In fact, the French, English, German, and other nations that are the model nation-states are the product of dynastic policies of consolidation and unification and not the product of some natural, inevitable force or process. As an example of this view of nations as natural and inevitable, consider the following: 'Helmuth Plassner called the Germans a "delayed nation". The French and English had managed to achieve political unity by the time of the high Middle Ages, whereas the Germans only became a nation in the nineteenth century, and even that did not include all Germans. What caused the delay?' Fuhrmann, *Germany*, p. 167.
71. Le Patourel, 'Plantagenet Dominions', p. 308.
72. It may well have been a conscious decision not to use the terms *imperium* and *imperator* in order to avoid conflict with the German emperors.
73. *Webster's Ninth New Collegiate Dictionary* (Springfield, MA, 1990), p. 408.
74. Le Patourel, 'Plantagenet Dominions', p. 294.
75. John Le Patourel, 'Angevin Successions and the Angevin Empire,' *Feudal Empires*, IX, p. 2.
76. Ibid.
77. On the Roman pattern of imperial governance: see Lintott, *Imperium Romanum*, pp. 186–7.
78. 'Bella gerant fortes; tu, felix Austria, nube.' *Quotations in History*, ed. Alan and Veronica Palmer (Hassocks, Sussex, 1976), p. 152.
79. *Irish Historical Documents 1172–1922*, ed. Edmund Curtis and R.B. McDowell, reprint ed (New York, 1968), p. 18; *Pontificia Hibernica*, 2 vols, ed. M.P. Sheehy (Dublin, 1965) 1:1–15.
80. J.A. Watt, *The Church and the Two Nations in Medieval Ireland* (Cambridge, 1970), p. 39: see also his *The Church in Medieval Ireland*, The Gill History of Ireland, vol. 5 (Dublin, 1972), pp. 35–9.
81. The English clergy might also have recalled that William, Duke of Normandy, had received a papal blessing on his planned invasion of England: see Blumenthal, pp. 146–8.
82. Curtis and McDowell, pp. 22–4 at pp. 22–3.
83. Gillingham, *Angevin Empire*, p. 26.
84. Ibid., pp. 23–4. In both cases, the language of superiority was that of feudalism, not empire. In practice, however, however, the consequences were the same.
85. Austin Lane Poole, *From Domesday Book to Magna Carta 1087–1216*, 2nd edn (Oxford, 1955), pp. 311–12.
86. Gillingham, *Angevin Empire*, p. 26.

87. 'Proposed Extension of English Law to the Native Irish', *Irish Historical Documents*, pp. 31–2.
88. Barlow, *William Rufus*, pp. 40–1.
89. For a survey of the debate about why William disposed of his properties as he did, see Barlow, *William Rufus*, pp. 40–50.
90. Barlow summed up the goals of William Rufus's reign as 'the *renovatio imperii Normannorum*', a striking phrase in view of the usual restriction of such *renovatio* to the German empire. Barlow, *William Rufus*, p. 434.
91. Le Patourel, 'Angevin Succession', p. 16.
92. As late as 1837, rule over Hanover passed from the English royal family to another branch of the family because Hanoverian law did not allow female succession.
93. Robert Fawtier, quoted in Charles Wood, *Appanages* (Cambridge, 1966), p. 150.
94. Strayer, *Medieval Origins*, p. 53.
95. In the sixteenth century, France had 'sixty general *coutumes* and close to three hundred local ones …'. Andrew Lossky, *Louis XIV and the French Monarchy* (New Brunswick, 1994), p. 8.

3   THE PAPAL CONCEPTION OF EMPIRE

1. Harold Berman, *Law and Revolution: the Formation of the Western Legal Tradition* (Cambridge, MA, 1983), p. 115.
2. Pennington, *The Prince and the Law*, p. 2.
3. See Richard Tuck's review of Pagden, *Lords of All the World* in *The Times Literary Supplement* (24 May 1996), p. 15. An important exception to this statement is R.W. and A.J. Carlyle, *A History of Mediaeval Political Thought in the West*, 6 vols (Edinburgh, 1903–36): on the importance of the legal tradition in general and the canonists in particular, see Carlyle 2:2–3. Most of the works on the Holy Roman Empire, books such as Bryce's *Holy Roman Empire* or on the concept of empire in general, Kroebner's *Empire* for example, make little or no mention of the canonists. Beginning 50 years ago, however, Stephan Kuttner created the modern study of canon law, a work carried on through the Institute of Medieval Canon Law and its journal, the *Bulletin of Medieval Canon Law* (1971–): see Brundage, *Medieval Canon Law*, pp. 231–4.
4. For the history and development of canon law, see Brundage, *Medieval Canon Law*, esp. ch. 3, 'Gratian and the Schools of Law in the Classical Period (1140–1375)'. On the popes as 'highly qualified jurists', see Walter Ullmann, *Law and Politics in the Middle Ages: an Introduction to the Sources of Medieval Political Ideas* (Ithaca, 1975), p. 140. Some doubt has been expressed, however, about the extent of the legal education of late-twelfth and early-thirteenth-century popes: see Kenneth Pennington, 'The Legal Education of Pope Innocent III', *Bulletin of Medieval Canon Law*, n.s. 4(1974):70–7; and John T. Noonan, Jr, 'Who was Rolandus'? in *Law, Church and Society: Essays in Honor of Stephan*

Kuttner, ed. Kenneth Pennington and Robert Somerville (Philadelphia, 1977), pp. 21–48.

5. Berman, p. 115.
6. Walter Ullmann, *Principles of Government and Politics in the Middle Ages* (London, 1961), p. 71. This theme runs through all of Ullmann's work on medieval papal and canonistic thought.
7. John Neville Figgis, *Political Thought from Gerson to Grotius: 1414–1625,* reprint (New York, 1960), p. 5. The book was originally titled *Studies of Political Thought from Gerson to Grotius: 1414–1625* (Cambridge, 1907). In recent years Figgis's work has become the subject of a great deal of scholarly interest, because he argued that modern constitutionalism was derived from the conciliar movement of the late Middle Ages. For a critique of the Figgis position, see Cary Nederman, 'Conciliarism and Constitutionalism: Jean Gerson and Medieval Political Thought', *History of European Political Ideas*, 12(1990):189–9. In response to Nederman, see Francis Oakley, 'Nederman, Gerson, Conciliar Theory and Constitutionalism: sed contra', *History of Political Thought* 16(1995):1–19.
8. In addition to Brundage, *Medieval Canon Law*, esp. ch. 3: see Berman, pp. 144–5; G. Le Bras, Ch. Lefebvre and J. Rambaud, *L'Age Classique 1140–1378: Sources et théorie du droit, Histoire du Droit et des Institutions de l'Eglise en Occident*, vol. 7 (Paris, 1965), pp. 78–99. Concerning the structure of the *Decretum*: see Stanley Chodorow, *Christian Political Theory and Church Politics in the Mid-Twelfth Century: the Ecclesiology of Gratian's Decretum* (Berkeley, 1972), pp. 7–16; *Histoire du Droit et des Institutions de l'Eglise en Occident*, vol. 7, *L'Age Classique 1140–1378*, pp. 78–99. There is a translation of the first 20 *distinctiones* and the ordinary gloss on it: see *The Treatise on Laws (Decretum DD 1–20)*, trans. Augustine Thompson and James Gordley, Studies in Medieval and Early Modern Canon Law, vol. 2 (Washington, DC, 1993). The theme of the *Decretum* was to bring order into the mass of materials dealing with ecclesiastical matters and to reconcile apparent contradictions among the existing canons: see Stephan G. Kuttner, *Harmony from Dissonance: an Interpretation of Medieval Canon Law* (Latrobe, PA, 1960).
9. *Decretum*, D. 96 c. 10. Gelasius is presented by way of a letter of Pope Gregory VII that contains Gelasius's words. For an English translation of Gelasius's text, see Tierney, *Crisis*, pp. 13–14.
10. For a discussion of Gelasius's letter and its influence in the early Middle Ages, see I.S. Robinson, 'Church and Papacy', in Burns, *The Cambridge History of Medieval Political Thought*, pp. 252–305 at pp. 288–300.
11. 'Humanum genus duobus regitur, naturali videlicet iure, et moribus.' *Corpus iuris canonici*, ed. E. Friedberg, 2 vols (Leipzig, 1879–81; reprint edn, Graz, 1959), vol. I, *Decretum*, D. 1. For a translation, see Tierney, *Crisis*, pp. 13–14; *Treatise*, ed. Thompson, p. 3.
12. Herrin, *The Formation of Christendom*, pp. 344–89.
13. See Chapter 1, p. 28.
14. Noble, *The Republic*, p. 291.

15. On the relation of the *Decretum* to the investiture controversy, see Chodorow, *Christian Political Theory*: see also Uta-Renate Blumenthal, *The Investiture Controversy: Church and Monarchy from the Ninth to the Twelfth Century*, 1988).
16. 'Imperator ius habet eligendi Pontificem.' D. 63 c. 22.
17. 'Electio Romani Pontificis ad ius pertinet imperatoris.' D. 63 c.23.
18. *Decretum*, D. 96 cc. 1, 2, 4–8.
19. Gregory VII's letters played a major role in shaping the canonistic tradition: see John Gilchrist, 'The Gregorian Reform Tradition and Pope Alexander III', *Miscellanea Rolando Bandinelli Papa Alessandro III*, ed. F. Liotta (Siena, 1986): pp.259–87.
20. Horst Furhmann, 'Konstantinische Schenkung und Sylvester-legende in neuer Sicht', *Deutsches Archiv* 15(1959): 523–40 at 523–4: see also his 'Konstantinische Schenkung und abendländisches Kaisertum', *Deutsches Archiv* 22(1966): 63–21. see also Domenico Maffei, *La donazione di Costantino nei giuristi medievali* (Milan, 1964), pp. 5–10. The text is translated in *Documents of the Christian Church*, ed. Henry Bettenson, 2nd edn (London, 1963), pp. 135–40. The Latin text is in C. Mirbt, *Quellen zur Geschichte des Papsttums und des römischen Katholizismus*, ed. C. Mirbt and K. Aland, 6th edn (Tübingen, 1967), pp. 251–6.
21. Walter Ullmann, *The Growth of Papal Government in the Middle Ages*, 2nd edn (London, 1962), pp. 58–9. For a critique of Ullmann's views, see Francis Oakley, 'Celestial Hierarchies Revisited: Walter Ullmann's Vision of Medieval Politics', *Past & Present* 60 (Aug. 1973): 3–48.
22. Janet Nelson, 'Kingship and Empire', Burns I, pp. 212–13.
23. Ibid., p. 231.
24. 'The Donation of Constantine', Henderson, pp. 319–29 at pp. 325–6: see also *Documents of the Christian Church*, ed. Henry Bettenson, 2nd edn (New York, 1963), pp. 135–40. The most famous discussion of the Donation as an eighth-century forgery was that of Lorenzo Valla, *The Profession of the Religious and the Principal Arguments from the Falsely-Believed and Forged Donation of Constantine*, trans. and ed. Olga Zorzi Pugliese (Toronto, 1985). This contains excerpts from Valla's critique of the Donation. For other Renaissance discussions of the Donation, see Joseph M. Levine, 'Reginald Pecock and Lorenzo Valla on the *Donation of Constantine, Studies in the Renaissance* 20(1973): 118–43; Louis B. Pascoe, 'Gerson and the Donation of Constantine: Growth and Development within the Church', *Viator* 5(1974): 469–85. There is a very useful brief discussion of the Donation in Herrin, pp. 385–7, 399–400. The standard work on the Donation is Domenico Maffei, *La donazione di Costantino nei giuristi medievali* (Milan, 1964).
25. Henderson, p. 328.
26. Concerning Constantine's grants to the Church and his role in the construction of the basilica of St John Lateran, see Richard Krautheimer, *Rome: Profile of a City, 312–1308* (Princeton, 1980), pp. 20–4.
27. Robert Grant, *Augustus to Constantine: the Rise and Triumph of Christianity in the Roman World* (New York, 1970; reprint 1990), p. 247.

28. The earliest Christian historians of Constantine's victory over his enemies at the Milvian Bridge, Lactantius (c.250–c.320) and Eusebius (c.260–c.339), attributed Constantine's victory to his heeding a vision explained in a dream that he would win if his soldiers wore a symbol representing Christ: see *A New Eusebius: Documents Illustrating the History of the Church to AD 337*, ed. J. Stevenson, rev. edn W.H.C. Frend (London, 1987), pp. 283–4.

29. Henderson, pp. 322–4.

30. Ullmann, *Growth*, pp. 55–9.

31. Henderson, pp. 327–8.

32. Heer, p. 46; Carlyle and Carlyle, 2:213; Maffei, pp. 15–16, 22.

33. For the text, see Walter Ullmann, *Growth*, pp. 241–2, note 1.

34. The *translatio* has been the subject of an extensive literature: see P.A. Van Den Baar, *Die kirchliche Lehere der Translatio Imperii Romani bis zur Mitte des 13. Jahrhunderts* (Rome, 1956); Werner Goez, *Translatio Imperii* (Tübingen, 1958).

35. Herrin, p. 387.

36. The Donation appears in the *Decretum* as D.96, c. 14. It was not included in Gratian's original text but added subsequently: see Valla, *The Profession*, p. 69; Carlyle and Carlyle, 2:209–13.

37. For a brief but comprehensive discussion of the *lex regia*, see Joseph Canning, *A History of Medieval Political Thought 300–1450* (London, 1996), pp. 8–9: see also Ullmann, *Law and Politics*, pp. 56–7.

38. The most important proponent of the view that the popes and canonists were hierocrats was Walter Ullmann. His views are presented at full length in *Principles of Government and Politics in the Middle Ages* (London, 1961). There have been a number of critiques of Ullmann's views: Alfons M. Stickler, 'Concerning the Political Theories of the Medieval Canonists', *Traditio* 7(1949–51): 450–63; Friedrich Kemp, 'Die päpstliche Gewalt in der mittelalterlichen Welt', *Miscellanea Historiae Pontificiae* 21(1959): 117–69; Brian Tierney, 'Some Recent Works on the Political Theories of the Medieval Canonists', *Traditio* 10(1954): 594–625; Francis Oakley, 'Celestial Hierarchies Revisited: Walter Ullmann's Vision of Medieval Politics', *Past & Present* 60 (August 1973): 3–48.

39. Luke 22:38; Matthew 26:52. See also J.A. Watt, 'Spiritual and Temporal Powers', Burns, *Cambridge History* I:367–423.

40. This use of the two-swords metaphor is found in the writings of Bernard of Clairvaux (1090–1153), *De Consideratione*, and those of his contemporaries, such as John of Salisbury (d. 1180), suggesting that it was becoming current around the middle of the twelfth century: see Carlyle and Carlyle, 4:333–6.

41. *Decretum*, C.23 q.8 *ante*. The most detailed analyses of this metaphor are to be found in the writings of A.M. Stickler: see his 'Der Schwerterbegriff bei Huguccio', *Ephemerides Iuris Canonici*, 3(1947):201–42; and 'Il "gladius" negli atti dei concili et dei RR. Pontifici sino Graziano e Bernardo di Clairvaux', *Salesianum* 13(1951):414–45.

42. Matthew 16: 18–19.

43. *Summa, ad Dist.* 22 c.1, pp. 47–8.
44. *Summa, ad Dist.* 22 c. 1: see Carlyle and Carlyle, 2:208. For the significance of Stephen of Tournai, see Stephan Kuttner and Eleanor Rathbone, 'Anglo-Norman Canonists in the Twelfth Century,' *Traditio* 7(1949–51): 279–358.
45. *Summa Omnis qui iuste, ad Dist.* 96 c. 6, Rouen Ms. 743. fol. 43(vb).
46. In spite of his importance, Huguccio's canonistic writings have never appeared in a printed edition, although many elements of his commentary on the *Decretum* are available. The best introduction to his work in English is Wolfgang P. Müller, *Huguccio: the Life, Works, and Thought of a Twelfth-Century Jurist,* Studies in Medieval and Early Modern Canon Law, vol. 3 (Washington, DC, 1994).
47. *Summa ad Dist.* 96. c. 6, '*Cum ad verum ventum*: usque adventum Christi iura temporalia et pontificalia erant indistincta, quia idem erat imperator et pontifex .... Set a Christo distincta sunt iura et officia imperatoris et pontificis et alia sunt attributa imperatori, scilicet temporalia, et alia, scilicet spiritualia, concessa sunt pontifici.' Stickler, 'Der Schwerterbegriff bei Huguccio', 210 n. 1. It is striking that Huguccio used the term 'emperor' not 'king' to describe Christ. See also Müller, *Huguccio*, pp. 10–12.
48. Medieval canonists discussed the powers that a bishop–elect could exercise until his consecration. By analogy, some of these lawyers extended this debate to the powers of the emperor-elect: see Robert L. Benson, *The Bishop-Elect* (Princeton, 1968), pp. 132, 140, 356.
49. *Summa ad Dist., officiis,* Stickler, 'Der Schwerterbegriff bei Huguccio', 211–212, n. 1.
50. Rufinus, *Summa ad Dist.* 22 c. 1, pp. 47–8.
51. Carlyle and Carlyle, 2:206–207.
52. Huguccio, *Summa ad* C.33 q.2 c.6, Stickler, 'Der Schwerterbegriff bei Huguccio', 222, n. 2.
53. Huguccio, *Summa ad Dist.*, Stickler, 'Der Schwerterbegriff bei Huguccio,' 220, n. 2.
54. *Summa Tractaturus magister ad Dist.* 96 c. 6, '*propriis...*'. A. Stickler, 'Imperator vicarius Papae', *Mitteilungen des Instituts für Österreichischen Geschichtsforschung,* 62(1954): 165–212, at 203, n. 69.
55. British Museum, Stowe 378 *ad Dist.* 22 c. 1, A. Stickler, '"Sacerdotium et Regnum" nei Decretisti et primi Decretalisti. Considerazioni metodologiche di ricerca e testi', *Salesianum* 15 (1953): 575–612 at 593.
56. *Summa Reverentia ss. canonum ad Dist.* 22 c. 1. *terreni simul...*', Stickler, 'Imperator vicarius Papae', 203–4, n. 69.
57. *Summa Reverentia ss. canonum ad Dist.* 10 c.8. '*dignitatibus distinctis...*', Stickler, 'Imperator vicarius Papae', 204, n. 69.
58. Benencasa d'Arezzo *ad Dist.* 22 c.1., *simul et terreni et celestis imperii ...*Stickler, ' "Sacerdotium et Regnum"', 602–3.
59. This distinction was to appear later in Innocent III's decretal *Venerabilem*, the fundamental papal statement on the relationship between the papacy and the empire.
60. *Summa Bambergensis ad Dist.* 22 c. 1, Stickler, 'Imperator vicarius Papae', 204, n. 69.

61. Caius College MS. 676 *ad Dist. 22. c. 1, fol. 12rb,* 'terreni simul ..'. See also Stickler, ' "Sacerdotium et Regnum"', 591.
62. Ullmann, *Papal Government*, pp. 428–30; M. Maccarrone, *Vicarius Christi: storia del titolo papale* (Rome, 1952).
63. The writer known as the Norman Anonymous is a partial exception to this in that he argued that Christ did possess both powers but that the temporal power is superior to the spiritual because Christ was King by virtue of His divinity but man in His role as Priest. Therefore, the spiritual power is instituted through the royal power and subject to it, a position diametrically opposed to the papal interpretation of the two powers: see M. Maccarrone, *Vicarius Christi: storia del titolo papale* (Rome, 1952): Lewis, *Medieval Political Ideas*, 2:563–6.
64. For the details of the conflict over the election, see David Abulafia, *Frederick II: a Medieval Emperor*, reprint edn (Oxford, 1992), pp. 89–93 and passim.
65. Denis Mack Smith, *History of Sicily. Medieval Sicily: 800–1713* (New York, 1968), p. 44.
66. Tierney, *Crisis*, p. 44, contains the text of the agreement.
67. Abulafia, *Frederick II*, p. 93.
68. *Das Register Papst Innocenz' III. Über den Deutschen Thronstreit*, 2 vols, ed. Walther Holtzmann (Bonn, 1947–48); *Regestum super negotio Romani Imperii*, ed. F. Kempf (Rome, 1947).
69. For an introduction to the debate about Innocent III, see *Innocent III: Vicar of Christ or Lord of the World?*, ed. James Powell, rev. edn (Washington, DC, 1994). Among the fundamental works on Innocent III are those of Michele Maccarrone: *Chiesa e stato nella dottrina di papa Innocenzo III* (Rome, 1940; *Vicarius Christi: Storia del titolo papale* (Rome, 1952); *Nuovi studi su Innocenzo III*, ed. Roberto Lambertini (Rome, 1995); see also Friedrich Kemp, 'Innocenz III. und der Deutsche Thronstreit', *Archivium Historiae Pontificiae* 23(1985): 63–91; Jane Sayers, *Innocent III: Leader of Europe 1198–1216* (London, 1994).
70. Manlio Bellomo, *The Common Legal Past of Europe 1000–1800*, trans. Lydia G. Cochrane (Washington, DC, 1995), p. 69.
71. *Decretales* 1.6.34; *Regestum*, 168–9.
72. Ibid.
73. Ibid.
74. Ibid.
75. Ibid.
76. Ibid.
77. Ibid.
78. Recently, Susan Reynolds called into question modern understanding of the language associated with feudalism. For her discussion of Adrian IV's use of the term *beneficium*, see her *Fiefs and Vassals: the Medieval Evidence Reinterpreted* (Oxford, 1994), pp. 443–4.
79. The texts of the relevant documents are in Tierney, *Crisis*, pp. 105–9. On the incident at Besançon, see Munz, 142–5.
80. Ibid., p. 119.

81. Huguccio, *Summa ad dist.* 96 c.6 in Stickler, 'Der Schwerterbegriff bei Huguccio', 201–42 at pp. 211–12, n.1.
82. Alanus, *ad dist.* 96 c.6 (second recension), in Alfons Stickler, 'Alanus Anglicus als Verteidiger des monarchischen Papsttum', *Salesianum* 21(1959): 346–406 at pp. 361–3.
83. *Decretales*, 1.6.34.
84. There was a *Glossa Ordinaria*, that is a basic commentary, on the *Decretum* and on the *Decretales*: see L.E. Boyle, 'Decretists', *New Catholic Encyclopedia*, 15 vols (New York, 1967) 4:711–13; A.M. Stickler, 'Joannes Teutonicus (Zemecke)', ibid., 7:998; L.E. Boyle, 'Decretalists', ibid., 4:705–7; J.M. Buckley, 'Bernard of Parma', ibid., 2:342.
85. *Glossa ordinaria* ad 1.6.34. The glossator cited a chapter of the *Decretum*, C.15 q.6 c.3 *Alius*, that explained that the ousting of the last Merovingian was not 'because of his sins ... but because of his uselessness' as a ruler. The concept of the incompetent, the useless king, the *rex inutilis*, has been explored at length in Edward M. Peters, *The Shadow King* (New Haven, 1970). The use of the term *imperium* in the *Glossa Ordinaria* reflects the multiple meanings of the term. Although the term is usually translated as 'empire', in fact the context would also allow it to be translated as 'power' or even as 'functional office'.
86. This was a common comparison but was often written incorrectly. The phrase 'king of a chess-set', *rex scaccariorum*, was written in a variety of erroneous ways, such as king of the Scots (*rex scottorum*) and king of the Franks (*rex francorum*): see Gaines Post, 'Some Unpublished Glosses (ca. 1210–1214) on the 'Translatio Imperii' and the Two Swords', *Archiv für katholisches Kirchenrecht* 117(1937): 403–29 at 408; and Charles Duggan, *Twelfth Century Decretal Collections* (London, 1963), pp. 9–11.
87. Tierney, *Crisis*, 20.
88. A miniature from the late-fourteenth-century manuscript illustrates Innocent III's conception of the right order of the world. It shows a pope seated upon his throne, presiding over a council. On his left hand, seated on a lower level, are the crowned kings of Europe and on the pope's right, on the same level as the kings, are cardinals and bishops. Between the kings and the pope, however, sits the emperor, above the kings but below the pope: see Geoffrey Barraclough, *The Medieval Papacy* (New York, 1968), p. 124.
89. On the papacy and Frederick II, see Abulafia, *Frederick II: a Medieval Emperor*, passim.

4 THE EMPEROR AS *DOMINUS MUNDI*

1. Dante, *Monarchy and Three Political Letters*, trans. Donald Nicholl and Colin Hardie (London, 1954), p. 11.
2. Franciscus de Vitoria, *De Indis et de iure belli relectiones*, ed. Ernest Nys, Classics in International Law (Washington, DC, 1917; reprint edn New York, 1964), p. 131.

3. For a concise examination of the legal revival, see Stephan Kuttner, 'The Revival of Jurisprudence', in *Renaissance and Renewal in the Twelfth Century*, pp. 299–323.
4. *Digest*, 14.2.9. 'Ego quidem mundi dominus.' Emperor Antoninus.
5. Pennington, *The Prince*, p. 30. This chapter owes a great deal to the work of Pennington and that of Joseph Canning cited below.
6. Hernan Cortés, *Letters from Mexico*, trans. and ed. A.R. Pagden (New York, 1971), Second Letter, p. 48; see also Pagden, *Lords*, p. 32.
7. Bryce, pp. 86–97. This book was written against the background of the re-establishment of a German empire, the first edition appearing in 1864 and the second in 1873.
8. Heer, pp. 284–5.
9. Pennington argues that this was not even a serious debate for the lawyers, that 'By the beginning of the thirteenth century, the jurists played rather than grappled with the idea of universal imperial sovereignty.' Pennington, *The Prince*, p. 36.
10. J.P. Canning, 'Introduction: Politics, Institutions and Ideas', Burns, *Cambridge History*, pp. 341–66 at p. 341.
11. The truth of this story is generally denied but, as Kenneth Pennington has written, 'if the story is not true, it should be'. Pennington, *Prince*, pp. 16–17. As an illustration of the nature of the emperor's universal claims, the story has an obvious heuristic function. In any event, the story underscores Barbarossa's interest in the Roman law and its implications for his rule.
12. For a survey of the views on this issue, see Peter Munz, *Frederick Barbarossa: a Study in Medieval Politics* (Ithaca, 1969), pp. 233–4 n. 2: see also Ferdinand Opll, *Friedrich Barbarossa* (Darmstadt, 1990), pp. 272–3.
13. *MGH, Legum*, sect. IV, Constitutiones, 1:182 in Carlyle and Carlyle 3:174 n. 1.
14. Carlyle and Carlyle, 3:175.
15. Robert Benson, '*Political renovatio*: Two Models from Roman Antiquity', *Renaissance and Renewal*: 339–86 at pp. 378–9.
16. The translation is in Tierney, *Crisis*, pp. 145–6 at p. 145.
17. Joseph Canning, *The Political Thought of Baldus de Ubaldus*, Cambridge Studies in Medieval Life and Thought, Fourth Series (Cambridge, 1987), p. 25.
18. Ibid.
19. Ibid., 27.
20. Dante, *Monarchy*, p. 4.
21. John M. Headley, *The Emperor and his Chancellor: a Study of the Imperial Chancellery under Gattinara*, Cambridge Studies in Early Modern History (Cambridge, 1983), p. 11.
22. Dante, *Monarchy*, p. 5.
23. Ibid., p. 9.
24. Ibid., p. 11.
25. Ibid., p. 12.
26. Augustine, *City of God*, bk 3 ch.6 [1:79–80].
27. Dante, *Monarchy*, pp. 32–3: for an extensive analysis of Dante's vision of the Empire, see Charles Davis, *Dante and the Idea of Rome* (Oxford, 1957), pp. 139–94.

28. Dante, *Monarchy*, p. 37.
29. Ibid., pp. 48–51.
30. Ibid., p. 51.
31. Ibid., p. 56.
32. Ibid., pp. 69–70. On the sun–moon analogy, see Canning, *History of Medieval Political Thought*, pp. 123, 151.
33. Dante, *Monarchy*, p. 76.
34. Ibid., p. 80.
35. Ibid., p. 83.
36. Ibid., p. 93.
37. Ibid., p. 94.
38. d'Entrèves, *Dante*, pp. 44, 47.
39. Headley, *The Emperor*, pp. 11, 95, 111–12; Pagden, *Spanish Imperialism*, p. 49.
40. Hugo Grotius, *The Law of War and Peace. De Jure Belli ac Pacis Libri Tres*, trans. Francis W. Kelsey, *The Classics of International Law* (Washington, DC, 1925; reprint edn Indianapolis, 1962), p. 352.
41. James Turner Johnson, *The Quest for Peace: Three Moral Traditions in Western Cultural History* (Princeton, 1987), p. 113.
42. *Decretum*, Dist. 1 c.12.
43. Skinner, *Foundations*, 2:54–5.
44. *Decretum*, c.7, q.1 c.41. Medieval men believed that beehives were headed by a king not by a queen, following Aristotle's position: see Aristotle, *Historia animalium*, 3 vols, trans. A.L. Peck (Cambridge, MA, 1965–70) 2:189 [bk V:21]; St Thomas Aquinas, *On Politics and Ethics*, ed. and trans. Paul E. Sigmund (New York, 1980), p. 18, n. 2.
45. Huguccio, *Summa ad* c.7 q.1 c.41; Mochi Onory, *Fonti*, 165.
46. Huguccio, *Summa ad* c.6 q.3 c.2; Mochi Onory, 166.
47. A major problem with Huguccio's work is that there is no standard edition of his *Summa* and there are numerous manuscripts containing all or parts of it written at different times: see Müller, *Huguccio*, pp. 4–8, 67–8.
48. Huguccio, *Summa ad Dist.* 21 c.12, Pembroke College MS. 72, fol. 130vb.
49. Huguccio, *Summa ad* c.15 q.6 c.3, ibid.
50. *App. Ecce vincit leo ad Dist.* 1 c.12. Text in Post, *Studies*, p. 460 n. 85.
51. Huguccio, *Summa ad Dist.* 21 c.12, Pembroke College MS. 72, fol. 130vb. *Summa Reginensis ad Dist.* 1 c.12 in Stickler, 'Vergessene Bologneser Dekretisten', *Salesianum* 14 (1952): 476–503 at 491.
52. Vacarius, *The Liber Pauperum*, ed. F. de Zulueta, Selden Society (London, 1927), pp. xiii–xxiii.
53. William Blackstone, *Commentaries on the Laws of England*, 4 vols (Oxford, 1765–69; reprint edn, Chicago, 1979), 1:18–19.
54. Ibid., 1:19–20.
55. F. Liebermann, 'Magister Vacarius', *English Historical Review* 11 (1896): 305–14 at 310–11.
56. H.A. Cronne, *The Reign of King Stephen 1135–54: Anarchy in England* (London, 1970), pp. 280–81.
57. A Spanish lawyer made a similar case for Spanish law in the thirteenth century. The 'liber iudiciorum of Leon forbade on the pain of death the

reception of the Roman law'. Post, *Studies*, p. 490, n. 189. It is important to note, however, that although it is often believed that Roman and
canon law had little influence on the growth of English law, in fact there
was significant influence. See Post, *Studies*, pp. 184–9.

58.   *Glossa ordinaria ad Dist.* 1 c.12, *Quod nulli.*
59.   Ibid., c.7 q.1 c.41, *Imperator.*
60.   Ibid., c.7 q.1 c.41, *Unus.*
61.   Tancred, *Comp.* III, *ad* I, vi,19 (*Decretales*, I,vi,34), Caius MS. 17, page
      162a, '*Transtulit*.' On the notion of '*imperium extra ecclesiam*', see James
      Muldoon, '*Extra ecclesiam non est imperium.* The Canonists and the
      Legitimacy of Secular Power', *Studia Gratiana* 9 (1966): 553–80. The
      excerpts from Tancred are at p. 562, n. 17.
62.   This concept has attracted a great deal of scholarly attention in recent
      years. Among the most important elements of this literature are: Brian
      Tierney, 'Some Recent Works on the Political Theories of the Medieval
      Canonists', *Traditio* 10 (1954): 594–625; Post, *Studies*, 453–82;
      F. Calasso, *I glossatori e la teoria della sovranita.* 3rd edn (Milan, 1957);
      Helmut G. Walther, *Imperiale Königtum Konziliarismus und
      Volkssouveränität* (Munich, 1976); Pennington, *The Prince.*
63.   *Decretum*, *Dist.* 2 c.4.
64.   *Summa Parisiensis*, ed. Terence McLaughlin (Toronto, 1952), *ad Dist.* 2
      c.4, p. 3.
65.   *App. Ecce vincit leo ad Dist.* 2 c.4, Trinity MS. 0.5.17, fol. 1 rb, '*quod
      tamen rex ...*'. See also Post, *Studies*, p. 460, n. 86.
66.   For the background to the decretal, see Tierney, *Crisis*, p. 129.
67.   *Decretales*, 4.17.13; Tierney, *Crisis*, pp. 136–8 at p. 136.
68.   Tierney, *Crisis*, p. 137.
69.   Alanus Anglicus *ad Dist.* 96 c.6 [second recension] '*cursu ....*' in Alfons
      Stickler, 'Alanus Anglicus als Verteidiger des monarchischen Päpsttums',
      Salesianum 21 (1959): 346–404 at 363; Tierney, *Crisis*, pp. 123–4 at p. 124.
70.   Ricardus Anglicus, gloss on *Compilatio I*, ed. F. Gillmann, 'Ricardus
      Anglicus als Glossator der Compilatio I', *Archiv für katholisches
      Kirchenrecht* 107 (1927): 575–655 at 626; Tierney, *Crisis*, pp. 161–2.
71.   In examining the materials discussed here, Post, *Studies*, pp. 434–93,
      found the roots of nationalism, a view that he recognized went against
      contemporary thought on the history of nationalism (p. 434, n. 1).
72.   *Glossa ordinaria ad Decretum ad Dist.* 63 c.22, '*Per singulos ....*'
73.   Post, *Studies*, pp. 488–91; Tierney, *Crisis*, p. 162.
74.   For other examples, see Tierney, *Crisis*, pp. 162–3.

5   EMPIRES – METAPHYSICAL AND MORAL

1.   George Berkeley, 'On the Prospect of Planting Arts and Learning in
     America', *1000 Years of Irish Poetry*, ed. Kathleen Hoagland (New York,
     1947), p. 333.
2.   Aeneas Sylvius (Pope Pius II), *De Ortu et Auctoritate Romani Imperii* in
     Lewis, *Medieval Political Ideas*, 2:504.

3.   When the Greek term 'monarchy' was translated into Latin, the term 'empire' was used. Aeneas Silvius Piccolomini, Pope Pius II (1458–64), for example, argued for a universal monarchy/empire in the following terms: 'individual rulers should be brought back under a single will, which the Greeks call monarchy and we call empire'. Cary Nederman, 'Humanism and Empire: Aeneas Silvius Piccolomini, Cicero and the Imperial Ideal', *The Historical Journal* 36 (1993): 499–515 at 510.

4.   *The Book of Daniel*, trans. Louis F. Hartman, C.SS.R., *The Anchor Bible* (Garden City, New York: Doubleday, 1978) 2:31–33, 37–40, 44 (pages 136–7). In the Jewish canon, the Book of Daniel 'was situated not among the Prophets ... but in the Hagiographia or the Writings.... The reason for this arrangement is not certain. It is possible that the rabbis did not consider the Book of Daniel as a prophetic writing.' On the other hand, 'In English Bibles edited by Christians, Daniel is placed among the Major Prophets ... as in the Greek witnesses ... and also in the Latin Vulgate.' Ibid., pp. 25–6.

5.   *Daniel*, Intro., p. 29. The editor discusses the historical context of the Book of Daniel and the prophecies it contains on pages 229–42. The Book appears to have been written in the second century BC (ibid., p. 25), although it discusses events that had occurred centuries earlier. In the Vulgate version of the Bible that St Jerome (c.347–c.419) prepared, the Book of Daniel contains the terms *rex* and *regnum*, king and kingdom, and not *imperator* and *imperium*, emperor and empire. Later writers, especially in the Middle Ages often, though not always, used *imperator* and *imperium*. Clearly, the large scope and great power of these kingdoms indicates that they were 'empires' in the later use of the term. In the Middle Ages and after, 'kingdom' referred to a unit of government smaller than an empire and, as we have seen, the title of emperor could be employed by a ruler who had conquered neighboring kingdoms, making him a king of kings or emperor.

6.   *Daniel*, p. 219.

7.   For the long-term significance of these ideas, see Norman Cohn, *The Pursuit of the Millennium*, rev. edn (New York, 1970).

8.   *Daniel*, Intro., p. 33.

9.   Ibid., p. 31.

10. Polybius, *Histories*, in Donald R. Kelley, *Versions of History from Antiquity to the Enlightenment* (New Haven, 1991), p. 37.

11. Ibid., p. 38.

12. Ibid.

13. Ernst Breisach, *Historiography: Ancient, Medieval & Modern* (Chicago, 1983), pp. 78, 83–4.

14. Augustine, *City of God*, 2 vols, trans. John Healey, ed. R.V.G. Tasker (London, 1945), 2:304–6.

15. Breisach, *Historiography*, p. 63.

16. Paulus Orosius in Kelley, p. 152.

17. Einhard and Notker the Stammerer, *Two Lives of Charlemagne*, p. 93; see also Janet Nelson, 'Kingship and Empire', Burns, *Cambridge History*, I:234.

18. Liutprand in Henderson, pp. 460–3.

19. Otto of Freising, *The Two Cities: a Chronicle of Universal History to the Year 1146 A. D.*, trans. Charles C. Mierow, ed. Austin P. Evans and Charles Knapp (New York, 1928), p. 166. For a discussion of the way in which Otto combined Augustine's view of history with that of Daniel, see ibid., pp. 27–33.

20. *The Two Cities*, pp. 167–8, 400–1.

21. Ibid., p. 283.

22. Ibid., pp. 353–4.

23. Van den Baar, pp. 62–3.

24. Janet Nelson, 'Kingship and Empire', Burns, *Cambridge History*, I:249.

25. *The Two Cities*, p. 354. It is important to realize that Augustine himself did not identify the City of God with the Church. On the subsequent development of Augustine's ideas to political life, see H.-X. Arquillière, *L'Augustinisme politique*, 2nd edn (Paris, 1955).

26. *The Two Cities*, p. 94.

27. Ibid., p. 97.

28. Ibid., p. 480.

29. There is an extensive literature on Joachim. Above all, see Marjorie Reeves, *The Influence of Prophecy in the Later Middle Ages* (Oxford, 1969). Norman Cohn has discussed the long-term significance of Joachim's conception of history in his well-known *The Pursuit of the Millennium*. His interpretation has been disputed: see Robert E. Lerner, *The Powers of Prophecy* (Berkeley, 1983), p. 195, esp. n. 16.

30. Cohn, *Pursuit*, pp. 109–10.

31. Ibid., p. 113.

32. Cohn, *Pursuit*, p. 113; Abulafia, *Frederick II*, pp. 428–35.

33. 'The work of the Roman emperors of antiquity was henceforth weighed with an eye to civic liberty, freed from the assumption that in the history of the Empire one had to recognize the hand of God.' Hans Baron, *The Crisis of the Early Italian Renaissance*, rev. edn (Princeton, 1966), p. 445. Critics of Baron's views have pointed out that humanists were as capable of defending empires as they were of defending republics: see Anthony Grafton, 'Humanism and Political Theory', Burns and Goldie, pp. 9–29, esp. pp. 15–20.

34. There is a selection of excerpts from other later medieval writers on empire in Lewis, *Medieval Political Ideas*, ch. VII, 'The Problem of Empire'. For a recent brief survey, see Anthony Black, *Political Thought in Europe, 1250–1450* (Cambridge, 1992), pp. 104–8.

35. The fundamental work for all modern consideration of the conciliar movement is Brian Tierney, *Foundations of the Conciliar Theory* (Cambridge, 1955).

36. Nicholas of Cusa, *The Catholic Concordance*, ed. Paul Sigmund (Cambridge, 1991), pp. 216–17.

37. Ibid., p. 234.

38. Dante, *Divine Comedy*, vol. I, *The Inferno*.

39. Baron, *Crisis* p. 445.

40. Skinner, *Foundations* I:168–9.

41. J.G.A. Pocock, *The Machiavellian Moment* (Princeton, 1975), p. 52.

42. Baron, *Crisis*, p. 16.

43. Ibid., p. 460.
44. Jacob Burckhardt, *The Civilization of the Renaissance in Italy*, trans. S.G.C. Middlemore (Greenwich, CN, 1965), p. 82.
45. It is well known that the views of Baron were influenced by his opposition to the rise of Hitler and his subsequent exile in the United States: see Albert Rabil, Jr, 'The Significance of "Civic Humanism" in the Interpretation of the Renaissance', *Renaissance Humanism: Foundations, Forms, and Legacy*, ed. Albert Rabil, Jr, 3 vols (Philadelphia, 1988) 1:141–74 at pp. 151–2.
46. Skinner, *Foundations*, esp. 1:xiv–xv; Pocock, esp. p. ix.
47. This section, as will become clear, owes a great deal to conversations and correspondence with Professors Cary Nederman of the University of Arizona and Constantin Fasolt of the University of Chicago who pointed out my failure to recognize humanist interest in imperial ideas in earlier versions of this work.
48. In spite of what Baron said about humanists and republicanism, the humanist-secretary was a common element of any princely court with pretensions to grandeur. For the role of such secretaries, see Paul Oskar Kristellar, *Renaissance Thought: the Classic, Scholastic, and Humanist Strains* (New York, 1961), pp. 11, 102–3.
49. For a survey of opinions about Aeneas Sylvius, see John B. Toews, 'The View of Empire in Aeneas Sylvius Piccolomini', *Traditio* 24 (1968): 471–87.
50. Nederman, 'Humanism and Empire', *The Historical Journal* 36 (1993): 499–515 at 500.
51. In support of the view that Aeneas Sylvius was simply re-stating outdated medieval views, it should be noted that as Pope Pius II he died on the way to lead a crusade against the advancing Turks. Given the overall course of expansion that the Ottoman Turks followed until the end of the seventeenth century, however, it would appear that he had a clearer grasp of the situation than did many of the leaders of the emerging 'states' of Europe. On Pius II, see Aziz S. Atiya, 'The Aftermath of the Crusades', *A History of the Crusades*, ed. K.M. Setton, vol. 3, *The Fourteenth and Fifteenth Centuries* (Madison, 1975), pp. 647–66 at pp. 658–60.
52. Lewis, *Medieval Political Ideas*, 2:502.
53. Ibid., 2:504.
54. Nederman, 'Humanism and Empire', 503.
55. Ibid., 504.
56. Ibid., 508.
57. Ibid., 510.
58. Thucydides, *The Peloponnesian War* became known once again in the fifteenth century when Lorenzo Valla translated it into Latin (1452), providing 'a basis for translation into modern languages.' Michael Grant, *The Ancient Historians* (New York, 1970), p. 390.
59. B.S. Capp, *The Fifth Monarchy Men: a Study in Seventeenth-Century English Millenarianism* (London, 1972); see also P.G. Rogers, *The Fifth Monarchy Men* (London, 1966).
60. Robertson, 'Union, State and Empire', p. 229.

6 THE GOLDEN AGE OF EMPIRE

1. Hernan Cortés, *Letters from Mexico*, trans. and ed. A.R. Pagden (New York, 1971), p. 48.
2. John Adams and Jonathan Sewall, *Novanglus and Massachusettensis* (Boston, 1819; reprint edn, New York, 1968), p. 143.
3. This fact is emphasized in Pagden, *Lords*, pp. 1–2.
4. Michael Hughes, *Early Modern Germany, 1477–1806* (Philadelphia, 1992), pp. 25–8.
5. Pope Leo X had opposed Charles's election, first supporting Francis I of France and, when that candidacy failed, supporting Frederick the Wise, Elector of Saxony: Brandi, *Charles V*, pp. 108–11. The pope and the emperor had differing interests at this point. Leo was primarily interested in stabilizing the political situation in Italy, while Charles was concerned with the larger situation, seeing himself in the tradition of the great emperors of the past who protected Christendom from its enemies, in this case, from the Lutherans within and the Muslims without. See also M.J. Rodriguez-Salgado, *The Changing Face of Empire: Charles V, Philip II, and Habsburg Authority, 1551–1559* (Cambridge, 1988). There is a useful introduction to the literature about Charles V in Martyn Rady, *The Emperor Charles V* (New York, 1988).
6. Hajo Holborn, *History of Modern Germany 1648–1840* (New York, 1966), p. 4.
7. Hedley Bull, 'The Importance of Grotius in the Study of International Relations', *Hugo Grotius and International Relations*, ed. H. Bull, B. Kingsbury, A. Roberts (Oxford, 1992), pp. 65–93 at 67; R.J. Vincent, 'Grotius, Human Rights, and Intervention', ibid., pp. 241–56 at 244.
8. Cortés, *Letters*, p. 48.
9. 'By the seventeenth century, the king of Castile was being referred to in semi-official publications as the "Emperor of America".' Pagden, *Lords*, p. 32.
10. Frances A. Yates, *Astraea: the Imperial Theme in the Sixteenth Century* (London, 1975; reprint edn, London, 1993), p. 23.
11. Sleidan, *History of the Reformation*, in Kelley, *Versions*, pp. 321–2.
12. Jean Bodin, *Method for the Easy Comprehension of History*, trans. Beatrice Reynolds (New York, 1945); reprint edn, New York, 1969), pp. 291–302; Kelley, *Versions*, pp. 391–2. On the notion of a *translatio ad Turcos*, see Ernst Werner, 'Translatio imperii ad Turcos: Päpstliche Renovatio und Weltkaiseridee nach dem Fall Konstantinopels', *Byzantinische Forschungen* 11(1987):465–72.
13. In the opinion of Friedrich Heer, the imperial conception that Gattinara espoused was rooted in the late medieval conceptions of empire that Maximilian I had encouraged: see Heer, *The Holy Roman Empire*, p. 141.
14. John M. Headley, *The Emperor and His Chancellor: a Study of the Imperial Chancellery under Gattinara* (Cambridge, 1983), p. 3.
15. Ibid., p. 11.
16. Ibid., p. 111; Yates, p. 26.

17.   Headley, *The Emperor*, p. 59.
18.   Brandi, *Charles V*, pp. 593–600.
19.   Peter Pierson, *Philip II of Spain* (London, 1975), p. 65. It is often over-
      looked that in addition to his other titles, Philip was also Philip I of
      England as a consequence of his marriage (1554) to Mary Tudor
      (1553–58). It was theoretically possible, as a consequence of this mar-
      riage, that a son of this marriage could inherit the English throne
      from his mother and the various Spanish thrones from his father. As
      Garrett Mattingly observed: 'This time, however, the magic formula,
      tu felix Austria, nube, failed. Mary bore no child. Even if she had done
      so, one may doubt whether the dynastic union would have succeeded.'
      Garrett Mattingly, *Renaissance Diplomacy* (Boston, 1955), pp. 189–90.
      Philip also considered marrying Elizabeth I after Mary's death,
      Prescott, *Philip II*, I:238–42. He also considered claiming the English
      throne by virtue of his descent from Edward III (1327–77) through his
      son, John of Gaunt (1340–99) who had married a daughter of the
      Castilian monarch, Peter the Cruel (1350–69). Their daughter married
      Henry III of Castile (1390–1406), the grandfather of Isabella of
      Castile: see O'Callaghan, *History of Medieval Spain*, pp. 526–8.
      Modern scholarship has reinforced Prescott's opinion: see, for
      example, John Lynch, *Spain under the Habsburgs*, 2 vols, 2nd edn
      (New York, 1984) 1:190–204.
20.   H.G. Koenigsberger, *Politicians and Virtuosi* (Rio Grande, Ohio, 1986),
      p. 82.
21.   Prescott's description of Philip II's work-habits sums up this point of
      view: 'He used to boast that thus hidden away from the world, with a
      little bit of paper he ruled over both hemispheres.' Prescott, *Philip II*,
      3:391.
22.   'The Dutch Republic originated in the opposition of the rational ele-
      ments of human nature to sacerdotal dogmatism and persecution – in
      the courageous resistance of historical and chartered liberty to foreign
      despotism.' John Lathrop Motley, *The Rise of the Dutch Republic*, 3 vols
      (New York, 1875), 1:v. For a more recent perspective, see J.H. Elliott,
      Europe Divided 1559–1598, Fontana History of Europe (London, 1968),
      pp. 125–44.
23.   John Elliott, *Imperial Spain 1469–1716* (New York, 1963; reprint edn,
      New York, 1966), p. 254.
24.   On the Aragonese empire, see O'Callaghan, pp. 382–406; Felipe
      Fernández-Armesto, *Before Columbus* (Philadelphia, 1987), pp. 11–42.
25.   D. A. Brading, *The First America* (Cambridge, 1991), pp. 2–3, 293–313.
26.   The situation was summed up in the saying: 'I obey but do not
      execute…'. C.H. Haring, *The Spanish Empire in America* (New York,
      1947), p. 123.
27.   Tanner, *Last Descendant*, p. 143.
28.   Chudoba, *Spain and the Empire*, p. 190.
29.   Tanner, *Last Descendant*, p. 178.
30.   Juan de Solórzano Pereira, *Disputatio de indiarum jure: sive, de justa
      indiarum occidentalium inquisitione, acquisitione et retentione*, 2 vols
      (Madrid, 1629, 1639; reprinted, Madrid, 1777). The most extensive

discussion of Solórzano's work is James Muldoon, *The Americas in the Spanish World Order* (Philadelphia, 1994); see also Muldoon, 'Boniface VIII as Defender of Royal Power: *Unam Sanctam* as a Basis for the Spanish Conquest of the Americas', *Popes, Teachers, and Canon Law in the Middle Ages*, ed. James Ross Sweeney and Stanley Chodorow (Philadelphia, 1989), pp. 62–73; and 'Solórzano's *De Indiarum iure*: Applying a Medieval Theory of World Order in the Seventeenth Century', *Journal of World History* 2(1991):29–45. For a discussion of Solórzano's work that places him in the context of Spanish governmental thought and practice in the Americas, see Brading, *First America*, pp. 215–27.

31. It is important to realize that this work appeared in two forms. It originally appeared in Latin. Subsequently it appeared in a Spanish version, *Política indiana* (Madrid: Ediciones Atlas, 1972). The Spanish version is not a translation, however, but a recasting of the original, leaving out some of the more critical observations about the Spanish government in the New World. The Latin version is very much in the tradition of the medieval scholastic treatise, reinforcing the conclusion that Solórzano placed the Spanish realms squarely in the medieval discussion of the nature of empire; see Muldoon, *The Americas*, pp. 8–12.

32. Solórzano, 1.16.51–5.

33. Ibid., 1.16.56: 'hoc tamen non solum hyperbolice, sed vere de diffusa Monarchia Hispani Imperii affirmare possumus; nam nascentis, & Occidentis Solis terminis, ut diximus, perstringit...'. See also 1.16.60: 'Et ita de Hispania nostra non solum illud praedicari potest, quod de Roma olim Virgil hyperbolice dixit: "Imperium Oceano, famam qui terminet astris."'

34. On Charles's abdications and the division of his lands and titles, see Brandi, *Charles V*, pp. 629–37.

35. Ibid., 2.21.18.

36. Ibid., 2.21.19. The reference is to the *Digest*, lib.14, tit. 2, *Deprecatio*.

37. Ibid., 2.21.25. The reference is to *Decretum*, C.7 q.1.cap. 41, *In apibus*.

38. Ibid., 2.21.27.

39. Ibid., 2.21.29. As we have seen, in fact, Conrad I never received imperial coronation.

40. Ibid., 2.21.30.

41. Ibid., 2.21.32.

42. Ibid., 2.21.35.

43. Ibid., 2.21.37.

44. Ibid., 2.21.38.

45. Ibid., 2.21.43.

46. Ibid., 2.21.44.

47. Ibid., 2.21.59.

48. Ibid., 2.21.60.

49. Ibid., 2.21.71.

50. Ibid., 2.21.73.

51. Ibid., 2.21.74–5.

52. Ibid., 2.21.76.

53. Ibid., 2.9.18: 'vere politicum vivendi modum'.

54.	Concerning the importance of Acosta, see Margaret T. Hodgen, *Early Anthropology in the Sixteenth and Seventeenth Centuries* (Philadelphia, 1964; reprint edn, 1971), pp. 313–15 and Pagden, *Fall of Natural Man*, pp. 146–200.
55.	Solórzano, 2.13.66. Here Solórzano refers to their 'ancient kingdoms and empires'. See also 2.12.25, 2.2.65.
56.	Ibid., 2.14.46.
57.	In addition, Solórzano discussed in various places the Roman Empire as found in Roman and canon law. He also described Christian society as the Christian Republic: ibid., 2.14.9.
58.	Concerning the military basis of the Aztec Empire, see Inga Clendinnen, 'The Cost of Courage in Aztec Society', *Past & Present*, no. 107 (May, 1985):44–89. For an introduction to the current literature on the Aztecs and the Incas, see the thoughtful review article by Benjamin Keen, 'Recent Writings on the Spanish Conquest', *Latin American Research Review* 20(1985): 161–71.
59.	The most recent edition of Vitoria's writings is Francisco de Vitoria, *Political Writings*, ed. Anthony Pagden and Jeremy Lawrence (Cambridge, 1991). Pagden's understanding of Vitoria has been severely criticized: see Brian Tierney, 'Aristotle and the American Indians – Again', *Cristianesimo nella Storia* 12(1991): 296–322.
60.	The 1647 edition of Solórzano's work was placed on the Index, because his discussion of Alexander VI's bull was seen as a rejection of papal authority: see Muldoon, *The Americas*, pp. 164.
61.	Brading, *First America*, p. 227.
62.	Ibid., pp. 535–60.
63.	On knowledge of Solórzano's work in the English world, see Muldoon, *The Americas*, p. 9; Pagden, *Lords*, pp. 38–9, 140–1.
64.	Act of Appeals, *The Tudor Constitution*, ed. G.R. Elton, 2nd edn (Cambridge, 1982), pp. 353–8 at p. 353.
65.	Ibid., pp. 360–3, at p. 360, pp. 364–5 at p. 364.
66.	Note that Daniel Leonard employed this conception of *imperium* as well. There is an extensive literature on Henry VIII's statement: see Kroebner, *Empire*, pp. 52–5, 61, and also his '"The Imperial Crown of this Realm": Henry VIII, Constantine the Great, and Polydore Vergil', *Bulletin of the Institute of Historical Research* 26(1953): 29–52; William Huse Dunham, Jr, 'The Crown Imperial', *Parliamentary Affairs* 6(1953): 199–206; Walter Ullmann, '"This Realm of England is an Empire"', *Journal of Ecclesiastical History* 30 (1979): 175–203.
67.	*Tudor Constitution*, pp. 37–9 at p. 37.
68.	This process was most effective within the contiguous regions of England (including Wales) and less so elsewhere.
69.	*Statutes of the Realm*, III, 563: 27 Henry VIII, c.26, in *Sources of English Constitutional History*, ed. Carl Stephenson and F.G. Marcham (New York, 1937): 314–15 at 314.
70.	Curtis and McDowell, pp. *Irish Historical Documents*, p. 77.
71.	R.F. Foster, *Modern Ireland 1600–1972* (Penguin, 1989), p. 3.
72.	Edmund Curtis, *A History of Ireland*, 6th edn (London, 1950; reprint edn, 1964), p. 168.

73. This bull has been the subject of a great deal of discussion and its authenticity even denied, although modern scholarship accepts it as authentic. For a survey of the literature concerning the bull, see James Muldoon, 'Spiritual Conquests Compared: *Laudabiliter* and the Conquest of the Americas', *In Iure Veritas: Studies in Canon Law in Memory of Schafer Williams*', eds Steven B. Bowman and Blanche E. Cody (Cincinnati, 1991): 174–86. For the debate about whether or not English possession of Ireland was in fact based on this bull, see ibid., 178–82.

74. Henry VIII's first Act of Succession and his will also referred to the 'imperial crown': see Stephenson and Marcham, pp. 310–11 at p. 310, pp. 323–4 at p. 324.

75. *Tudor Constitution*, pp. 372–7 at pp. 372–3.

76. Ibid., p. 375.

77. Ibid., pp. 423–8; Elizabeth's response is on pp. 428–31 at p. 428.

78. This would seem to reinforce John Adams's argument that the use of imperial language was not founded on legal and constitutional bases but on literary and journalistic bases.

79. Yates, *Astraea*, pp. 38–9.

80. Ibid., pp. 42–3.

81. Ibid., p. 51.

82. Ibid., p. 4.

83. P.G. Rogers, *Fifth Monarchy Men* (London, 1966), p. 15; see also J.C.D. Clark, *The Language of Liberty 1660–1832* (Cambridge, 1994), pp. 225, 227.

84. 'Royal Proclamation for Virginia (13 May 1625)', W.F. Craven, *Dissolution of the Virginia Company: the Failure of Colonial Experiment* (New York, 1932; reprint edn Gloucester MA, 1964). The text of the act is in *English Historical Documents*, vol. IX, *American Colonial Documents to 1776*, Merrill Jensen (New York, 1955), pp. 235–7 at p. 235.

85. For the text of the agreement, see *The Treaty of Union of Scotland and England 1707*, ed. George S. Pryde (London, 1950; reprint edn Westport, CN, 1979), pp. 81–102.

86. Ibid., pp. 83, 84.

87. Ibid., p. 83.

88. Charles H. McIlwain traced the basis of what he called 'the theory of the imperial commonwealth' to the act of the Long Parliament (1649) that abolished the monarchy and asserted the jurisdiction of the English Parliament not only over England but also over 'the dominions thereunto belonging'. This was, MacIlwain argued, 'apparently the first formal assertion by a Parliament of its authority beyond the realm'. Charles H. McIlwain, *The American Revolution: a Constitutional Interpretation* (New York, 1923; reprint edn Ithaca, 1958), p. 9. McIlwain's views have received little attention from scholars. As H. Trevor Colbourn has observed: 'The value of McIlwain's study remains uncontested, even though his approach awaits scholarly exploitation...'. *The Lamp of Experience* (Chapel Hill, NC, 1965), p. 188, note 18. The Parliamentary act to which McIlwain referred was the 'Act declaring England to be a Commonwealth', *Select Documents of*

English Constitutional History, ed. G.B. Adams and H.M. Morse (New York: Macmillan, 1904), p. 400.

89. The text is in Curtis and McDowell, 83; see also Foster, *Modern Ireland*, pp. 23–4.

90. William Molyneux, *The Case of Ireland Stated: Irish Writings from the Age of Swift*, vol. 5 (1698; reprint edn, Dublin, 1977), p. 46.

91. Ibid., p. 34.

92. Curtis and McDowell, p. 186.

93. Ibid., pp. 316–17 at p. 317.

94. MacDonald, p. 317.

95. 'Into the political connexion between Great Britain and Hanover there entered no element of federal relations of any sort or kind.' Adolphus William Ward, *Great Britain & Hanover: Some Aspects of the Personal Union* (Oxford, 1899; reprint edn New York: Haskell House, 1971), p. 2.

96. At least some English officials were aware of the importance of the Spanish model in the governance of far-flung imperial possessions and even cited Solórzano as an expert on colonial matters: see for example, James Abercromby, *Magna Carta for America*, ed. J.P. Greene, C.F. Mullett, E.C. Papenfuse (Philadelphia: American Philosophical Society, 1986), pp. 70, 184, 199, 312.

97. John Adams and Jonathan Sewall, *Novanglus and Massachusettensis* (Boston, 1819; reprint edn, New York: Russell & Russell, 1968), p. 143.

98. Ibid., p. 171.

99. John Adams, *Life and Works*, ed. Charles Francis Adams, 10 vols (Boston, 1850–56), 4: 37.

100. Ibid., 114.

101. According to A.G. Stapleton, the private secretary and biographer of George Canning: 'His late Majesty, George III, was advised, at the time of the Union with Ireland, in compensation for H.M.'s abandonment, then voluntarily made, of the title King of France ... to assume the title of Emperor of the British and Hanoverian Dominions; but his late Majesty felt that his true dignity consisted in his being known to Europe and the world by the appropriated and undisputed style belonging to the British Crown.' A.G. Stapleton, *Political Life of George Canning* II (1831), pp. 361–2 note, in *English Historical Documents 1783–1832*, eds A. Aspinall and E. Anthony Smith (New York: Oxford University Press, 1959), p. 83. The Act of Union with Ireland speaks of both 'the British empire' and 'the imperial crown of the said united kingdom, and of the dominions thereunto belonging'. See Curtis and McDowell, pp. 208–13 at 209.

CONCLUSION: EMPIRE AND STATE

1. Aubrey de Sélincourt, *The World of Herodotus* (Boston, 1962), p. 276.

2. Leonardo Bruni, 'Panegyric to the City of Florence', trans. B.J. Kohl, in *The Earthly Republic: Italian Humanists on Government and Society*, ed. Benjamin G. Kohl and Ronald G. Witt (Philadelphia, 1978), pp. 135–75 at pp. 151, 154.

3.   Bernard Bailyn, *The Ideological Origins of the American Revolution* (Cambridge, MA 1967), p. 26.

4.   Ronald Reagan, *Public Papers* for 8 March 1983, and 8 June 1982.

5.   J.G.A. Pocock, *Virtue, Commerce and History* (Cambridge, 1985), p. 86.

6.   Bernard de Voto, *The Course of Empire* (Boston, 1952).

7.   Francis Fukuyama, *The End of History and the Last Man* (New York, 1992), p. xi.

8.   Irving Kristol, 'The Emerging American Imperium', *Wall Street Journal*, Monday, 18 August 1997, section A, p. 14.

9.   The use of imperial language in connection with these petty rulers might remind one of the lengthy list of titles of the ruler of Lilliput: 'most mighty Emperor of Lilliput, delight and terror of the universe … monarch of all monarchs … at whose nod the princes of the earth shake their knees …'. Jonathan Swift, *Gulliver's Travels and Other Writings*, ed. Miriam Kosh Starkman (New York, 1962), p. 58.

10.   Strayer, *On the Medieval Origins*, p. 53.

11.   One reason was that the German rulers employed the term, and that possession of the imperial title was in the gift of the papacy, a relationship that the French kings seem anxious to avoid. Another was that the French monarchs had not acquired rule over any other kings.

12.   The Golden Bull was 'a bundle of laws and ordinances', old and new, affecting the election of the King of Germany who would expect to be elevated to the imperial office by the pope: see Joachim Leuschner, *Germany in the Late Middle Ages*, trans. Sabine MacCormack (Amsterdam, 1980), p. 155. The text is in Henderson, *Select Historical Documents*, pp. 220–61.

13.   James B. Collins, *The State in Early Modern France* (Cambridge, 1995), p. 5.

14.   John H. Elliott, 'A Europe of Composite Monarchies', *Past & Present*, no. 137 (Nov. 1992): 48–71 at 71.

15.   As early as the thirteenth century, an English settler in Ireland complained '"that just as we are English as far as the Irish are concerned, likewise to the English we are Irish, and the inhabitants of this island and of the other assail us with an equal degree of hatred."' Seán Duffy, *Ireland in the Middle Ages* (New York, 1997), p. 101.

16.   David Armitage, 'Making the Empire British', *Past & Present*, no. 155 (May 1997): 34–63 at 34.

17.   Note that Daniel Leonard employed this conception of *imperium* as well. There is an extensive literature on Henry VIII's statement: see Kroebner, *Empire*, pp. 52–5, 61, and also '"The Imperial Crown of this Realm:" Henry VIII, Constantine the Great, and Polydore Vergil', *Bulletin of the Institute of Historical Research* 26 (1953): 29–52; William Huse Dunham, Jr, 'The Crown Imperial', *Parliamentary Affairs* 6(1953) 199–206; Walter Ullmann, '"This Realm of England is an Empire"', *Journal of Ecclesiastical History* 30 (1979): 175–203.

18.   It is important to note that the papacy did not give up its own claim to a kind of universal legal jurisdiction through its canon law.

19.   Adams, *Works*, IV, pp. 278–81 at p. 280.

20.   R.C.K. Ensor, *England 1870–1914* (Oxford, 1936), p. 39.

Bibliography

Abbreviations

Burns – Burns, J.H. *The Cambridge History of Medieval Political Thought c.350–c.1450*. Cambridge: Cambridge University Press, 1988.
Burns and Goldie – Burns, J.H. and Mark Goldie. *The Cambridge History of Political Thought 1450–1700*. Cambridge: Cambridge University Press, 1991.
Imperial State – *An Imperial State at War: Britain from 1689 to 1815*, ed. Lawrence Stone. London and New York: Routledge, 1994.
MGH – *Monumenta Germaniae Historica*.
NCE – *New Catholic Encyclopedia*. New York: McGraw-Hill, 1967.
Renaissance and Renewal – *Renaissance and Renewal in the Twelfth Century*, ed. Robert L. Benson and Giles Constable. Cambridge: Harvard University Press, 1982.

Manuscripts

Caius College (Cambridge) MS. 17.
Huguccio, *Summa*. Pembroke College (Cambridge) MS. 72.
Summa Omnis qui iuste. Rouen Ms. 743.

PRINTED SOURCES

Abercromby, James. *Magna Carta for America*, ed. J.P. Greene, C.F. Mullett, E.C. Papenfuse. Philadelphia: American Philosophical Society, 1986.
Adams, John. *Life and Works*, ed. Charles Francis Adams, 10 vols. Boston: Little Brown, 1850–56.
—— and Jonathan Sewall. *Novanglus and Massachusettensis*. Boston: Hews & Goss, 1819; reprint edn, New York: Russell & Russell, 1968.
Aquinas, Thomas. *On Politics and Ethics*, ed. and trans. Paul E. Sigmund. New York: Norton, 1980.
Aristotle. *Historia animalium*. 3 vols, trans. A.L. Peck. Cambridge, MA: Harvard University Press, 1965–70.
Augustine. *City of God*, 2 vols, trans. John Healey, ed. R.V.G. Tasker. London: J.M. Dent, 1945.
Bede. *Opera Historica* 2 vols, ed. C. Plummer. Oxford: Clarendon Press, 1896; reprint edn, 1 vol. 1946.
Blackstone, William. *Commentaries on the Laws of England*, 4 vols. Oxford: Clarendon Press, 1765–69; reprint edn, Chicago: University of Chicago Press, 1979.
Bodin, Jean. *Method for the Easy Comprehension of History*, trans. Beatrice Reynolds. New York: Columbia University Press, 1945; reprint edn, New York: W.W. Norton, 1969.

——. *The Six Books of a Commonweal*, trans. Richard Knolles, ed. Kenneth D. McRae. Cambridge, MA: Harvard University Press, 1962.

Capitularia Regum Francorum, 2 vols, ed. A. Boretius. *MGH Legum*. Hanover: Hahn, 1883–97.

Comnena, Anna. *The Alexiad*, trans. Elizabeth A.S. Dawes. London: K. Paul, Trench, Trubner, 1928; reprint edn, New York: Barnes & Noble, 1967.

Corpus iuris canonici, ed. E. Friedberg, 2 vols. Leipzig, 1879–81; reprint edn, Graz: Akademische Druck-U. Verlagsanstalt, 1959.

Cortés, Hernan. *Letters from Mexico*, trans. and ed. A.R. Pagden. New York: Grossman, 1971.

The Crisis of Church and State 1050–1300, ed. Brian Tierney. Englewood Cliffs, NJ: Prentice-Hall, 1964.

Daniel, The Book of, trans. Louis F. Hartman, C.SS.R. *The Anchor Bible*. Garden City, New York: Doubleday, 1978.

Dante. *Monarchy and Three Political Letters*, trans. Donald Nicol and Colin Hardy. New York: Noonday Press, 1954.

Documents of the Christian Church, ed. Henry Bettenson, 2nd edn. London: Oxford University Press, 1963.

Documents of German History, ed. Louis L. Snyder. New Brunswick: Rutgers University Press, 1958.

Eagle, the Crescent, and the Cross: Sources of Medieval History, vol. I *c.250–c.1000*, ed. Donald White. New York: Appleton-Century-Crofts, 1967.

Einhard and Notker the Stammerer. *Two Lives of Charlemagne*, trans. Lewis Thorpe. Harmondsworth: Penguin, 1969.

English Historical Documents 1660–1714, ed. Andrew Browning. *English Historical Documents*, vol. 8. New York: Oxford University Press, 1953.

English Historical Documents: American Colonial Documents to 1776, ed. Merrill Jensen. *English Historical Documents*, vol. 9. New York: Oxford University Press, 1955.

English Historical Documents 1783–1832, eds A. Aspinall and E. Anthony Smith. *English Historical Documents*, vol. 11. New York: Oxford University Press, 1959.

Epistolae Karolini Aevi, ed. P. Kehr, vol. 7. *MGH* Berlin: Weidmannos, 1928.

Familiar Quotations, ed. John Bartlett, 15th edn. Boston: Little Brown, 1980.

Great Issues in Western Civilization, ed. Brian Tierney, Donald Kagan, and L. Pearce Williams, 3rd edn, New York: Random House, 1976.

Grotius, Hugo. *The Law of War and Peace. De Jure Belli ac Pacis Libri Tres*, trans. Francis W. Kelsey. *The Classics of International Law*. Washington, DC: Carnegie Endowment for International Peace, 1925; reprint edn, Indianapolis: Bobbs-Merrill, 1962.

Imperial Lives and Letters of the Eleventh Century, trans. Theodor E. Mommsen and Karl F. Morrison, ed. Robert L. Benson. New York: Columbia, 1962.

Innocent III. *Das Register Papst Innocenz' III. Über den Deutschen Thronstreit*, 2 vols, ed. Walther Holtzmann. Bonn: Universitäts-Verlag, 1947–48.

——. *Regestum super negotio Romani Imperii*, ed. F. Kempf. Rome: Pontificia Università Gregoriana, 1947.

Irish Historical Documents 1172–1922, eds Edmund Curtis and R.B. McDowell. London: Methuen, 1943; reprint edn, New York: Barnes & Noble, 1968.

Kelley, Donald R. *Versions of History from Antiquity to the Enlightenment*. New Haven: Yale University Press, 1991.

Lewis, Ewart. *Medieval Political Ideas*, 2 vols New York: Knopf, 1954.

Molyneaux, William, *The Case of Ireland Stated*. Dublin, 1698: reprint edn, Dublin: Cadenus Press, 1977.

New Eusebius: Documents Illustrating the History of the Church to AD 337, ed. J. Stevenson, rev. edn, W.H.C. Frend. London: SPCK, 1987.

Nicholas of Cusa. *The Catholic Concordance*, ed. Paul Sigmund. Cambridge: Cambridge University Press, 1991.

Otto of Freising. *The Two Cities: a Chronicle of Universal History to the Year 1146 A.D.* Records of Civilization, trans. C.C. Mierow, ed. Austin P. Evans and Charles Knapp. New York: Columbia University Press, 1928.

Pontificia Hibernica, 2 vols, ed. M.P. Sheehy. Dublin: M.H. Gill, 1962, 1965.

Procopius. *The Secret History*, trans. and ed., G.A. Williamson. Harmondsworth: Penguin, 1966; reprint edn, 1981.

Quellen zur Geschichte des Papsttums und des römischen Katholizismus, ed. C. Mirbt and K. Aland, 6th edn, Tübingen: J.C. Mohr, 1967.

Rufinus. *Summa Decretorum*, ed. H. Singer. Paderborn: F. Schoningh, 1902; reprint Aalen: Scientia Verlag, 1963.

Select Charters and Other Documents Illustrative of American History 1606–1775, ed. William MacDonald. New York: Macmillan, 1899.

Select Documents of English Constitutional History, ed. G.B. Adams and H.M. Morse. New York: Macmillan, 1904.

Select Historical Documents of the Middle Ages, ed. Ernest F. Henderson. London: G. Bell and Sons, 1925.

Son of Charlemagne: a Contemporary Life of Louis the Pious, trans. Allen Cabaniss. Syracuse: Syracuse University Press, 1961.

Sources of English Constitutional History, eds Carl Stephenson and F.G. Marcham. New York: Harper & Brothers, 1937.

Summa Parisiensis, ed. Terence McLaughlin. Toronto: Pontifical Institute of Medieval Studies, 1952.

1000 Years of Irish Poetry, ed. Kathleen Hoagland. New York: Grosset & Dunlap, 1947.

Tocqueville, Alexis de. *Democracy in America*, ed. J.P. Mayer trans. George Lawrence. Garden City, NY: Doubleday, 1969.

Treatise on Laws (Decretum DD 1–20), trans. Augustine Thompson and James Gordley. Studies in Medieval and Early Modern Canon Law, vol. 2. Washington, DC: Catholic University of America, 1993.

Treaty of Union of Scotland and England 1707, ed. George S. Pryde. London: T. Nelson and Sons, 1950; reprint edn, Westport, CN: Greenwood Press, 1979.

Tudor Constitution, 2nd edn, ed. G.R. Elton. Cambridge: Cambridge University Press, 1982.

Vacarius. *The Liber Pauperum*, ed. F. de Zulueta. Selden Society. London: Quaritch, 1927.

Valla, Lorenzo. *The Profession of the Religious and the Principal Arguments from the Falsely-Believed and Forged Donation of Constantine*, trans. and ed.

Olga Zorzi Pugliese. Toronto: Centre for Reformation and Renaissance Studies, 1985.

Virgil. *The Aeneid*, trans. Rolfe Humphries. New York: Scribner's Sons, 1951.

Vitoria, Francisco de. *Political Writings*, ed. Anthony Pagden and Jeremy Lawrence. Cambridge: Cambridge University Press, 1991.

Vitoria, Franciscus de. *De Indis et de iure belli relectiones*, ed. Ernest Nys. *Classics in International Law*. Washington, DC: Carnegie Institution, 1917; reprint edn, New York: Oceana, 1964.

Widukind. *Rerum Gestarum Saxonicarum*, ed. G. Waitz and K.A. Kehr, 5th edn rev. Paul Hirsch and H.-E. Lohman, *MGH*, Scriptores Rerum Germanicarum in Usum Scholarum. Hannover: Hahnsche Buchhandlung, 1935.

SECONDARY SOURCES

Abulafia, David. *Frederick II: a Medieval Emperor*. Penguin Press: Allen Lane, 1988: reprint edn, Oxford: Oxford University Press, 1992).

Akehurst, Michael. *A Modern Introduction to International Law*, 5th edn, London: George Allen and Unwin, 1984.

Allen, J.W. *A History of Political Thought in the Sixteenth Century*, rev. edn, London: Methuen, 1957; reprint, 1960.

Arquillière, H.-X. *L'Augustinisme politique*, 2nd edn, Paris: J. Vrin, 1955.

Atiya, Aziz S. 'The Aftermath of the Crusades', *A History of the Crusades*, ed. K.M. Setton, vol. 3, *The Fourteenth and Fifteenth Centuries*. Madison: University of Wisconsin Press, 1975: 647–66.

Bailyn, Bernard. *The Ideological Origins of the American Revolution*. Cambridge, MA: Harvard University Press, 1967.

Barlow, Frank. *William Rufus*. Berkeley: University of California Press, 1983.

Baron, Hans. *The Crisis of the Early Italian Renaissance*, rev. edn, Princeton: Princeton University Press, 1966.

Barraclough, Geoffrey. *The Origins of Modern Germany*, 2nd edn, Oxford: Basil Blackwell, 1947.

——. *The Medieval Papacy*. Harcourt, Brace & World: New York, 1968.

Bartlett, Robert. *The Making of Europe*. Princeton: Princeton University Press, 1993.

——. and Angus MacKay (eds). *Medieval Frontier Societies*. Oxford: Clarendon Press, 1989; reprint edn, 1992.

Becker, Carl L. *The Heavenly City of the Eighteenth-Century Philosophers*. New Haven: Yale University Press, 1932.

Bellomo, Manlio. *The Common Legal Past of Europe 1000–1800*, trans. Lydia G. Cochrane. Washington, DC: Catholic University of America, 1995.

Benson, Robert L. 'Political *Renovatio*: Two Models from Roman Antiquity', *Renaissance and Renewal*: 339–86.

——. *The Bishop-Elect*. Princeton: Princeton University Press, 1968.

—— and Giles Constable, eds. *Renaissance and Renewal in the Twelfth Century*. Cambridge, MA: Harvard University Press, 1982.

Berman, Harold. *Law and Revolution: the Formation of the Western Legal Tradition*. Cambridge, MA: Harvard University Press, 1983.

Black, Anthony. *Political Thought in Europe, 1250–1450*. Cambridge: Cambridge University Press, 1992.

Blumenthal, Uta-Renate. *The Investiture Controversy: Church and Monarchy from the Ninth to the Twelfth Century*. Philadelphia: University of Pennsylvania Press, 1988.

Bowlus, Charles R. *Franks, Moravians, and Magyars: the Struggle for the Middle Danube, 788–907*. Philadelphia: University of Pennsylvania Press, 1995.

Boyle, L.E. 'Decretists', NCE 4: 711–13.

——— 'Decretalists', NCE 4: 705–7.

Brading, D.A. *The First America: the Spanish Monarchy, Creole Patriots, and the Liberal State 1492–1867*. Cambridge: Cambridge University Press, 1991.

Brandi, Karl Brandi. *The Emperor Charles V*, trans. C.V. Wedgwood. London: Jonathan Cape, 1939; reprint edn, 1968.

Breisach, Ernst. *Historiography: Ancient, Medieval & Modern*. Chicago: University of Chicago Press, 1983.

Brewer, John. 'The Eighteenth-Century British State: Contexts and Issues', *Imperial State*: 52–71.

Brown, T.S. 'Louis the Pious and the Papacy: a Ravenna Perspective.' *Charlemagne's Heir: New Perspectives on the Reign of Louis the Pious (814–840)*. Oxford: Oxford University Press, 1990: 297–307.

Brundage, James A. *Medieval Canon Law*. London: Longman, 1995.

Bryce, James. *The Holy Roman Empire*, rev. edn, New York: A.L. Burt, 1886.

Buckley, J.M. 'Bernard of Parma', *NCE*, 2: 342.

Bull, Hedley. 'The Importance of Grotius in the Study of International Relations', *Hugo Grotius and International Relations*, ed. H. Bull, B. Kingsbury, A. Roberts. Oxford: Clarendon Press, 1992: 65–93.

Bullough, Donald. *The Age of Charlemagne*. New York: Putnam, 1966.

Burns, J.H. *The Cambridge History of Medieval Political Thought c.350–c.1450*. Cambridge: Cambridge University Press, 1988.

———. and Mark Goldie. *The Cambridge History of Political Thought 1450–1700*. Cambridge: Cambridge University Pres, 1991.

Calasso, F. *I glossatori e la teoria della sovranita*. 3rd edn, Milan, Giuffrè, 1957.

Canning, Joseph. *A History of Medieval Political Thought 300–1450*. London: Routledge, 1996.

———. *The Political Thought of Baldus de Ubaldus*, Cambridge Studies in Medieval Life and Thought, Fourth Series. Cambridge: Cambridge University Press, 1987.

———. 'Introduction: Politics, Institutions and Ideas', Burns: 341–66.

Capp, B.S. *The Fifth Monarchy Men: a Study in Seventeenth-Century English Millenarianism*. London: Faber, 1972.

Carlyle, R.W. and A.J. Carlyle. *A History of Mediaeval Political Theory in the West*, 6 vols. Edinburgh and London: William Blackwood & Sons, 1903–36.

Chodorow, Stanley. *Christian Political Theory and Church Politics in the Mid-Twelfth Century: the Ecclesiology of Gratian's Decretum*. Berkeley: University of California Press, 1972.

Chudoba, Bohdan. *Spain and the Empire*. Chicago: University of Chicago Press, 1952.

Clark, J.C.D. *The Language of Liberty 1660-1832*. Cambridge: Cambridge University Press, 1994.

Clendinnen, Inga. 'The Cost of Courage in Aztec Society', *Past & Present*, no. 107 (May 1985): 44-89.

Cohn, Norman. *The Pursuit of the Millennium*, rev. edn, New York: Oxford University Press, 1970.

Colbourn, H. Trevor. *The Lamp of Experience*. Chapel Hill: University of North Carolina Press, 1965.

Coronation of Charlemagne: What did it Signify?, ed. Richard E. Sullivan. Problems in European Civilization. Boston: D.C. Heath, 1959.

Cronne, H.A. *The Reign of King Stephen 1135-1154: Anarchy in England*. London: Weidenfeld and Nicolson, 1970.

Curtis, Edmund. *A History of Ireland*, 6th edn, London: Methuen, 1950; reprint edn, 1964.

Davis, Charles. *Dante and the Idea of Rome*. Oxford: Clarendon Press, 1957.

d'Entrèves, A.P. *Dante as a Political Thinker*. Oxford: Oxford University Press, 1952.

David, Paul A. 'Clio and the Economics of QWERTY', *The American Economic Review* 75 (1985): 332-7.

Duggan, Charles. *Twelfth Century Decretal Collections*. London: University of London, Athlone Press, 1963.

Dunham, William Huse, Jr. 'The Crown Imperial', *Parliamentary Affairs* 6 (1953): 199-206.

Elliott, J.H. *Europe Divided 1559-1598*. Fontana History of Europe. London: Fontana/Collins, 1968.

——. *Imperial Spain 1469-1716*. New York: St. Martin's Press, 1963; reprint ed. New York: New American Library, 1966.

Empress Theophano: Byzantium and the West at the Turn of the First Millennium, ed. Adelbert Davids. Cambridge: Cambridge University Press, 1995.

Fanning, Steven. 'Bede, *Imperium*, and the Bretwaldas', *Speculum* 66 (1991): 1-26.

——. 'Imperial Diplomacy between Francia and Byzantium: the Letter of Louis II to Basil I in 871', *Cithera* 34 (1994): 3-17.

Fernández-Armesto, Felipe. *Before Columbus*. Philadelphia: University of Pennsylvania Press, 1987.

Figgis, John Neville. *Political Thought from Gerson to Grotius 1414-1625*, 2nd edn, Cambridge, Cambridge University Press, 1916; reprint edn, New York: Harper & Row, 1960.

Folz, Robert. *The Concept of Empire in Western Europe from the Fifth to the Fourteenth Century*, trans. Sheila Ann Ogilve (London: Edward Arnold, 1969).

——. *L'Idée d'Empire en occident du Ve au XIVe Siècle*. Paris: Aubier, 1953.

Foster, R.F. *Modern Ireland 1600-1972*. Harmondsworth: Penguin, 1989.

Franklin, Julian H. 'Sovereignty and the Mixed Constitution: Bodin and His Critics.' Burns and Goldie: 298-328.

Furhmann, Horst. 'Konstantinische Schenkung und Sylvesterlegende in neuer Sicht'. *Deutsches Archiv* 15 (1959): 523-40.

——. 'Konstantinische Schenkung und abendländisches Kaisertum', *Deutsches Archiv* 22 (1966): 63-178.

Geary, Patrick J. *Before France and Germany: the Creation and Transformation of the Merovingian World*. New York: Oxford University Press, 1988.

Gilbert, A. *Machiavelli's 'Prince' and its Forerunners*. Durham, NC: University of North Carolina Press, 1938.

Gilchrist, John. 'The Gregorian Reform Tradition and Pope Alexander III', *Miscellanea Rolando Bandinelli Papa Alessandro III*, ed. F. Liotta. Siena: Accademia senese degli intronati, 1986: 259–87.

Gillingham, John. *The Angevin Empire*. New York: Holmes & Meier, 1984.

Gillmann, F. 'Ricardus Anglicus als Glossator der Compilatio I', *Archiv für katholisches Kirchenrecht* 107 (1927): 575–655.

Goez, Werner. *Translatio Imperii*. Tübingen: J.C.B. Mohr [Paul Siebeck], 1958.

Goffart, Walter. *Barbarians and Romans*. Princeton: Princeton University Press, 1980.

Grafton, Anthony. 'Humanism and Political Theory'. Burns and Goldie: 9–29.

Grant, Michael. *The Ancient Historians*. New York: Charles Scribner's Sons, 1970.

Grant, Robert. *Augustus to Constantine: the Rise and Triumph of Christianity in the Roman World*. New York: Harper & Row, 1970; reprint edn, 1990.

Haring, C.H. *The Spanish Empire in America*. New York: Oxford University Press, 1947.

Hatton, Ragnhild. *George I, Elector and King*. Cambridge MA: Harvard University Press, 1978.

Hay, Denys. *Europe: The Emergence of an Idea*. Edinburgh, University of Edinburgh Press, 1957; reprint edn, New York, Harper & Row, 1966.

Headley, John M. *The Emperor and his Chancellor: a Study of the Imperial Chancellery under Gattinara*. Cambridge Studies in Early Modern History. Cambridge: Cambridge University Press, 1983.

Heer, Friedrich. *Charlemagne and His World*. New York: Macmillan, 1975.

——. *The Holy Roman Empire*, trans. Janet Sondheimer. New York: Praeger, 1968.

Herrin, Judith. *The Formation of Christendom*, reprint rev. edn, Princeton: Princeton University Press, 1989.

Hexter, J.H. '*Il Principe* and *lo stato*.' *Studies in the Renaissance* 4 (1957): 113–38; reprinted in his *The Vision of Politics on the Eve of the Reformation: More, Machiavelli and Seyssel*. London: Allen Lane, 1973: 150–78.

Hobbes, Thomas. *Leviathan*. Oxford: Basil Blackwell, 1957.

Hodgen, Margaret T. *Early Anthropology in the Sixteenth and Seventeenth Centuries*. Philadelphia: University of Pennsylvania Press, 1964; reprint edn, 1971.

Holborn, Hajo. *History of Modern Germany 1648–1840*. New York: Knopf, 1966.

Hughes, Michael. *Early Modern Germany, 1477–1806*. Philadelphia: University of Pennsylvania Press, 1992.

'Imperialismus'. *Geschichtliche Grundbegriffe*, ed. Otto Brunner, Werner Conze, Reinhart Koselleck, 6 vols. Stuttgart: Klett-Cotta, 1972–1990, 3: 171–88.

Imperial State at War: Britain from 1689 to 1815, ed. Lawrence Stone. London and New York: Routledge, 1994.

Innocent III: Vicar of Christ or Lord of the World?, ed. James Powell, rev. edn, Washington, DC: Catholic University of America, 1994.

Irish Historical Documents 1172–1922, ed. Edmund Curtis and R.B. McDowell. London: Methuen, 1943; reprint edn, New York: Barnes & Noble, 1968.

James, Edward. *The Origins of France: from Clovis to the Capetians, 500–1000*. London: Macmillan, 1982.

Jedin, Hubert. *Ecumenical Councils of the Catholic Church*, trans. Ernest Graf. New York: Paulist Press, 1960.

Johnson, James Turner. *The Quest for Peace. Three Moral Traditions in Western Cultural History*. Princeton: Princeton University Press, 1987.

Keen, Benjamin. 'Recent Writings on the Spanish Conquest', *Latin American Research Review* 20 (1985): 161–71.

Keir, David L. *The Constitutional History of Modern Britain since 1485*, 8th edn, Princeton: Van Nostrand, 1966.

Kemp, Friedrich. 'Die päpstliche Gewalt in der mittelalterlichen Welt'. *Miscellanea Historiae Pontificiae* 21 (1959): 117–69.

——. 'Innocenz III. und der Deutsche Thronstreit', *Archivium Historiae Pontificiae* 23 (1985): 63–91.

Koenigsberger, H.G. *Politicians and Virtuosi: Essays in Early Modern History*. Rio Grande, Ohio: Hambleton, 1986.

Krautheimer, Richard. *Rome: Profile of a City, 312–1308*. Princeton: Princeton University Press, 1980.

Kristellar, Paul, Oskar. *Renaissance Thought: the Classic, Scholastic, and Humanist Strains*. New York: Harper & Row, 1961.

Kroebner, Richard. '"The Imperial Crown of this Realm": Henry VIII, Constantine the Great, and Polydore Vergil', *Bulletin of the Institute of Historical Research* 26 (1953): 29–52.

——. *Empire*. Cambridge: Cambridge University Press, 1961.

Kuttner, Stephan G. *Harmony from Dissonance: an Interpretation of Medieval Canon Law*. Latrobe, PA: Archabbey Press, 1960.

——. 'The Revival of Jurisprudence'. *Renaissance and Renewal*: 299–323.

——. and Eleanor Rathbone, 'Anglo-Norman Canonists in the Twelfth Century', *Traditio* 7 (1949–51): 279–358.

Lapsley, G.T. *The County Palatine of Durham*. Cambridge MA: Harvard University Press, 1924.

Lasko, Peter. *Ars Sacra 800–1200*, 2nd edn, New Haven: Yale University Press, 1994.

Le Bras, G., Ch. Lefebvre, and J. Rambaud. *L'Age Classique 1140–1378: Sources et théorie du droit, Histoire du Droit et des Institutions de l'Eglise en Occident*, vol. 7. Paris: Sirey, 1965.

Lerner, Robert E. *The Powers of Prophecy*. Berkeley: University of California Press, 1983.

Levine, Joseph M. 'Reginald Pecock and Lorenzo Valla on the Donation of Constantine'. *Studies in the Renaissance* 20 (1973): 118–43.

Levison, Wilhelm. *England and the Continent in the Eighth Century*. Oxford: Clarendon Press, 1946.

Leyser, Karl. *Communications and Power in Medieval Europe: the Carolingian and Ottonian Centuries*, ed. Timothy Reuter London: Hambledon Press, 1994.

——. *Rule and Conflict in an Early Medieval Society: Ottonian Saxony.* Bloomington: Indiana University Press, 1979.

——. 'Ends and Means in Liudprand of Cremona', in Leyser, *Communications and Power*: 125–42.

Liebermann, F. 'Magister Vacarius', *English Historical Review* 11 (1896): 305–14.

Lintott, Andrew. *Imperium Romanum: Politics and Administration.* London: Routledge, 1993.

——. 'What was the "Imperium Romanum"?' *Greece & Rome* 28 (1981), 53–67.

Lossky, Andrew. *Louis XIV and the French Monarchy.* New Brunswick: Rutgers University Press, 1994.

Lotter, Friedrich. 'The Crusading Idea and the Conquest of the Region East of the Elbe', *Medieval Frontier Societies*, ed. Robert Bartlett and Angus MacKay. Oxford: Clarendon Press, 1989; reprint edn, 1992: 267–306.

Loyn, H.R. *Anglo-Saxon England and the Norman Conquest.* London: Longman, 1962.

Luchaire, A. *Innocent III*, 6 vols. Paris: Hachette et Cie, 1904–8, vol. 5, *Les royautés vassales du Saint-Siège.*

Lynch, John. *Spain under the Habsburgs*, 2 vols, 2nd edn, New York: New York University Press, 1984.

Maccarrone, Michele. *Chiesa e stato nella dottrina di papa Innocenzo III.* Rome: Facultas Theologica Pontificii Athenaei Lateranensis, 1940.

——. *Nuovi studi su Innocenzo III*, ed. Roberto Lambertini. Rome: Istituto storico Italiano per il medio evo, 1995.

——. *Vicarius Christi: Storia del titolo papale.* Rome: Facultas Theologica Pontificii Athenaei Lateranensis, 1952.

McCormick, Michael. *Eternal Victory: Triumphal Rulership in Late Antiquity, Byzantium, and the Early Medieval West.* Cambridge: Cambridge University Press, 1986.

Maitland, F.W. *Roman Canon Law in the Church of England.* London: Methuen, 1898.

Maffei, Domenico. *La Donazione di Cosantino nei Giuristi Medievali.* Milan: Giuffrè, 1964.

McIlwain, Charles H. *The American Revolution: a Constitutional Interpretation.* New York: Macmillan, 1923; reprint edn, Ithaca: Cornell University Press, 1958.

McKitterick, Rosamund. *The Frankish Kingdom under the Carolingians.* London: Longman, 1983.

Mattingly, Garrett. *Renaissance Diplomacy.* Boston: Houghton Mifflin, 1955.

Melloni, Alberto. *Innocenzo IV: La concezione e l'esperienza della cristianità come regimen unius personae.* Genoa: Marietti, 1990.

Mitteis, H. *The State in the High Middle Ages*, trans. H.F. Orton. Amsterdam: North-Holland, 1975.

Mochi Onory, Sergio. *Fonti canonistiche dell'idea moderna dello stato.* Milan: Vita e Pensiero, 1951.

Morrison, Karl. 'Canossa: a Revision.' *Traditio* 18 (1962): 121–48.

Motley, John Lathrop. *The Rise of the Dutch Republic*, 3 vols. New York: Harper, 1875.

Muldoon, James. *The Americas in the Spanish World Order.* Philadelphia: University of Pennsylvania Press, 1994.

——. 'Boniface VIII as Defender of Royal Power: *Unam Sanctam* as a Basis for the Spanish Conquest of the Americas', *Popes, Teachers, and Canon Law in the Middle Ages*, ed. James Ross Sweeney and Stanley Chodorow. Philadelphia: University of Pennsylvania Press, 1989: 62–73.

——. 'Solórzano's *De indiarum iure*: Applying a Medieval Theory of World Order in the Seventeenth Century', *Journal of World History* 2 (1991): 29–45.

——. 'The Contribution of the Medieval Canon Lawyers to the Formation of International Law', *Traditio* 28 (1972): 483–97.

——. '*Extra ecclesiam non est imperium*. The Canonists and the Legitimacy of Secular Power', *Studia Gratiana* 9 (1966): 553–80.

——. 'The Indian as Irishman', *Essex Institute Historical Collections* 111 (1975): 267–289.

——. 'Spiritual Conquests Compared: *Laudabiliter* and the Conquest of the Americas'. *In Iure Veritas: Studies in Canon Law in Memory of Schafer Williams*, eds. Steven B. Bowman and Blanche E. Cody. Cincinnati: University of Cincinnati College of Law, 1991: 174–86.

Müller, Wolfgang, P. *Huguccio, The Life, Works, and Thought of a Twelfth-Century Jurist.* Studies in Medieval and Early Modern Canon Law, vol. 3. Washington, DC: Catholic University of America, 1994.

Munz, Peter. *Frederick Barbarossa: a Study in Medieval Politics.* Ithaca: Cornell University Press, 1969.

Nederman, Cary. 'The Politics of Mind and Word, Image, and Text: Retrieval and Renewal in Medieval Political Theory', *Political Theory* 25 (1997): 716–32.

——. 'Conciliarism and Constitutionalism: Jean Gerson and Medieval Political Thought'. *History of European Political Ideas*, 12 (1990): 189–209.

——. 'Humanism and Empire: Aeneas Silvius Piccolomini, Cicero and the Imperial Ideal', *The Historical Journal* 36 (1993): 499–515.

Nelson, Janet L. *Charles the Bald.* London: Longman, 1992.

——. 'Kingship and Empire', Burns: 211–51.

——. 'The Frankish Kingdoms, 814–898: The West'. *New Cambridge Medieval History*, ed. Rosamund McKitterick. Cambridge: Cambridge University Press, 1995, 2: 110–41.

New Catholic Encyclopedia, 15 vols. New York: McGraw-Hill, 1967.

Nicol, Donald M. Nicol. 'The Byzantine View of Western Europe', *Greek, Roman and Byzantine Studies* 8 (1967): 315–39 at 317–18; reprinted in Donald M. Nicol, *Byzantium: Its Ecclesiastical History and Relations with the Western World.* London: Variorum, 1972.

Noble, Thomas F.X. *The Republic of St. Peter.* Philadelphia: University of Pennsylvania Press, 1984.

Noonan, John T. 'Who was Rolandus?', *Law, Church and Society: Essays in Honor of Stephan Kuttner*, ed. Kenneth Pennington and Robert Somerville. Philadelphia: University of Pennsylvania Press, 1977: 21–48.

Norman, Donald A. *The Psychology of Everyday Things.* New York: Basic Books, 1988.

Oakley, Francis. 'Nederman, Gerson, Conciliar Theory and Constitutionalism: sed contra'. *History of Political Thought* 16 (1995): 1–19.

——. 'Celestial Hierarchies Revisited: Walter Ullmann's Vision of Medieval Politics', *Past & Present* 60 (Aug. 1973): 3–48.

Obolensky, Dimitri. *The Byzantine Commonwealth: Eastern Europe, 500–1453.* New York: Praeger, 1971.

O'Callaghan, Joseph F. *A History of Medieval Spain.* Ithaca: Cornell University Press, 1975; reprint 1983.

Ohnsorge, Werner, 'The Coronation and Byzantium', *The Coronation of Charlemagne: What did it Signify?*, ed. Richard E. Sullivan, Problems in European Civilization. Boston: D.C. Heath, 1959: 80–91.

——. *Das Zweikaiserproblem im früheren Mittelalter.* Hildesheim, A. Lax, 1947.

Opll, Ferdinand. *Friedrich Barbarossa.* Darmstadt: Wissenschaftliche Buchgesellschaft, 1990.

Ostrogorsky, G. *History of the Byzantine State*, rev. edn, New Brunswick, Rutgers University Press, 1969.

Pagden, Anthony. *European Encounters with the New World.* New Haven: Yale University Press, 1993.

——. *The Fall of Natural Man: the American Indian and the Origins of Comparative Ethnology*, 2nd edn, Cambridge: Cambridge University Press, 1986.

——, *Lords of All the World: Ideologies of Empire in Spain, Britain and France c.1500–c.1800.* New Haven: Yale University Press, 1995.

——. *Spanish Imperialism and the Political Imagination.* New Haven: Yale University Press, 1990.

Pascoe, Louis B. 'Gerson and the Donation of Constantine: Growth and Development within the Church'. *Viator* 5 (1974): 469–85.

Patourel, John le. 'Angevin Successions and the Angevin Empire', *Feudal Empires Norman and Plantagenet*, London: Hambledon Press, 1984, IX.

——. *Feudal Empires Norman and Plantagenet.* London: Hambledon Press, 1984, VIII.

——. 'The Plantagenet Dominions', *History* 50 (1965) 289–308.

Pennington, Kenneth. 'The Legal Education of Pope Innocent III', *Bulletin of Medieval Canon Law*, n. s. 4 (1974): 70–77.

——. *The Prince and the Law.* Berkeley: University of California Press, 1993.

Peters, Edward M. *The Shadow King: Rex Inutilis in Medieval Law and Literature, 751–1327.* New Haven: Yale University Press, 1970.

Phillips, J.R.S. *The Medieval Expansion of Europe.* Oxford: Oxford University Press, 1988.

Pierson, Peter. *Philip II of Spain.* London: Thames and Hudson, 1975.

Pocock, J.G.A. *The Machiavellian Moment.* Princeton: Princeton University Press, 1975.

Poole, Austin Lane. *From Domesday Book to Magna Carta. 1087–1216*, 2nd edn, Oxford: Clarendon Press, 1955.

Post, Gaines. '"Blessed Lady Spain" – Vincentius Hispanus and Spanish National Imperialism in the Thirteenth Century.' *Speculum* 29 (1954): 198–209.

——. 'Some Unpublished Glosses (ca. 1210–1214) on the "Translatio Imperii" and the Two Swords,' *Archiv für katholisches Kirchenrecht* 117 (1937): 403–29.

——. *Studies in Medieval Legal Thought.* Princeton: Princeton University Press, 1964.

Prescott, William H. *Philip II*. 3 vols. London: Routledge, 1881.

Quotations in History, ed. Alan and Veronica Palmer. Hassocks, Sussex: Harvester Press, 1976.

Rabil, Albert, Jr. 'The Significance of "Civic Humanism" in the Interpretation of the Renaissance', *Renaissance Humanism: Foundations, Forms, and Legacy*, ed. Albert Rabil, Jr, 3 vols. Philadelphia: University of Pennsylvania Press, 1988, 1: 141–74.

Rady, Martyn. *The Emperor Charles V*. London: Longman, 1988.

Reuter, Timothy. *Germany in the Early Middle Ages c.800–1056*. London: Longman, 1991.

Reynolds, Susan. *Fiefs and Vassals: the Medieval Evidence Reinterpreted*. Oxford: Clarendon Press, 1994.

Richardson, J.S. '*Imperium Romanum*: Empire and the Language of Power', *Journal of Roman Studies* 81 (1991): 1–9.

Riché, P. *Daily Life in the World of Charlemagne*, trans. J.A. McNamara. Philadelphia: University of Pennsylvania Press, 1978.

Robertson, John. 'Union, State and Empire', *Imperial State*: 224–57.

Robertson, William. *History of the Reign of Charles the Fifth*, 2 vols. London: George Routledge and Sons, 1878.

Robinson, I.S. 'Church and Papacy', Burns: 252–305.

Rodriguez-Salgado, M.J. *The Changing Face of Empire: Charles V, Philip II, and Habsburg Authority, 1551–1559*. Cambridge: Cambridge University Press, 1988.

Rogers, P.G. *The Fifth Monarchy Men*. London: Oxford University Press, 1966.

Rowe, John Howland, 'The Renaissance Foundations of Anthropology,' *American Anthropologist* 65 (1965): 1–20.

Rubinstein, Nicolai, 'Italian Political Thought', Burns and Goldie: 30–65.

Sabine, George H. *A History of Political Theory*, 3rd edn, New York, Holt, Rinehart and Winston, 1961.

Sayers, Jane. *Innocent III: Leader of Europe*. London: Longman, 1994.

Schulze, Hagen. *States, Nations and Nationality: from the Middle Ages to the Present*, trans. William E. Yuill. Cambridge MA: Blackwell, 1996.

Sherwin-White, A.N. *The Roman Citizenship*, 2nd edn, Oxford: Clarendon Press, 1973.

Skinner, Quentin. *Machiavelli*. Oxford: Oxford University Press, 1981.

——. *The Foundations of Modern Political Thought*, 2 vols. Cambridge: Cambridge University Press, 1978.

Smith, Denis Mack. *History of Sicily. Medieval Sicily: 800–1713*. New York: Viking Press, 1968.

Smith, Julia M.H. '*Fines Imperii: the Marches*', *The New Cambridge Medieval History*, vol. II c.700–c.900, ed. Rosamund McKitterick. Cambridge: Cambridge University Press, 1995: 169–89.

Smyth, Alfred P. *King Alfred the Great*. Oxford: Oxford University Press, 1995.

Solórzano Pereira, Juan de. *Disputatio de indiarum jure: sive, de justa indiarum occidentalium inquisitione, acquisitione et retentione*, 2 vols. Madrid, 1629, 1639; reprinted, Madrid, 1777.

——. *Política indiana*. Madrid: Ediciones Atlas, 1972.

Stenton, F.M. *Anglo-Saxon England*, 3rd edn, Oxford: Clarendon Press, 1971.

Stickler, A. 'Alanus Anglicus als Verteidiger des monarchischen Papsttum', *Salesianum* 21 (1959): 346–406.

——. 'Concerning the Political Theories of the Medieval Canonists'. *Traditio* 7 (1949–51): 450–63.

——. 'Il "gladius" negli atti dei concili et dei RR. Pontifici sino Graziano e Bernardo di Clairvaux', *Salesianum* 13 (1951): 414–45.

——. 'Imperator vicarius Papae', *Mitteilungen des Instituts für Österreichischen Geschichtsforschung*, 62 (1954): 165–212.

——. 'Joannes Teutonicus (Zemecke)', NCE, 7:998.

——. '"Sacerdotium et Regnum" nei Decretisti et primi Decretalisti. Considerazioni metodologiche di ricerca e testi', *Salesianum* 15 (1953): 575–612.

——. 'Der Schwerterbegriff bei Huguccio', *Ephemerides Iuris Canonici* 3 (1947): 201–42.

——. 'Vergessene Bologneser Dekretisten', *Salesianum* 14 (1952): 476–503.

Stone, Lawrence, ed. *An Imperial State at War: Britain from 1689 to 1815*. London and New York: Routledge, 1994.

Strayer, Joseph R. *On the Medieval Origins of the Modern State*. Princeton: Princeton University Press, 1970.

Thompson, John A.F., *Popes and Princes, 1417–1517*. London: George Allen & Unwin, 1980.

Tierney, Brian. *Foundations of the Conciliar Theory*. Cambridge: Cambridge University Press, 1955.

——. *Religion, Law, and the Growth of Constitutional Thought, 1150–1650*. Cambridge: Cambridge University Press, 1982.

——. 'Hierarchy, Consent, and the "Western Tradition."' *Political Theory* 15 (1987): 646–52.

——. 'Some Recent Works on the Political Theories of the Medieval Canonists', *Traditio* 10 (1954): 594–625.

——. 'Aristotle and the American Indians – Again', *Cristianesimo nella Storia* 12 (1991): 296–322.

——. 'Hierarchy, Consent, and the "Western Tradition",' *Political Theory* 15 (1987): 646–52.

Toews, John B. 'The View of Empire in Aeneas Sylvius Piccolomini', *Traditio* 24 (1968): 471–87.

Tuck, Richard. 'Grotius and Selden', Burns and Goldie: 499–529.

Ullmann, Walter. '"This Realm of England is an Empire"', *Journal of Ecclesiastical History* 30 (1979): 175–203.

——. *The Growth of Papal Government in the Middle Ages*, 2nd edn, London: Methuen, 1962.

——. *Principles of Government and Politics in the Middle Ages*. London: Methuen, 1961.

——. *Law and Politics in the Middle Ages: an Introduction to the Sources of Medieval Political Ideas*. Ithaca: Cornell University Press, 1975.

Van Den Baar, P.A. *Die kirchliche Lehere der Translatio Imperii Romani bis zur Mitte des 13. Jahrhunderts*. Rome: Apud Aedes Universitatis Gregorianae, 1956.

Vincent, R.J. 'Grotius, Human Rights, and Intervention', *Hugo Grotius and International Relations*, ed. H. Bull, B. Kingsbury, A. Roberts. Oxford: Clarendon Press, 1992: 241–56.

Viroli, Maurizio. *From Politics to Reason of State: the Acquisition and Transformation of the Language of Politics 1250–1600*. Cambridge: Cambridge University Press, 1992.

Vogt, Joseph. *The Decline of Rome*, trans. Janet Sondheimer. New York: Praeger, 1969.

Wallach, Liutpold. *Alcuin and Charlemagne: Studies in Carolingian History and Literature*. Ithaca: Cornell University Press, 1959.

Walther, Helmut G. *Imperiale Königtum Konziliarismus und Volkssouveränität*. Munich: Wilhelm Fink Verlag, 1976.

Ward, Adolphus William. *Great Britain & Hanover. Some Aspects of the Personal Union*. Oxford: Oxford University Press, 1899; reprint edn, New York: Haskell House, 1971.

Watt, J.A. *The Church in Medieval Ireland*. The Gill History of Ireland, vol. 5. Dublin: Gill and Macmillan, 1972.

——. *The Church and the Two Nations in Medieval Ireland*. Cambridge: Cambridge University Press, 1970.

Werner, Ernst. 'Translatio imperii ad Turcos: Päpstliche Renovatio und Weltkaiseridee nach dem Fall Konstantinopels', *Byzantinische Forschungen* 11 (1987): 465–72.

Wilks, Michael J. *The Problem of Sovereignty in the Later Middle Ages*. Cambridge: Cambridge University Press, 1963.

Wood, Charles. *The French Apanages and the Capetian Monarchy, 1224–1328*. Cambridge: Harvard University Press, 1966.

Yates, Frances A. *Astraea: the Imperial Theme in the Sixteenth Century*. London: Routledge & Kegan Paul, 1975; reprint edn, London: Pimlico, 1993.

Index